the Jazz Harmony BOOK

A Course in Adding Chords to Melodies

by David Berkman

Graphic Design - Attila Nagy

©2013 Sher Music Co., P.O.Box 445, Petaluma, CA 94953
www.shermusic.com. No part of this book or audio CD may be reproduced
in any form without written permission from the publisher.
All Rights Reserved. International Copyright Secured.
ISBN 1-883217-79-2

CONTENTS

Introduction: ii

PART 1 – THE HARMONIC UNIVERSE OF A KEY

Chapter 1: The First Circle: I, IV and V7 Chords 1

Chapter 2: The Second Circle: Diatonic Seventh Chord Substitutes for I, IV and V7 13

Chapter 3: The Third Circle: Secondary Dominant Seventh and Related ii Minor7 chords.... 18

Chapter 4: Understanding the Geography of Standard Tunes: Jazz Cadences and Turnarounds. 34

Chapter 5: The Fourth Circle: Passing Chords 40

Chapter 6: The Fifth Circle: Modal Interchange Chords 51

Chapter 7: The Last Circle: Tritone Substitutes............................... 67

Chapter 8: The Harmony of Minor Tunes 84

Chapter 9: Another Approach to Jazz Harmony Using Diminished Chords 89

Chapter 10: Deep Structure, the Right Changes and Re-Harmonization............ 107

PART 2 – BEYOND THE HARMONIC UNIVERSE: RULES FOR NON-FUNCTION

Chapter 11: Eleven Organizing Principles of Non-functional Chord Progressions 121

Chapter 12: Same Root, Different Chord Quality 124

Chapter 13: Slash Chords 128

Chapter 14: Harmonizing a Bass Line 136

Chapter 15: Chords Built in Fourths 139

Chapter 16: "Giant Steps" 145

Chapter 17: Color Chords 150

Chapter 18: Parallel Chords that use Exact Transposition (planing) 154

Chapter 19: Pedals 161

Chapter 20: Chord Subtraction 166

Chapter 21: Unavailable Tensions 171

Chapter 22: Incomplete Chords 176

Chapter 23: Conclusions 182

Appendix A: Tips for Composers 187

Appendix B: Piano Basics 197

I like to think of harmonizing as a process that can be studied through an ever widening set of concentric circles, each circle expressing some key part of harmony, or a process of harmonization. The first circle is the most basic, central harmony—the simplest most elemental way a melody can be harmonized using western musical tonal principles. As we move outward from the center circle, we add harmonic possibilities, and have a larger and larger palette of chords available to use in our harmonizations of melodies.

INTRODUCTION

Today, the jazz world is in a particularly rhythm-focused period. Of course, interest in rhythm is nothing new—jazz has always been about rhythm. Swinging, grooving, 'over-the-bar playing' or cross rhythms, African influences, Afro-Cuban clave and samba—all these rhythmic elements have been shaping jazz since its birth around the beginning of the 20th century. Harmony and melody have always been, and continue to be, a significant part of that story as well, but recently, the focus of many younger musicians has been rhythmic above all else and innovations in rhythm, particularly improvising over odd meter and mixed meter forms have been driving most of the innovations in contemporary jazz of the last 15 years.

This was not always the case. Many jazz players who came of age in the 60s and 70s played mostly, if not entirely in 4/4, 3/4 and 6/8. It's important for younger players to take note of the fact that the musicians that shaped and developed jazz, players from Lester Young and Charlie Parker to John Coltrane, Sonny Rollins, Thelonious Monk and countless others played entirely in these meters. (That is not to say that there weren't experiments in different meters, from Don Ellis to Dave Brubeck and many jazz fusion players in the 70s and beyond, but this was, by and large, an exception to the general trend among mainstream jazz musicians.)

From the 40s through the 60s, rhythms in jazz evolved and changed but it's probably fair to say that harmony was leading the way. The harmonic innovations of bebop musicians (the use of chromaticism in scales, the superimposition of chords, secondary dominants and tritone substitutions, the use of more exotic scales and emphasis on unusual sounding altered tensions on chords) were followed by the harmonic innovations of modal music, Coltrane and "Giant Steps" chord progressions, free jazz players and the open-ended and mysterious playing of the late 60s Miles Davis Quintet. Players like Herbie Hancock and McCoy Tyner re-defined the harmonic palette of jazz piano with influences drawn from 20th Century classical music and African pentatonic scales.

Well, so be it. Time marches on and tastes change. Personally, as a jazz pianist and composer, I continue to be fascinated by harmonic color: from the whole tone flourishes and chains of secondary dominants of Thelonious Monk, Bud Powell and Art Tatum; the passing chords, parallel voicings and moving inner voices that resolve through altered tensions to chord tones in great players such as Hank Jones, Bill Evans and Keith Jarrett; the diminished and near-diminished sounds you hear in Herbie Hancock's playing, as well as the world of classically-influenced harmony drawing on Ravel, Bartok, Hindemith and others. I am, of course, also fascinated by rhythm, but for a while now I've been noticing that my students are out of touch with the subtle manipulation of harmony that has been the stock and trade of most great jazz pianists, guitarists and arrangers of the past.

One reason for this is that most students first encounter standards in fake books nowadays. They often play with (other young) players who have also learned standards from books. Learning standards from fake books leads toward more agreement about the changes of the tune—young players play the changes they've learned and they play them more or less the same way every time they play the tune, chorus after chorus.

It was not always like this. When musicians learned standards on the bandstand from each other, there was a lot of negotiation of the harmony. In many cases a consensus of what the basic changes were emerged, but each playing of the tune (and sometimes each chorus of the performance) might contain subtle changes of the underlying chord structure. I was struck by this recently, while watching a video of Hank Jones on YouTube. In an interview, he demonstrates the tune "How High the Moon" using changes that one would never find in a fake book. Diatonic passing chords, diminished chords, chromatic passing chords, secondary dominants, modal interchange chords and tritone substitutes are available for him to use or not, as he chooses to express the harmony in the moment. This is not usually how my students play a tune like this. They play the same changes each chorus, and if there is a G major7 for 2 bars in the lead sheet version of the tune, they play G major7 for two bars. With the passing of musical giants like Hank Jones, this living, breathing sense of the harmony of songs is threatened. However, my primary motive here is really not to preserve something that we are in danger of losing. There are always great young players who use harmony with a lot of nuance and awareness of both historical and contemporary approaches. The point is that you should join this club if you are interested, and hopefully, this book will help you do so.

Jazz pianists like Teddy Wilson, Oscar Peterson, Duke Ellington, Art Tatum, Erroll Garner, Hank Jones, Cedar Walton, Red Garland, Bill Evans, Wynton Kelly, Tommy Flanagan, Barry Harris, Ahmad Jamal, Thelonious Monk, Phineas Newborn, Herbie Hancock, Richie Beirach, Mulgrew Miller, Bud Powell, Lennie Tristano, McCoy Tyner, Chick Corea, Keith Jarrett and Brad Mehldau made (or make) an art of reinterpreting the harmony of standards to create their own personal statements on these songs.

One other point here is worth mentioning. Many young players spend most of their time with musician's tunes and originals instead of jazz standards, aka songs from the Great American Songbook (Gershwin, Porter, Berlin, Van Heusen, Rogers, etc.) Tunes like "Giant Steps" or "Inner Urge" are great songs and wonderful vehicles for improvisation and of course, original compositions extend the boundaries of jazz and creative music. However, there is something that playing standard tunes teaches us about harmony that can't be learned from playing originals and "jazz tunes". It's as simple as the fact that almost everyone plays the exact same chord changes to "Giant Steps" but "Bye, Bye Blackbird" and "Embraceable You" are likely to contain subtle variations when performed by different musicians. Understanding these variations teaches you a lot about how tonal harmony works in jazz.

What I find in my classes on harmony (I teach in the Jazz M.M. Program at Queens College in New York) is not that students don't understand the techniques for re-harmonization (for the most part). Most of my students understand what a tritone substitute or a diatonic passing chord is before they take a class from me. However, knowing theoretically what these harmonic devices are is useless without practice employing them on tunes. When you hear a particularly artful or surprising use of harmony, knowing the name of the device used isn't the point. These moments may be very simple conceptually, but something grabs you: you hear a tune that you thought you knew in a new dress.

Harmony is all about drama. What do you want to say at a particular point in a tune? If I add a passing chord or secondary dominant it can make the next chord more important by preparing it, or it can make the next chord less interesting by giving away the surprise. Changing harmony slows down the forward motion of the tune down by making destination points in the song, or speeds it up by creating tension and momentum pushing toward a resolution. Using substitute chords can make part of the tune feel dark and gloomy or light and cheerful. Harmony takes the black and white outlines of the melody, and bathes them in color. Harmony is like lighting in a theatrical play. Students who haven't listened for the "harmonic message" that chords tell, often write and arrange music that feels leaden and arbitrary. My goal in writing this book is to help students become more sensitive to the story that chords are telling and the nuances of movement, tension and resolution that they suggest.

To become more harmonically sensitive you need to spend time with each of the techniques that you may already know, employing them over many different types of tunes.

Coming up as a young jazz player in Cleveland in the 70s and 80s, I used to hear older players playing unusual changes on familiar tunes, changes that weren't in fake books. They traded their discoveries on standards, savoring a chord change that was unexpected and challenging each other by inventing new chord progressions on the spot. I often didn't understand what they were doing but was intrigued by the "slightly wrong" changes that they were using to "hipify" the standard tunes they played. Playing together on steady gigs that might last years, pianists and bassists built a personal vocabulary of their arrangements. When I'd work with an older bassist, he would keep me on my toes, showing me different ways through the labyrinth of chord changes on a tune.

So now in my harmony classes, I try to sensitize students to this harmonic landscape. We start with simple hymns and Christmas carols and then move up to the world of standards. It's a cliche to say that I learn more from my students than they learn from me (and how would I know that anyway?) but I've learned a lot about harmony by preparing for these classes and from the responses that I get from students. I've been teaching jazz harmony classes for several years now and this has caused me to continually re-investigate my harmonic understanding and to expand my sense of what is possible a little further each time. At a clinic at a school where I was teaching, the great sax player and educator Dave Liebman was talking about the difficulty in teaching students to swing and play with a deep sense of groove and he said," Harmony is easy. Anyone can teach you harmony." Well, I agree with that. Harmony is easier to teach than how to swing. But this doesn't make the study of harmony any less interesting. In fact, it makes the lack of sensitivity to harmony even more regrettable, because it is something that any musical person can learn with a little commitment and attention. I think that jazz students in general and non-pianists in particular can benefit from trying to develop a stronger and more nuanced sense of how jazz harmony works.

This book is about the process of putting chord changes to melodies and the study of how chord progressions work. I need to stress that here—this book is not about soloing over chord changes and other aspects of jazz theory. It's a book about the different chords that can be used (and have been used by great pianists and arrangers of the past and present) to harmonize melodies.

This book consists of two main sections. The first part of the book discusses the key elements that make up the tonal universe (or the world of a key). Inside this universe, diatonic or functional harmonic relationships are present. This part of the book is concerned with the kind of harmonic manipulations that one finds the great pianists, guitarists and arrangers of the mainstream jazz tradition (Hank Jones, Thad Jones, Art Tatum, Oscar Peterson, etc.) using most of the time in their arrangements. The second part of the book deals with harmonic approaches that aren't, strictly speaking, functional, although to an extent, functionality in harmonic settings is, to quote a Dewey Redman record title, in the "ear of the behearer." These approaches help explain some additional harmonic moves of mainstream jazz players, as well as some of the harmonic techniques that we see in modern jazz pianists like Herbie Hancock, Richie Beirach and others. Finally, there are two appendices—first, tips for composing and second, a very essential piano primer for those needing a little help with piano voicings, since the best way for non-pianists to develop their harmonic sensitivity is to learn to play piano better.

One word of caution: I start at the beginning with how chords are constructed and some will be tempted to skip over the earlier sections of this book. I urge you not to skip over the "simple" parts of this book. (Okay, you can skip how to make seventh chords if you already know that, but don't skip the basic steps in harmonizing songs.) Skipping over things that you know already leads you away from the kind of in-depth exploration of harmonic techniques that I have in mind. As I said above, the harmonic tools are relatively easy to understand but are extremely beautiful and surprising when employed in just the right places.

This, like so many things, reminds me of a story. Many years ago, I was living in Boston and car-pooling to weekly lessons with a teacher who lived an hour north of the city. The other student that rode up with me had been studying jazz piano with this teacher for 3 years. One week, a snowstorm kept us from making the trip so we headed over to a practice room at Berklee and showed each other what we were working on. I played a re-harmonization of a standard that I was working on and the other student was confused by a simple diatonic substitution. I told him that I was just substituting one tonic chord for another and he said: "Tonic chords? What are those?" It amazed me that he could have come so far in music without this kind of basic knowledge. But it goes beyond not knowing the concept. Even if you already have some familiarity with the basic concept, ask yourself, 'do I use this device in my own playing?' That's the thing about complex jazz harmony: it comes on the back of simple jazz harmony and in almost every complex harmonic situation, it's the combination of complexity and simplicity that creates the richness of the mix. So if you are using slash chords, but have never employed a tritone substitute or used a 6th chord instead of a major 7th, you may find some new tools here for composing and arranging.

Try to approach the study of harmony with curiosity and an open mind. A few years back, the great jazz saxophonist Donny McCaslin took some piano lessons from me. Doing re-harmonizations and working at the keyboard was something he thought would help him and it was a pleasure to work with such a strong player, watching him use his impressive musical intelligence and diligent practice technique on an instrument that he didn't know as well as the saxophone. I've had a lot of great students, but it was very interesting seeing how this already developed saxophonist applied himself to the piano. Donny eventually got busy with other things, but I am sure he is still pursuing new directions and challenging himself to further his musical explorations. We can all benefit from taking a page from his book.

How to Use this Book

This book loosely follows the two semester graduate course in Jazz Harmony I teach at Queens College in New York. After each chapter, I encourage you to try to apply the harmonic approaches on as many tunes as you can. I've included written piano voicings for most of the examples. If you don't have a lot of piano skills these written voicings provide adequate versions of the harmony studied. I tried to walk a line here—hopefully not making the voicings so complicated that non-pianists couldn't manage to play them (at least most of the time), but not to making the voicings so simplistic that they wouldn't convey the mood that I was trying to create. In the accompanying CD you can hear all of these recorded examples. Study and listen to these examples and go over the material in Appendix B (on piano voicings) and try to develop the minimal keyboard knowledge that is necessary for understanding the harmonic concepts discussed. If the piano is unfamiliar to you, you can write out voicings in a notation program and listen to the results. Try hard not to skip any of the steps, but apply each concept: modal interchange chords, say, or diminished passing chords, over many, many standards. This material can only be internalized by doing the work at the keyboard, but it will reward you many times over with a deeper understanding of the harmonic foundations of jazz and modern music.

I've been told that I am asking a lot of the reader, but there's really no other way to master this material. Anyone who is serious about developing a deeper understanding of how jazz harmony works, and is willing to do some study, should be able to get a handle on most of the important concepts discussed here. Finally, though, let me urge you to take whatever is of value in this text and ignore the things that are not useful for you. This book is not a method book. It is a course in jazz harmony, specifically about the process of adding chords to melodies and it is filled with suggestions that serious students of jazz—players, arrangers and composers—may wish to try to deepen their understanding of jazz harmonic nuance.

Chapter 1 – The First Circle: I, IV and V7 chords

Creating Chords in a Key

Before we can talk about basic harmonization, we have to create the chords that we use to harmonize. We start with a major scale.

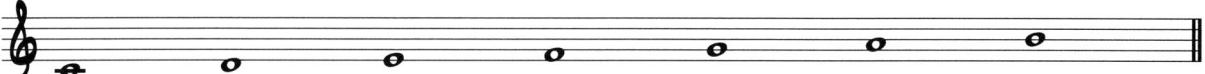

We can create chords built on each one of the degrees of a major scale. To make a triad (a 3-note chord) play the first note of a major scale, then skip the second note, play the third note, skip the fourth and play the fifth. (This chord is called the I chord because it is built on the first degree of the scale.) In a similar way, you can build a triad on the second degree of the scale by playing the second, fourth and sixth notes of the major scale (called the ii chord). To make a chord built on the third note of the major scale you'd play the third, fifth and seventh note of the scale. In this way, working upward, playing alternating notes of the scale, you can build triads starting on each note of the scale.

Because the major scale is not symmetrical, meaning it is composed of both half steps and whole steps that don't occur in an even pattern, these chords are not all the same type of chord. The I, IV and V chords are major triads (three note chords comprised of the interval of a major third between the bottom two notes and the interval of a minor third between the top two notes), the ii, iii and vi chords are minor triads (three note chords comprised of the interval of a minor third between the bottom two notes and the interval of a major third between the top two notes) and the vii chord is a diminished triad (a three note chord comprised of two minor thirds). Following common practice, I use upper case roman numerals for major chords (and augmented) and lower case roman numerals for all other chord types. The three major triads are the most centrally important chords of a key. They can be combined into cadences, which are the basic harmonic building blocks of songs.

Basic Cadences

Cadences are harmonic phrases, the "sentences" that music is written in. The most common cadence, the "full" cadence is the famous I IV V I cadence that defines so much harmonic movement in western harmony. As you can see, it begins on the I chord. This chord occupies the home position in a key—the most resolved and free of tension place in the harmony; the root, the key center—home base. The I chord is the name of the chord (since it is built on the first degree of the major scale) but the quality that I am describing is called the "function" of the chord. To say that a chord has a function in a progression or in a key means that the chord is behaving in the way that we expect it to behave, leading somewhere or returning from somewhere. The function of the I chord, defining where home base is, is called the "tonic" function, and the I chord is referred to as a "tonic-functioning" chord or "tonic" chord for short. The IV chord comes next in our cadence and it has a feeling of moving away from home, but it isn't a particularly tense chord and so doesn't require immediate resolution. This function is traditionally called "subdominant" or "dominant preparation" and is characterized by a feeling of moving away from the I or tonic, but without an intense desire to resolve back to the tonic. The V chord, or "dominant", which comes next in the cadence, has a very strong pull back toward the tonic. Songs rarely end on the dominant, but lead back to the I chord (home); the tonic or tonal center of the key.

So we have these three chords with three important functions. They can be combined in several different sorts of cadences:

1. **I, IV, V, I**
2. **I, IV, I**
3. **I, V, I**
4. **I, IV, V**

Think of the first cadence (the above-mentioned "full" cadence) as the most essential, like a noun/verb/object kind of sentence in prose. We start on home base, take a step away from home, go to a new place where we are feeling a strong pull back toward home and then—we return home.

This may be the most common cadence, but it would be boring to have only one type of cadence to work with. It's as if we only had one type of sentence to write prose with:

"The dog ate the piano." "The bigamist hit the cow." "The piranha taught French." "The teacher drew a boomerang." "The antelope expressed regret."

This is a very limiting way to write. We need different types of sentences: some compound, some simple. Even sentence fragments. Haven't you noticed that it changes the flow of a paragraph to end on a question from time to time?

So, for variety's sake, we have different types of sentences in prose and different types of cadences in music. The second kind of cadence, (#2 above) is called a plagal cadence, most famously, the Amen chord at the end of a hymn. The IV chord has a much weaker pull back to the tonic, but there is **some** pull toward resolution and so in the end we return to I and that gives this cadence it's breathy, somewhat less urgent quality. We sit on the IV chord for a moment, and without tremendous hurry, we resolve back to the I. ("Ahhhhhhh"—IV chord—"men"—I chord.)

THE FIRST CIRCLE: I, IV AND V7 CHORDS   CHAPTER 1

The third cadence, I V I, is like the ending of a traditional symphony piece—think of tympani banging out the I, V, I, V, I, V again and again, delaying the final resolution. With each reiteration of the I we think we might be finished but the V comes back and then we know we're going to have to resolve to the I chord again——we need to get back home, we can't just stay on the V. Also, a V to I cadence can be thought of as a kind of sketchier form of the full cadence. It's a full cadence with the IV chord left out (the least important chord of the cadence). I V I is a "just the facts, mam" kind of cadence.

The fourth cadence listed above is a different sort. It's a half-cadence, meaning that it ends on the dominant chord. It's like ending on a question, isn't it? By ending some phrases on the dominant, there is a strong pull toward the beginning of the next phrase. Songs almost never end with a half-cadence, but a section that ends on a half-cadence sets up the next phrase and keeps things moving.

These cadences and these three chords are enough to play most basic songs, as anyone with a very small knowledge of guitar and the desire to play "Jimmy Crack Corn" can tell you. When I first learned the G, C and D triads on my Stella Harmony guitar in Junior High School, I had the keys to the kingdom (as long as the kingdom consisted of songs like "Jimmy Crack Corn"). Some of these songs might sound better with more than three chords, but most simple folk songs, hymns and simple diatonic songs like traditional Christmas carols can be harmonized effectively with these few basic chords.

Let's try some examples and see. Here is the melody of "O Christmas Tree".

The song is in F major so you should try to harmonize it using only the I, IV and V chords of F which are F, Bb and C. Most people, given only these three chords to work with, will harmonize this tune more or less as I've done below. There may be some different versions of the third bar of the tune (which is repeated three times in the form.) I've opted for IV to V in this bar, but some might prefer just the V (I V I instead of I IV V I) but that's a minor point. The main point is that the melodies of these songs have a kind of built-in harmonic structure for which there is (more or less) general agreement.

CHAPTER 1

THE FIRST CIRCLE: I, IV AND V7 CHORDS

(CD TRACK 1)

THE FIRST CIRCLE: I, IV AND V7 CHORDS   CHAPTER 1

I want to point out that I am not thinking analytically here. Just use your ear and put the I, IV and V triads where you think they sound best. Finding where the tonic, subdominant and dominant functions occur on a simple melody is something that most musical people can do. The chords will be suggested by the melody of the song and your memory of how it is usually played. Notice that in the above harmonization of "O Christmas Tree" I used mostly I and V chords. I added a IV chord before the V chord in bar 15 (this bar has the same melody that I harmonized with just a V chord in bars 3 and 7.) As I mentioned above, this is often an option, to add or subtract a sub-dominant chord before the V chord. I added it here because I think some of you will harmonize the melody that way.

I am doing this without thinking too much about what note is occurring on each chord. If you analyze the melody, you will notice that the melody often lands on chord tones (1, 3 and 5) of the chords you chose. But again, I'm not thinking too much about these details—I'm just letting my intuition tell me where to place I, IV and V.

Try this on your own. Harmonize the following well-known tunes with I, IV and V chords only. Those of you who have minimal knowledge of the piano can refer to my simple piano voicings for the tune above. Keep in mind with piano voicings that root position chords (1,3,5 in stacked thirds) have a tendency to get muddy lower on the instrument and can be avoided by leaving out notes in the harmony that are doubled in the melody or by putting the third (the 1, **3**, 5) in the right hand below the melody (1,5 **10**). Occasionally I doubled the root of the chord in octaves for a little variety, but this isn't necessary to hear these chord qualities.

"Happy Birthday"

CHAPTER 1

THE FIRST CIRCLE: I, IV AND V7 CHORDS

SILENT NIGHT

You probably had something like the following (again, with variations in the use of IV **and** V or just V to harmonize some bars).

THE FIRST CIRCLE: I, IV and V7 chords CHAPTER 1

(CD TRACK 2)　　　　　　　"HAPPY BIRTHDAY"

CHAPTER 1

THE FIRST CIRCLE: I, IV AND V7 CHORDS

(CD TRACK 3) "Silent Night"

8

THE FIRST CIRCLE: I, IV AND V7 CHORDS CHAPTER 1

Notice in the above cases that several different kinds of cadences occur in these songs. For example, "Silent Night" begins with an extended period (4 bars) of I chord. Bars 5 and 6 have a V to I cadence, but bars 9 through 16 are plagal cadences, or IV for two bars followed by I for two bars. I have bar 17 as a V chord—although if you had it as a IV chord leading to a V chord in bar 18 that also makes a lot of musical sense. (Classical theorists might have issues with this liberal approach to adding I, IV and V chords wherever you hear them and if you study classical harmony, these harmonic choices are discussed in a lot greater detail particularly in relation to harmonizing melody notes that aren't chord tones. However, as I said above, you can do this by ear— you don't have to be aware of all the rules of chorale harmony to apply I, IV and V triads to folk tunes. You can start by seeing what sounds good and natural to you, since whether you know it or not, you have been absorbing the "rules" of functional harmony unconsciously all of your life.)

Creating Sixth and Seventh Chords

Harmonizing using triads provides a strong clear statement of the basic harmony, but triads aren't the only type of chord available to us and they aren't the type of chord most often used in jazz, so you may have felt a little limited by having only triads to work with. Four-note chords, called seventh chords, are constructed in the same way we built triads above, by stacking the notes of the scale in thirds. So, the I triad becomes a four-note chord by adding the next note of the scale a third above. This chord is called a I major7th chord. (The "Δ" symbol is commonly used as a designation for major so a "CΔ7" means C major7) . If we add a note a third above a IV chord we get a IV major7 and if we add a note a third above a V chord (a minor third above this time,

9

CHAPTER 1

THE FIRST CIRCLE: I, IV AND V7 CHORDS

due to the asymmetrical distribution of half-steps in the major scale) we get a V7. (This last type of seventh chord is called a dominant seventh). Jazz harmony differs from classical harmony in that these seventh chords don't always need to resolve: the I major7 is considered a stable, tonic sound. However, the major7 does have some dissonance that I may not want as the resolution point of a given cadence. This dissonance is especially pronounced when the melody lands on the root of the chord (as it often is at the end of a song) so we have additional four-note chords available to us: the major6 is constructed by adding the 6th (a whole step above the 5th) instead of the 7th note of the chord. (I major 6th and IV major 6th chords are common, but the V6 is not.)

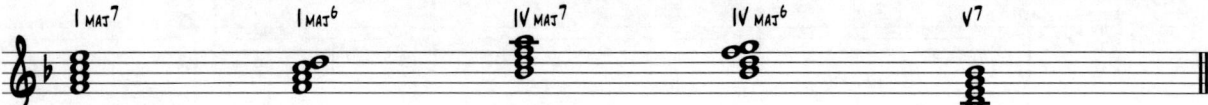

I've built all these chords by thinking of a major scale and using every other note as I stack the scale in thirds. However, it's usually more useful to be able to visualize these chords as independent of scales. So it's worth noting that any major7th is a major triad plus a note that is an interval of a major 7th above the root, and that a dominant seventh is a major triad plus a note that is an interval of a minor 7th above the root. When we are viewing chords as *qualities* (meaning, types of chords, so all major 7th chords or all dominant 7th chords) we speak of the chord tones as 1, 3, 5, and 7 for these stacked thirds above the root. If I want to be more precise I can relate these numbers to a major scale so a dominant seventh chord would have these chord tones: 1, 3, 5 and b7 because the 7th you find on a C dominant7 is a half step lower than the seventh note of a C major scale.

I've grouped these seventh chords together because that makes it easier to explain how they are constructed, but actually, the dominant7 is a more fundamental sound than the I major7 or IV major7 chords. In most triadic situations, the dominant chord is a dominant7 and not a dominant triad. (Again, those of you with very limited guitar ability will know this, since you learned G, C and D7 among your first chords, or maybe A, D and E7.) That's because the addition of the seventh to the dominant triad makes its function as a dominant chord **clearer**. The dominant 7th chord is a chord with an inherent instability to it—which is a fancy way of saying it wants to resolve. It wants to resolve because it contains the interval of a tritone between the 3rd and 7th of the chord. This is a very unstable sound, a dissonance, which, in traditional classical harmony, has an urgent need to resolve. The notes of the tritone each want to resolve to important notes of the I chord.

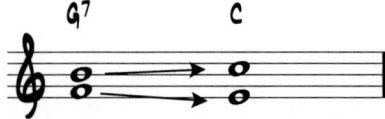

The addition of a 7th or a 6th to a major triad in major7 or major6 chords, softens our sense of the chord's function—meaning that a I major triad is the most tonic sound and I major6 or I major7 are slightly softer expressions of the tonic. The dominant seventh however, with its internal tritone, is the strongest expression of the dominant function of the V chord, stronger than the V major triad. (This is also why you rarely see V major 6th chords—the major 6th sound makes the chord feel (or in more musical terms, function) less like dominant.

CHAPTER 1

The First Circle: I, IV and V7 chords

Harmonizing Melodies with Seventh Chords

Let's look at the first few bars of "Silent Night" harmonized with seventh and sixth chords.

(CD TRACK 4)

You can see in the above example, that we have more harmonic options now, even though the function of the chords, that is, where I, IV and V occur, is the same as in the simpler triadic harmonization of this song. This illustrates a very important point: as you re-harmonize, it's important to keep in mind what the fundamental I, IV and V relationships are of the song's basic structure. You can substitute chord changes that have the same function more easily than chord changes that have a different function. That's because, as we saw above, the tonic, subdominant and dominant functions are written into the DNA of the melody. When you re-harmonize songs and ignore the expected harmonic functions of chords usually associated with a particular melody, you do so at your peril and risk chord progressions that feel random and arbitrary.

So this is the first of our concentric circles: the most basic ways songs can be harmonized using only the I, IV and V7.

One more thing should be mentioned before we move on to other diatonic seventh chords. All of the chords we've discussed so far have had the root of the chord on the bottom, so a C major triad had a C in the bass (the lowest note of the voicing). Of course, we can change the order of the notes of a chord, putting a different note in the bass if we wish. These re-orderings are called inversions of a chord. A triad can appear in root position, with the root of the chord in bass, in first inversion with the 3rd in the bass or in second inversion with the 5th of the chord in the bass.

A 7th chord can appear in four different inversions: root position with the root of the chord in the bass, 1st inversion with the 3rd of the chord in the bass, 2nd inversions with the 5th of the chord in the bass and 3rd inversion with the 7th of the chord in the bass.

The most common reason for inverting a chord is to create a more melodic line in the bass voice. Because the bass note of the chord is so important, inversions feel different from root position chords and they have a slightly different sense of harmonic function, which we'll get to in the next chapter.

CHAPTER 2 – THE SECOND CIRCLE: DIATONIC SEVENTH CHORD SUBSTITUTES FOR I, IV AND V7

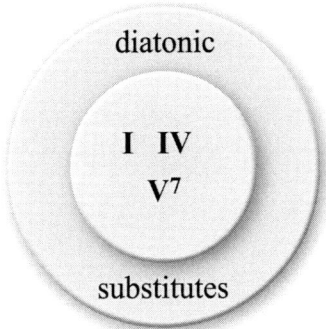

The next circle gives us the rest of the chords that are built on the scale degrees of the major scale: the ii minor triad, the iii minor triad, the vi minor triad and the vii diminished triad. If we add sevenths to these triads we get the following: ii minor7, iii minor7, vi minor7 and vii minor7 b5 (or half-diminished7). (Minor is often notated using the symbol " – ", so a C minor7 is commonly written as a C-7.)

Diatonic Sevenths in C major

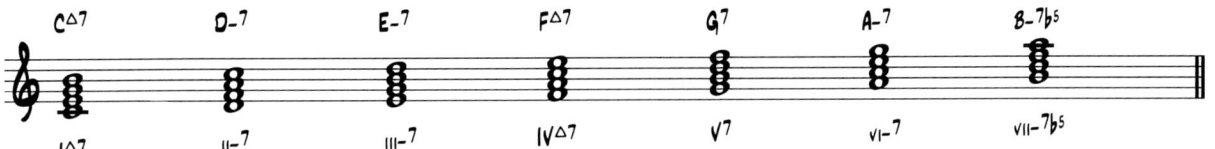

Note that these seventh chords come in two chord qualities that we haven't seen yet: minor7, a minor triad with a fourth note added a minor seventh (interval) above the root and minor7 b5, a diminished triad with a fourth note added a minor seventh (interval) above the root.

These new chords all act either like a tonic chord, a subdominant chord or a dominant chord. That means that we can plug them into our cadences substituting tonic chords for the I chord, subdominant chords for the IV chord and dominant chords for the V7. These substitutions give us more harmonic options, variety and changes of color while still maintaining the logic of the harmonic phrase. It's like the difference between the sentences, "My armadillo is sad." and "My armadillo is consumed by an existential depression." They mean essentially the same or at least a similar thing, but the nuance is different.

The tonic chords are I major7 or major6, iii-7 and vi-7. Subdominant chords are IV major7 and ii-7. Dominant chords are V7 and vii-7b5.

    Tonic: I major7, I major6, iii-7, vi-7
    Subdominant: IVmajor7, ii-7
    Dominant: V7, vii-7b5

CHAPTER 2

THE SECOND CIRCLE: DIATONIC SEVENTH CHORD SUBSTITUTES FOR I, IV AND V7

Using All of the Diatonic Chords to Harmonize Songs

So now we have a lot of choices for how to harmonize a simple song. We can use I, IV and V in triadic, seventh or (in the case of the I chords) 6th forms, we can also use ii minor7, iii minor 7, vi-7 and vii-7b5. So from the basic full cadence:

    I IV V I

We can create myriad variations by using the following diatonic substitutes:

    I IV V vi
    I IV V iii
    iii IV V I
    vi IV V I
    iii IV V iii
    iii IV V vi
    vi IV V vi
    vi IV V iii
    I ii V I
    I ii V iii
    I ii V vi
    iii ii V I
    iii ii V vi
    vi ii V I
    vi ii V iii
    vi ii V vi
    I IV vii I
    I IV vii iii
    I IV vii vi
    iii IV vii I

and that's not including the ones I left out because of my mediocre mathematical ability. I didn't even get to variations mixing triads, 7ths and 6ths chords. I could also add inversions. There are a LOT more possibilities now.

I keep mentioning Christmas Carols, but tunes like "Silent Night" have passed into the world of popular song. Chorales are good illustrations of these cadences functioning in their pure form such as this excerpt from the first chorale of Book I (4-Part Chorales of J.S.Bach.)

THE SECOND CIRCLE: DIATONIC SEVENTH CHORD SUBSTITUTES FOR I, IV AND V7

(My apologies to classical theory students, to avoid a discussion of classical methods of labeling inversions, I used the jazz method of labeling inversions, the chord followed by a slash and the scale degree of the bass note. I'm not advocating this technique, but it simplifies things by avoiding introducing another system of analysis and labeling at this point.)

This is one of Bach's simpler Chorales, harmonically speaking. Most of the cadences are variations on I IV V I with inversions used to create more melodically interesting parts for voices. In the second full bar (bar 3) we have a I V vi cadence (much like our I V I cadence in that it has no subdominant and the final I chord is replaced by a different tonic triad, the vi.) Bar 4 has a IV V I cadence following the vi triad on beat 3 of the third bar. Bar 5 has a V to I cadence, and in bar 6 the vii chord replaces the V in a I V I type cadence (so I vii I). Bar 7 is a full cadence with the ii-7 (note the note G held over in the alto voice from the first beat of the measure) replacing the IV chord. You'll notice that even though there is a lot of variety in the bass notes of these chords due to the use of inversions, the basic cadences are similar to what we've discussed above. The use of the vi, vii and ii chords as substitutes provide additional harmonic color.

As I mentioned above, these diatonic substitutes are not exact equivalents of the tonic, subdominant and dominant chords that they replace—but they have a logic similar to the I, IV and V harmonizations we did above. Some of these substitutes are easier to use than others. For example, in a jazz context, ii-7 to V7 to I major7 is a more common cadence than IV to V7 to I major. In fact, in the world of jazz, the IV chord is more of a substitute for ii minor7 than the other way around. In either case, the substitution of a IV for a ii chord is usually less of a dramatic shift than the substitution of a vii minor7 b5 for V7 chord. In this case, the vii-7b5 often feels like an awkward choice for a V7 (in part because the minor7 b5 occurs much more often with a different function, as the ii chord in minor, as we shall see later.) The substitution of iii-7 and vi-7 for I is common, but (especially in contexts where the I major7 is particularly expected—say at the end of a tune) it can feel like a fairly radical change of color. All this is just a way of saying that you have to check out these sounds carefully and be sensitive to the different colors these substitutes provide and not just blindly substitute tonic for tonic, subdominant for subdominant and dominant for dominant.

Now, with these new substitutes available to us, we can return to "Silent Night". Even though I, IV and V provided a marginally adequate harmonization of the song, you may have felt that something was missing when you compared the harmony that we came up with to your own memory of the way the tune is normally played. That's because the use of harmonic substitutes is so clearly etched into your sense of how the song goes.

Here's one possible harmonization:

Chapter 2

The Second Circle: diatonic seventh chord substitutes for I, IV and V7

(CD TRACK 5)

THE SECOND CIRCLE: DIATONIC SEVENTH CHORD SUBSTITUTES FOR I, IV AND V7   CHAPTER 2

If you refer to simple first circle chords "Silent Night" you'll see that most of the substitutes followed the I, IV, V harmony with a few exceptions. In bars 5, 10 and 14, I added a ii minor7 to the V7 to lead back to the tonic chord. Still, this re-harmonization follows, more or less, the harmonic functions of the original harmony. It's not impossible to change the function of a chord and put a tonic chord where a dominant usually goes—never, say never—but this kind of manipulation often makes a re-harmonization feel more arbitrary.

I could create many variations of the harmony of "Silent Night" and each one will be slightly different, with a slightly different mood or color, depending on which diatonic substitutes I employ.

Inversions can often mimic the function of chords that are built on a particular bass note. Thus, in the key of C, a C/E is a tonic chord variation on the I chord a bit similar in feeling to the iii-7, and a C/G acts a bit like a dominant (in classical harmony, the cadential 6 4 is a I chord in 2nd inversion that usually leads to a dominant.) Classical music is filled with inversions and inversions ARE used in jazz harmony as well, although not to the same extent as in classical music. This is probably because so much of jazz harmony is conceived in relationship to the root of the chord, particularly as chords become filled with "tensions" or the upper-structure notes of the chord. The more complex a chord becomes, the more likely it is that it will have a root in the bass.

Now would be a good time to go back to the other songs that you harmonized with I, IV and V and add diatonic substitutes. See if you can come up with more than one harmonic variation that you like for each of these songs, without changing the harmonic function of these progressions.

Chapter 3 – The Third Circle: Secondary Dominant Seventh and Related ii Minor7 Chords

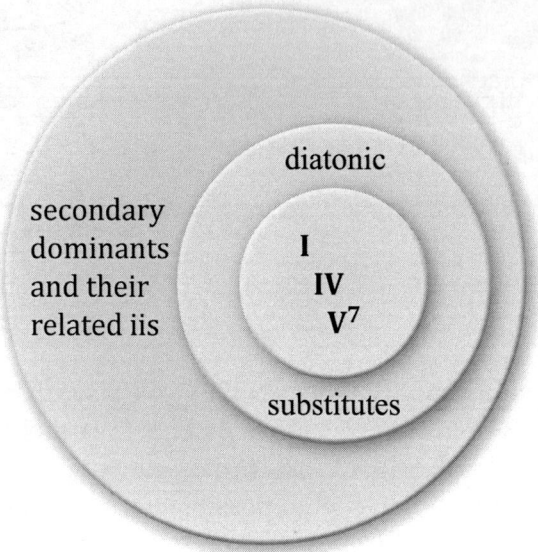

One defining element of the first two harmonic circles is that all of the notes of all the chords come from the major scale. All of the other circles that we are studying will contain chords that have notes that are not found in the major scale. These circles cause us to move outward into a larger and larger pool of available notes, and yet, all of these chords **function** in the key, meaning, that these chords with their notes from outside of the scale still behave like tonic, subdominant and dominant chords (more or less). These chords from outside the scale behave in ways that create the network of harmonic relationships that defines the harmony of a key.

The harmony of the third circle comes about because of the centrality of the V7 to I relationship in western harmony. You could say that the V7 chord resolving to the I chord is the engine that drives tonal harmony. Subdominant function is important, but ultimately the progression builds toward the V7 that will lead to I. V7 defines where I is by making the arrival at this point of resolution a target or destination.

For this reason, the first chords that we are going to add to our diatonic harmony are the dominant7 chords that lead to the diatonic seventh chords built on the degrees of the major scale other than I. These chords are called "secondary dominants", because they are not the dominant7 chord of the key, (the V7) but rather the V7's of each of the other diatonic seventh chords. So (in the key of C) A7 is the V7 of the ii chord, D-7; B7 is the V7 of the iii chord, E-7; C7 is the V7 of the IV chord, F major7; D7 is the V7 of the V chord, G7; E7 is the V7 of the vi chord, A-7 and F#7 is the V7 of the vii chord (although it tends to be used less than the other secondary dominant chords), B-7b5. (Secondary dominants are usually written with the dominant on the left side of a forward slash and the target chord on the right, so, for example, V7 of ii is written as V7/ii.)

THE THIRD CIRCLE: SECONDARY DOMINANT SEVENTH AND RELATED II MINOR7 CHORDS — CHAPTER 3

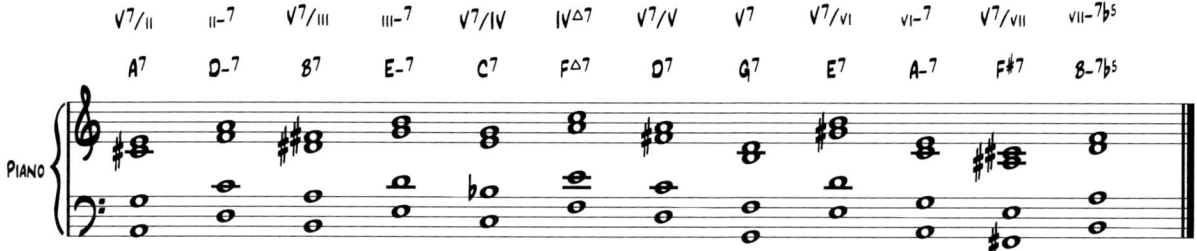

To repeat, it's logical that, if we are going to start adding non-diatonic chords to our list of chords available to harmonize melodies with, the first chords we add are dominant sevenths of the diatonic chords that we are already using. These secondary dominants point to the chord that they are the dominant of. They do this because they have that same strong desire to resolve to those target chords that the dominant7 of the key (the V7) has to resolve to the I chord.

So, if the progression D minor7 to G7 to C major7 is changed to D7 to G7 to C major7, there's a little more of a push in that first chord to resolve to the G7. This secondary dominant (in this case: V7 of V) also makes G7 a little more of a destination point, because it is the target of the D7 chord change. The difference can be explained like this: D-7 prepares us for the G7 that resolves to the C major7, but D7 propels us to the G7 that resolves to the C major7. I can use these secondary dominants to add more movement to any progression: C major7, D-7, G7, C maj7 becomes C major7, A7, D-7, D7, G7, C major 7; or C major7, E7, A minor7, A7, D-7, D7, G7, C major7. Working backwards from the target chord, I can even leave out the first C major7 and begin my re-harmonization with a secondary dominant: B7, E minor7, E7, A minor7, etc.

Whether or not I can use the secondary dominant (as with any harmonic substitution) depends on how the new chord works with the melody. Dominants tend to be quite flexible because there are a lot of possible notes that can be played over them (see below: available tensions on seventh chords).

Used in this way, secondary dominants have a lot of power to transform a progression. This simple harmonic principle tends to be under-utilized by jazz students. In many solo recordings by Art Tatum, Oscar Peterson, Hank Jones and Thelonious Monk (to name a few of the many jazz pianists who employ this technique often), we hear loads of secondary dominants, making chains of altered chords that start in surprising places but eventually lead to a target chord or cadence point in the original harmony of the tune.

Along with these secondary dominants, we can add the ii minor7 chords associated with them, as we did above when we added the C-7 to the F7 in "Silent Night". These minor7 chords are alled "related ii minor7s". They are the ii minor7 chords in the key of the secondary dominant. Adding these chords creates something like a small modulation to a new key, but for such a brief amount of time that we don't really feel it as a modulation. It's just a quick harmonic movement that sets up the target chord. So in the progression D-7 to G7 to C major7, we can precede the D-7 with an A7 (V7/ii). We can precede the A7 with the ii chord of D minor. However, the ii chord in a minor key is not a minor7. The ii chord in a minor key is a ii-7b5, so we can add an E-7b5 before the

CHAPTER 3
THE THIRD CIRCLE: SECONDARY DOMINANT SEVENTH AND RELATED II MINOR7 CHORDS

A7. (This isn't very complicated. To find the ii chord in a minor key you just have to build diatonic 7th chords using the notes of the natural minor scale. For example, the key of C minor has 3 flats: Bb, Eb and Ab. If you build a seventh chord on the second degree of the scale (a ii chord) you get a D minor7b5—the fifth, the A, is flat in this key. I'm fudging a little bit here to avoid a more lengthy discussion of minor scales, but the important point is this: the ii chord that belongs with a dominant7 of a minor chord is a ii-7b5.)

So the secondary dominant and related ii chords in C major are:

E minor7b5 to A7 to D minor7 (ii-7b5/ii, V7/ii)
F# minor7b5 to B7 to E minor7 (ii-7b5/iii V7/iii)
G minor7 to C7 to F major7 (ii-7/IV V7/IV)
A minor7 to D7 to G7 (ii-7/V V7/V)
B minor7 to E7 to A minor7 (ii-7b5/vi V7/vi)
C# minor7b5 to F#7 to B-7b5 (ii-7b5/vii V7/vii)

Available Tensions on Chords

We have been treating seventh chords as four-note chords and of course they **are** four-note chords in the sense that they have four "chord tones" (1, 3, 5, 7 for sevenths and 1, 3, 5, 6 for 6th chords). These chord tones give the fundamental sound of the chord. However, there are other notes that may be added to these chord tones to give the chord more harmonic color. These notes are called tensions (sometimes referred to as "extensions" or "upper-structure" notes of the chord). Tensions are added to chords in a similar way to the way chords are built, by stacking thirds. If I continue stacking thirds as I build the chord upwards from 1, 3, 5 and 7, I get 9ths, 11ths and 13ths. These notes are essentially the same as 2nds, 4ths and 6ths but by convention when we are thinking of them as part of a chord (built vertically) we use these larger numbers to continue the progression of stacked thirds: 1, 3, 5, 7, 9, 11 and 13.

So how do I know what type of third (major or minor) to use when stacking 9ths, 11ths and 13ths on to a chord? Or in other words, when do I use b9, #9, natural 9, 11 or #11, b13 or 13? In our earlier chord building we simply used the major scale to find all of the chord tones, but that isn't always a suitable method when I am thinking vertically. Using the notes of a major scale to choose the tensions for diatonic chord types will often add dissonance, more dissonance than we commonly hear on these chords. One way of addressing this problem is to think of every chord type as having certain standard tensions that are used. Just as it's important to be able to construct seventh chords without referring to a major scale (a triad + a seventh) it's also important to be able to recognize and easily find the commonly used available tensions on each chord independent of any scale or key center.

Actually, it's fairly easy to find the appropriate tensions on a chord, because for most chords, one simple rule applies. The standard tensions for most sevenths are found one major 9th interval (a whole step + an octave) above the root, 3rd and 5th of each chord (and in the case of diminished sevenths, above the root, 3rd, 5th and 7th of the chord).

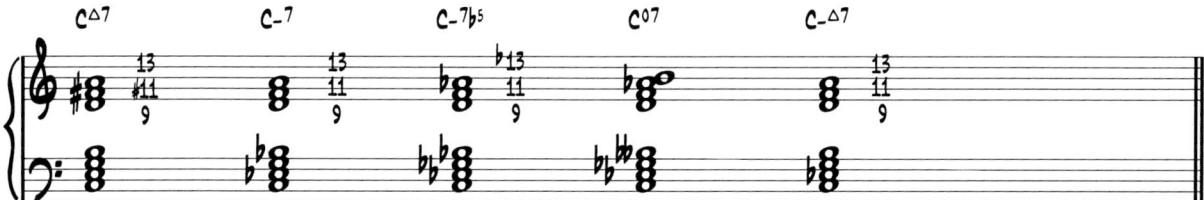

So, looking at the available tensions above, you can see that C major7 (and, of course, any major7) has a ninth that would be found a whole step (+ an octave) above its root, or in C, a D. This note is called a "9". The 11th that you find for this same chord located one whole step (+ an octave) above the 3rd of the chord is an interval of a #11th above the root, so this note is called the #11. The appropriate 13th is a whole step (+ an octave) above the fifth of the chord and is called a "13".

I started playing jazz piano when I was pretty young, 12 or so, but I wasn't terribly serious about if for several years. I always had a fairly incomplete sense of harmony until I went to Berklee for a few semesters when I was 19. Before that, I had wondered why you use an F# on a C major7 when a C major scale has no F# in it. The reason is that when we are thinking about available tensions (vertically, like a chord built from the root as opposed to horizontally, like a scale) we harmonize the chord with tensions that are consonant and usually avoid b9 intervals. The F natural of the C major scale adds a sound that would be inappropriate in most mainstream jazz settings because it is a b9 interval above the third of the chord and so creates an unappealing dissonance. While this dissonance may occasionally be used (and we'll discuss this down the line when we get to "unavailable tensions" on chords used by contemporary players) one can say that in the traditional jazz language, the language of Oscar Peterson, Bud Powell and Bill Evans, the natural 11 occurs rarely on major7 chords. (We do find F naturals played on C major chords, but they occur as passing melody notes, brief melodic dissonances that resolve, most often to the third of the chord. This is different from a tension, which is considered a stable part of the chord sound, not a melodic passing note.).

For the C minor7 chord change the appropriate 9th is once again a whole step (+ an octave) above the root, the appropriate 11th is a whole step (+ an octave) above the minor 3rd and the appropriate 13th is whole step (+ an octave) above the 5th. So we have 9, 11 and 13 available to use on these chords.

For the C minor7b5 chord change, the appropriate 9th is once again a whole step (+ an octave) above the root, the appropriate 11th is again a whole step (+ an octave) above the minor 3rd and the thirteenth is a whole step (+ an octave) above the flatted 5th. 9, 11 and b13 are available on this chord type.

For the C diminished7 chord change, the appropriate tensions are found a whole step (+ an octave) above each of the chord tones. Due to the special nature of diminished chords (they have an 8 note symmetrical scale, rather than a 7 note asymmetrical scale), which we will discuss later, these tensions aren't usually referred to as 9ths, 11ths, and 13ths, but the important thing to notice here is that the same rule applies and the color tones of the chord—the tensions—are found a whole step above the chord tones.

If you are unfamiliar with this theory, I'd recommend that you practice the above voicings at the piano, slowly, in every key, starting with C major then F, Bb, Eb, Ab, Db, Gb, B, E, A, D and G. This intervallic movement is called the circle of 5ths because each chord is the 5th of the next chord and is the same intervallic movement we find in secondary dominants. (C is the V of F, F is the V of Bb, Bb is the V of Eb, etc. See Appendix B, Piano Basics for more suggestions of keyboard/harmony exercises to practice.)

We've talked about the available tensions for all of the chord types we've been studying but we left out a very important chord type, dominant7th chords. That's because the easy-to-apply rule given above, that tensions are located a whole step above the 1, 3rd and 5th of the chord, doesn't suffice to give a list of the available tensions for dominant7ths. That's because there are a lot more available tensions on dominant7ths than on other chords.

Dominant sevenths have the same tensions available that the above chords have, the tensions located a whole step above the root, 3rd and 5th of the chord (the natural 9, #11, and 13) but they also have what are usually called "altered" tensions, the b9, #9 and b13. These tensions create stronger dissonances when played against the chord tones of the dominant chord. All of these color notes increase the dissonance of the dominant 7th, but they don't undermine our sense of the chord's function. The dominant7th which has a lot of tension built into it (the tritone interval that defines the dominant7th) can take on additional tension without losing its function as a dominant7th. When we hear this tense chord we expect them to resolve up a fourth to the I chord (or target of a secondary dominant) eventually.

THE THIRD CIRCLE: SECONDARY DOMINANT SEVENTH AND RELATED II MINOR7 CHORDS — CHAPTER 3

These are the available tensions on dominant 7th chords:

Some of these tensions are more tense than others: the natural 9 and natural 13 are warm and relaxed sounds, the altered tensions: b9, #9 and b13 are darker, more dissonant colors. The #11 is an edgy tense sound. These associations are dependent on musical context and to some extent are subjective, but you need to become very sensitive to the sound of each of these tensions, because using these tensions selectively has a large impact on the harmony of your writing and arranging. The sound of altered tensions on dominant 7th chords is one of the defining sounds of jazz harmony.

Tensions tend to come in certain combinations: we find b9 and #9 together, but not natural 9 and b9 or natural 9 and #9. The same goes for b13 and 13, they are rarely played together, and when b13 is found in a chord, generally the 5th of the chord is not present. (The natural 5th tends to be an expendable note that doesn't add a lot of color to seventh chords). The reason for this is that we commonly find the b9 interval on dominant7th chords only between the root of the chord and the b9 tension. Other intervals of the b9 (for example, between the 3rd and the natural 11th, the b9 and natural 9th or the 5th and the b13th) are deemed to be too dissonant for common usage.

Which tensions are chosen on dominant7ths is, to a large extent, dependent on the chord that follows the dominant7th. Since we are talking about secondary dominants in this chapter, the dominant7ths here are acting like V7 chords, resolving to a target chord up a fourth. In this situation, the altered tensions are often used, especially if the target chord of the dominant7th is a minor chord.

There are lots of rules for which tensions you should use on which dominant7th chords and we'll discuss some of these a bit more later, but more important than remembering theoretical rules is getting a sense of what all of these tensions sound like. Then, of course, you can make your own choices for which tensions you wish to use on them. In general, altered tensions tend to create more dissonance and a stronger desire for the dominant7th chord to resolve up a fourth to a target chord. Natural 9ths and 13ths tend to soften dominant7ths a bit, adding colors that don't create as strong a need for resolution. They are often used instead of altered tensions in dominant7th chords that don't resolve up a fourth, dominant7ths that are followed by a chord a different interval away.

Once again, if you are not familiar with all of the available tensions I've been discussing you should refer to the available tensions on major 7ths, minor 7ths, minor7b5s, diminished 7ths and dominant 7ths listed below and practice them slowly in all keys. (See "the complete set of seventh chords and their available tensions", below). Play the chord tones in your left hand and the tensions in your right, taking them through the circle of fifths.

23

One last point should be stressed about available tensions on chords. "Available" means just that, that these tensions are available to you if you want to use them. "Available" tensions are like available spices in your spice rack—if you own them, they're available to you. But having purchased a bottle of celery seed or fennel doesn't make you a great cook and using those particular spices in your next batch of chocolate chip cookies might be a questionable decision, available or not. So, you can use any or all of these tensions on seventh chords. You should look for opportunities to use all these different types of tensions in order to become familiar with the effects that they have, and where they fit or don't fit on tunes.

However, it should also be mentioned that (in most mainstream jazz contexts) tensions are used constantly on all types of chords. It's possible that you might occasionally want to use only chord tones on a particular voicing, but this occurs a lot less often than most of my harmony students seem to think. It's pretty rare to hear a dominant seventh in a mainstream jazz setting without some tension (or tensions) on it. In addition to this, adding tensions to chords usually makes them flow better in a progression by softening their functionality. (You'll remember from our discussion of tonic, subdominant and dominant chords that the I triad was the most tonic functioning chord and that adding the seventh softened that function a bit by adding a subtle color (and a subtle dissonance). This is also true of tensions, which add more colors to functional harmonic contexts.)

The Complete Set of Seventh Chords and Their Available tensions

I've been introducing seventh chords slowly until now—that is, introducing them as we encountered them in each circle—and now we've encountered most of the chord qualities that commonly occur on standard tunes. It's necessary to become familiar with a lot of chord qualities as you continue studying harmony. We'll talk more about some of the less common chord qualities more as we encounter them in musical situations, but for general reference's sake, here's a more complete set of chord qualities and the available tensions found on them. You can refer to this page whenever you are in doubt about which tensions are found on which chords. It would be very helpful to memorize these in all keys.

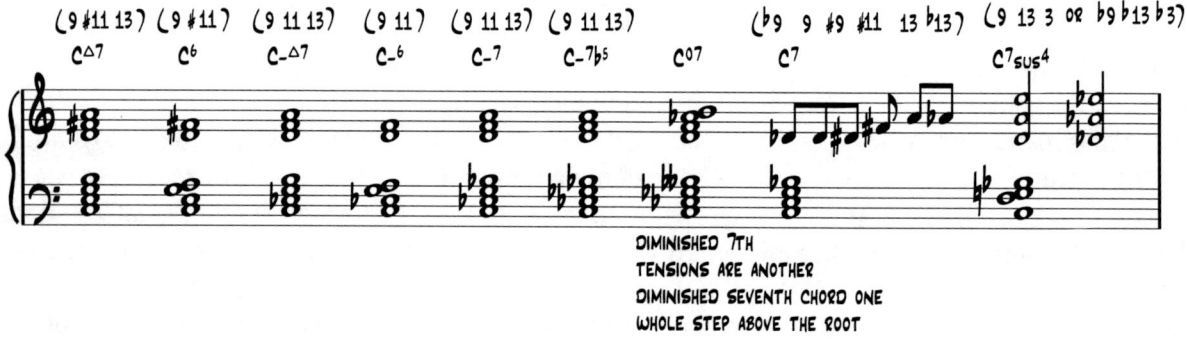

Okay, that was a heap of theory so let's try to get back to some practical examples that you can play and hear. In general, when people read a paragraph that is filled with sentences like "the appropriate 11th is found a whole step and an octave above the third of the chord" their eyes glaze over and they start thinking about funny commercials they've seen or YouTube videos of cats playing the piano, so it's important to take all of this information and apply it in simple ways in real musical situations as soon as you can.

Let's return to "Silent Night". (This chapter **wa**s written during the Christmas season, but that's not why I keep coming back to this song. Christmas carols give us a lot of basic cadences to work with on songs that don't modulate.) Here's a version that brings in the secondary dominants that we've been discussing, along with the diatonic substitutes that we looked at earlier.

Chapter 3

The third circle: secondary dominant seventh and related ii minor7 chords

(CD TRACK 6)

You can see that adding secondary dominants and their related ii chords adds a lot of interesting color to this harmonization of the tune, but it's not just color that these chords are adding—it's harmonic direction and logic. These chords bring clear direction to the progression and they signal important cadence points. For example, in bar 4, the F-7 Bb7 (a secondary dominant and its related ii-7 chord that leads to IV) signals that we are moving to a new harmonic area, leaving the tonic. In bar 7, the use of the triad in first inversion gives us another tonic variation (Bb/D feels like a color variation of the iii-7 chord, D minor7.). Bar 10 is particularly strong—introducing a ii-7b5-V7 up a half-step from the Eb major7 chord. If you compare this to the previous harmonization, in which the Eb major7 lasted for bars 9 and 10, you can see that there's a lot more forward motion created, movement that leads to the D-7 in bar 11 more forcefully than in the simpler version. Of course, you might not want that movement—I am trying to characterize the quality of forward motion that certain harmonic progressions create, not make value judgments about which progressions are better than others. In your composing and arranging sometimes you'll want the harmony to create forward motion and sometimes you'll want the harmony to drift along without implying what might come next. The important thing is to try to build your appreciation of the nuances of different harmonies.

You should also notice that in bar 7, I added a C7 before the F-7 in the next bar. In this case, the C7 is a V7 of the related ii chord of a ii-V leading to Ebmaj7, the IV chord (or a V7 of ii/IV). This is how secondary dominants work to make chains of chords—I can work backward from any chord, preceding it by a dominant 7th a fourth away, but we'll get to more of that later.

The chords in the above harmonization don't have a lot of added tensions in them (with the exception of the places where the melody note is a tension as in bar 1 beat 3, bar 4 beat 1, bar 5 beat 1, etc.) As I said above, adding tensions to minor7ths, minor7th b5s and major 7ths adds richness and color and can create nuance by softening the sense of harmonic direction these logically placed chords are bringing. This is a subtle distinction, but I think this is an important point that students often miss. I want to add logic to my progressions but adding chords back to back without tensions can feel a little clunky and heavy handed. It's a little like painting using colors right out of the tube—the grass is green and the sky is blue. Adding tensions allows me to blend the colors more, softening the edge between the green and blue border, making aquamarine, sky blue and all those other tints you see at a paint store, slightly blurring the distinction between chords. Dominants have a rich palette of tensions associated with them and since we are using so many secondary dominants we have a lot of chances to add harmonic color by using altered tensions (b9, #9, b13). Here's another harmonization of "Silent Night" using the same harmony as above, but adding tensions to the chord changes.

Chapter 3

The Third Circle: Secondary Dominant Seventh and Related II Minor7 Chords

(CD TRACK 7)

You can see that in this version, there's a lot more harmonic color. I've added natural 9ths in bars: 1, 2, 3, 6, 7, 9, 11, 13, 15, 16, 17 and 21. I've added altered tensions to all of the secondary dominants, occasionally adding a natural tension that changes to an altered tension (9 to b9 or 13 to b13) as the harmony holds (bars 12 and 20). Getting control of these tension options is an important step in furthering your awareness of harmonic nuance. However, the more notes I add, the more complex the piano arrangement becomes. Students who leave out tensions because of poor piano skills do themselves a disservice. If playing the piano is a struggle for you, then you should study these piano arrangements and get a feel for how piano voicings are made. I've tried to keep to a few simple rules, generally keeping 1 and 7 in the bass (adding the 3rd in the left hand from time to time if I need it there to support tensions in the right hand). I don't usually place tensions below the 3rd in the voicing (except the 9, which is fine below the third, whether flatted or natural—sharp nine can be a little problematic because of the half step, but it's possible.) I rarely double the root in these voicings. I did add a few 5ths in the left hand to make the voice-leading a little more logical, but the arrangement would have been adequate without it. (To pursue this further, see Appendix B, Piano Basics.)

Please notice in the above harmonization that natural 9ths tend to be the easiest tension to add to a voicing.

Notice also that piano voicings are notated in treble and bass clef. Most people tend to view these as corresponding to the right hand (treble clef) and left hand (bass clef) but that's not necessarily the case. For certain voicings, such as the last chord of the piece, it's impossible for the left hand to play all of the notes in the bass clef, but the right hand can easily play those notes (and should.) The other option is to write out lots of ledger lines below the treble clef, preserving the distinction between the two hands, but making the piece harder to read. I prefer the former, but there is no absolute right or wrong here.

Notice also that I have followed the usual convention of labeling chords when adding tensions. The common practice is that if you add a natural tension, say a 9th to a G minor7, this chord is now called a G-9. If I add an 11 and a 9, it's called an 11. (There is a little ambiguity if I've only added an 11 and no 9th, that chord too is called an 11. If I want to be clear I will call the chord G-11(9), using the largest tension in the chord for the chord name and whatever other tensions are found in the chord in parentheses. You may also see G-11(add 9) and G-11 (no 9). You should probably avoid the label G-7+9 because the "+" sign is sometimes used to indicate a #9. For altered tensions on dominant chords, label the chord "7" and add the altered tension in parentheses, as in Bb7 (b9,#11) or without the parenthesis if the font that you are using allows you to add these tensions clearly next to the chord symbol.

Having said all that, you will no doubt encounter a lot of variations in chord labeling so you should take the above nomenclature with a grain of salt. I've tried to be consistent in my own labeling, but I've probably slipped up here and there. When labeling chords that are comprised of chord tones and the usual available tensions, some people prefer to the simpler name, so, for example, refer to a G-11 (9) as a G-7 because you get the 9 and 11 for free in this chord if you wish. (I often do this when labeling chords for my own arrangements and compositions when I am primarily the person who is interpreting the harmony. However I've opted for more specificity in this book.) It's always important to use your harmonic knowledge of available tensions to make your own decisions about which tensions to add to chords as well as to check the suggestions of the author of any set of chord symbols.

Okay, let's leave the world of tension options and return to our use of secondary dominant chords. I could have been even more extreme in my use of secondary dominants on "Silent Night". Let's just look at the first two bars of the song and consider a few different possibilities. Here, I harmonized the first bar differently from the versions above.

(CD TRACK 8)

I've skipped the first I major7 chord, and that creates a surprising beginning to a well-known tune. Part of the drama comes from the fact that in the I IV V version of the tune, the melody was almost entirely composed of chord tones, whereas in this version, two important melody notes are now altered tensions on the dominant7th chords—the b13 on the A7 (V7/V7/vi) and the #9 on the D7 (V7/vi). The progression still feels logical because we are heading to a tonic chord in the second bar but the unusual colors and the unexpected starting chord add a lot of surprise.

I could be even more extreme.

(CD TRACK 9)

I changed the rhythm of the melody to allow me to use three chords divided evenly into the measure. Now I am starting on an E7b9, a V7/V7/V7 of vi, followed by the A7, a V7/V7/vi followed by a D7 (V7/vi) and eventually G-7 (vi). Of course, you can overdo a good thing. If almost every chord is an altered dominant (a dominant 7 with b9, #9 or b13) they tend to lose their impact.

You should also notice that even though secondary dominants and their related ii chords can often be added to songs, there are many situations in which the melody will make it impossible. Going back to our earlier version of "Silent Night", with a iii-7 chord in bar 3—D-7—I can't add a secondary dominant anywhere in the bar before it because the D in the melody will clash with the 3rd of the V7/iii (A7). In this case, the melody is sitting on the natural 11 of our potential secondary dominant, and this note is not one of the available tensions on that chord.

Just to walk through this process one more time, here are a few versions of Auld Lang Syne that use secondary dominants and their related ii chords.

The first version has a moderate amount of secondary dominant sounds which you can compare to the first circle chords of I, IV and V7 suggested by the most basic harmonization of the melody.

(CD TRACK 10)

The second version shows a more extreme use of secondary dominants.

Chapter 3
The Third Circle: Secondary Dominant Seventh and Related II Minor7 Chords

(CD TRACK 11)

The second version will work better at a slower tempo so that the listener can take in the more complex harmony.

Overall, I find these kind of harmonizations very satisfying. The logic that secondary dominants bring, along with the richness of all the altered dominant sounds that are available, make even extreme usages of these chords palatable. Secondary dominants and diatonic substitutes taken together can create harmonic progressions that convey a sense of earnestness and sincerity, at least that's the feeling I get from them. For those with more piano skills, you'll notice that the above harmonizations are improved by good voice-leading in the inner voices of the chords. If this were a jazz piano book, I would have taken that several steps further, but I am trying (I really am trying, believe it or not) to keep these piano realizations of the harmony playable by non-pianists. In the above harmonizations, I am attempting to walk the line between the normal amount of tensions that I would usually add to these chords and what a non-pianist can look at without giving up. (If you do give up on playing these yourself, you can always listen to the CD to hear what these harmonizations sound like. While listening to the example on the CD, you should follow the written musical examples, stopping to check on a particular voicing or harmony that you want to understand in greater detail.)

Now that we've worked through the process of adding secondary dominant and related ii chords to "Silent Night", and "Auld Lang Syne", you can go back and go through the same process with "Happy Birthday", "O Christmas Tree" and any other hymns ("Amazing Grace", "We Shall Overcome", "Swing Low, Sweet Chariot", whatever you like) or simple chorale-like melodies and folk tunes. I'll say it again, and it won't be the last time, that you get conversant with these techniques by applying them over and over again on different songs. So challenge yourself to go through this process many, many times on different pieces.

Chapter 4 – Understanding the Geography of Standard Tunes: Jazz Cadences and Turnarounds

Our discussion of cadences above was based (albeit somewhat loosely) on chorale harmony. The type of cadences that one finds in Christmas carols and hymns follows this type of harmony and is constructed of various cadences, deceptive resolutions (meaning resolution to a diatonic substitute chord), inversions and secondary dominants and their related ii chords. Jazz and popular tunes of the 30s through the 60s (show tunes and tin pan alley songs by composers like George Gershwin, Jerome Kern, Cole Porter, Jimmy Van Heusen and Irving Berlin, sometimes referred to collectively as the Great American Songbook) use elements that come from this classical chorale harmony but contain significant differences.

Perhaps most significantly, the chord progressions of jazz standards tend to be somewhat more repetitive and occur with a harmonic rhythm that is more regular than, say, a Bach Chorale. A lot of this has to do with the fact that chorales were written in a 4-part counterpoint writing style for voices (and contain lots of inversions, suspensions and passing tones as we saw above.) Jazz standards are far more root-based, containing complex relationships between the chord tones and tensions of a given chord but a simpler role for the bass in primarily sticking with the root of the chord. (One further reason for the simpler root-oriented progressions of standard tunes when contrasted with classical chorales is that the role of the bass, whether "walking"—playing a quarter note line derived from the chord changes—or playing some other bass texture, is created by the bassist or arranger in a given arrangement and so complexity is added at the arrangement stage of the process.)

The most common form for these popular tunes is AABA in which each section is 8 bars long. The A sections may have subtle variations in them, but they are essentially the same material repeated, often with differences in the 1st and 2nd ending, occasionally, with a third ending as well (most often, the 2nd and 3rd endings are the same or similar.) The B section contains contrasting harmonic material and often modulates to one or more different keys. Examples of AABA songs include "I Got Rhythm" and "Body and Soul", to name two of the many, many songs that have been written using this form. The next most common form is the ABAC song form, again in 8 bar sections. Sometimes the B and C sections are nearly identical, but they can also vary greatly from each other. Two examples of this form are "On Green Dolphin Street" and "But Not For Me," although once again, I am picking from thousands of tunes that employ this structure.

ABCD tunes, such as "Stella By Starlight" and "Bye Bye Blackbird" (where the D section recaps some of the melodic material from the first A section) are less common although this and many other combinations of these 8 bar sections can be found in standard tunes. 8 bar sections are extremely prevalent in standards, but variations in the number of bars in sections and extensions of phrases are also quite common and can be seen in such familiar tunes as "All the Things You Are," and "Alone Together" and "the Nearness of You".

When I say that these songs are more repetitive than a Bach chorale, I don't just mean because the first section is repeated 3 times in an AABA song form. (Bach Chorales also have repeated sections.) I should perhaps clarify what I mean by repetitiveness, because it's not meant as a value judgment of popular song forms as somehow less intrinsically interesting than Bach

UNDERSTANDING THE GEOGRAPHY OF STANDARD TUNES: JAZZ CADENCES AND TURNAROUNDS — CHAPTER 4

Chorales. It's meant more as a statement about the regularity of the harmony that occurs in jazz standards. The harmony is a little boxier, has a more regular harmonic rhythm, with modular units that you see re-appearing in different tunes. (Of course, chorales have their repeated pieces of harmony as well, but the counterpoint tends to make the harmony more irregular beat to beat, with a cadence occurring in the middle of a measure, or on the second beat of a bar.) Take "Heart and Soul", the Hoagy Carmichael song that beginning pianists (and an awful lot of non-pianists) have played at one point or another. The chord progression for the A sections is a simple repeated cadence: I major, vi minor, ii minor, V major (the cadence is of the same type, functionally, as our most basic full cadence: I IV V I. In this case we have two tonic chords, I and vi-, followed by a subdominant chord, ii-, and a dominant chord, V, which leads back to the I at the start of the repeat of this phrase). This kind of progression is called a "turnaround" in jazz terminology and even though most tunes are not as repetitive as Heart and Soul (fortunately) turnarounds appear in many, many songs.

Turnarounds are important to recognize for two reasons:
1) They have a similar function whenever they occur.
2) There are a lot of variations in standard turnarounds which can be substituted for each other as you wish, as long as the one you choose works with the melody of the song.

So what is a turnaround, functionally? A turnaround is a kind of placeholder in a song. It centers on the tonic, so it happens in the part of a song that is based on the I chord. This sort of tonic section occurs in many standards. The song might begin with several bars of the I chord, and we just sit there, in a kind of static way. "Silent Night" is this sort of tune, starting with four bars of the I chord. "Bye, Bye Blackbird" and "I Got Rhythm" are tunes that begin on the I chord, and the common variations in the chord progression of these tunes are variations in whether turnarounds are employed, and if so, which ones are used.

A turnaround is essentially treading water in a key. The choice between resting on the I chord or using a turnaround is like the difference between standing at a bus stop waiting for a bus and pacing in a circle at a bus stop waiting for a bus. The harmony is really about the tonic, either taking a few small steps away from the tonic and then returning to it, or just waiting on the tonic chord.

So a turnaround can occur in a part of a tune that is harmonized by the I chord:

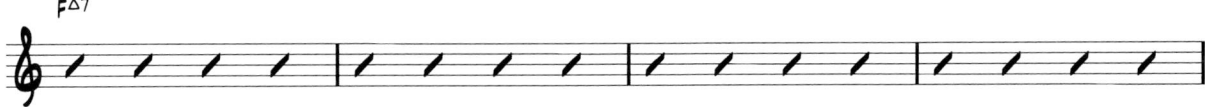

I can add a ii-V7 to the 2nd and 4th bars and I get a less static, more cyclical feeling in the harmony. We are going somewhere and returning to the I chord instead of just staying on the I.

A "Heart and Soul" type turnaround makes the changes feel even more like a cycle. The I major7, vi-7, ii-7, V7 turnaround is perhaps the most common. All of the changes are diatonic to the key center.

Replacing the vi-7 chord with a V7/ii gives a little more forward momentum toward the ii-7 chord in the 2nd and 4th bars. It also gives me the opportunity to add altered tensions if I wish and so I am able to bring more non-diatonic harmonic sounds to this progression.

Substituting iii-7 for the I chord is a common variation. This makes the turnaround feel even more circular because we are resolving to a less final feeling tonic chord than the I chord. I can also replace the ii-7 chord with a V7/V. This gives me more opportunities for adding non-diatonic chord tones and tensions to the progression.

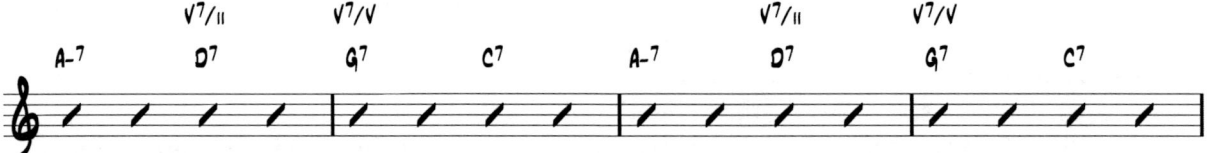

Or I can add related ii chords to my secondary dominants. Progressions like this that speed up the harmonic rhythm may only be available on slower tunes. At any rate, turnarounds with this sort of irregular harmonic rhythm are far less common.

More variations can be created using these approaches and there are many other variations of turnarounds that we will encounter that utilize harmonic principles that we haven't studied yet (such as passing chords, modal interchange chords and tritone substitutes) but for now, try some of these variations on songs that you know. Examples of tunes that have extended tonic or turnaround sections in them include: "Bye Bye Blackbird", "I Got Rhythm", "Secret Love", "Heart and Soul", "Mean to Me", "St. Thomas", "Polka Dots and Moonbeams", "Smile", "The Song is You", "You Took Advantage of Me" and countless others.

Being able to recognize turnaround sections in a tune and play turnaround variations of your own choosing is particularly important for soloists on rhythm changes (the chord progression of "I Got Rhythm"). This tune is 4 bars of turnarounds (chords moving two beats per bar) followed by a ii-V to the IV chord (or some other functionally similar connector to the IV chord) and then a turnaround back to the top (although the turnaround for the second and third A sections are a bit different but that's a small detail). Students who learn this tune chord by chord instead of functionally don't see that they can solo over ANY of the turnaround possibilities that they know and

UNDERSTANDING THE GEOGRAPHY OF STANDARD TUNES: JAZZ CADENCES AND TURNAROUNDS — CHAPTER 4

will be stuck trying to "paint by the numbers" instead of creating freely within the functional boundaries of the tune. So if the first two bars of rhythm changes are Bb G-7/C-7 F7/ to you, you may end up playing a Bb major scale for that whole section, whereas if you know that you can substitute secondary dominants for the vi-7 or ii-7 chord, you have a lot more options.

Just as songs contain turnaround sections that are centered on the tonic, they also contain sections that are centered on the dominant. These are the half cadences of the tune, phrases that end on the dominant and eventually lead back to the I chord at the beginning of the next phrase. These sections of tunes are functionally V7 sections, but generally are more commonly harmonized as ii-Vs. (As noted above, the addition of a ii-7 to a V7 is extremely common).

Songs including: "Perdido", "Body and Soul", "If I were a Bell", "Secret Love", "Scrapple from the Apple", "Sweet and Lovely", "Honeysuckle Rose", "Our Love is Here to Stay" and "But Not For Me" all feature extended ii-7 V7 sections. Afro-Cuban music often features extended improvisational sections (and devices such as montuno) over ii-7 V7 vamps.

So, a V7 part of a tune might just sit on the V7 chord

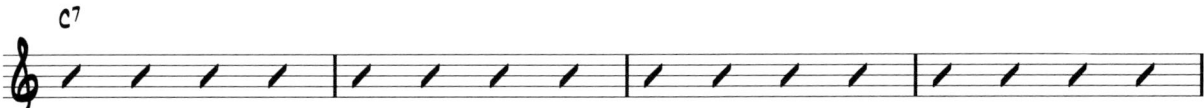

Or we could add a ii-7.

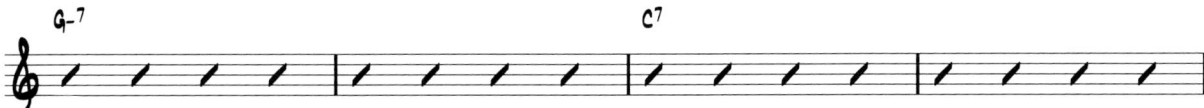

I can shorten the harmonic rhythm further and adding a second ii-7 V7.

Or shorten it further adding more ii-Vs.

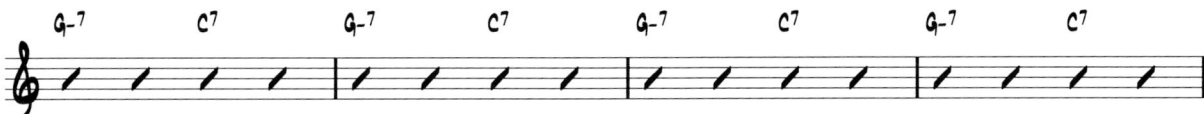

I can replace some of the dominants with V7/ii-7s, as happens in the first two bars of "Body and Soul".

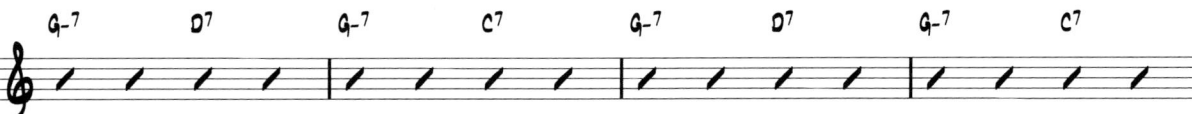

Or I can replace the ii-7 chords with V7sus4 chords.

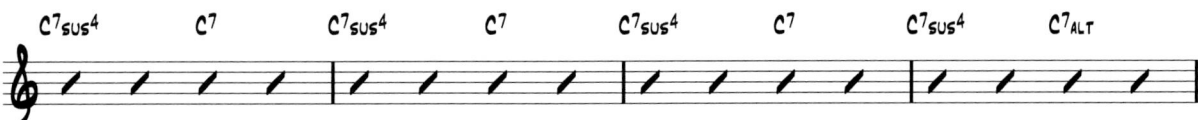

We haven't talked about the dominant7 suspended 4 chord yet so now is our chance to do so. A dominant7 suspended 4 is a chord with the following chord tones: 1, 4, 5, b7. Instead of the 3rd that we normally find in dominant 7th chords, this chord has a 4th. Historically, this chord was a dominant seventh with one non-chord tone in it. The non-chord tone, called a "suspension" resolved to the chord tone (in this case the third) after the point of the chord change. However, even though historically the fourth of this chord required resolution, the dominant7th sus4 chord in jazz is considered a stable entity which doesn't necessarily require resolution. When it DOES resolve, as in the example above, the 4 resolving to the 3rd is the same key note (in this case, F) that resolves down a step (to E) in a ii-V in that key: 7 of the ii-7 chord (F) resolves to the 3rd of a dominant7 (E). We can think of a C7sus4 to a C7, as a G-7/C to a C7.

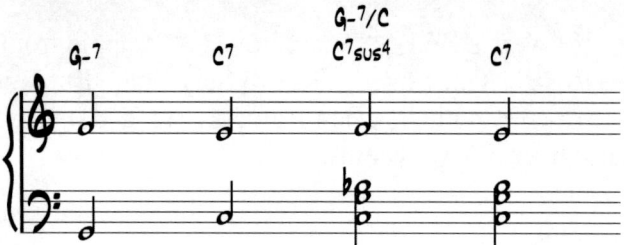

The first two notes, the F to the E that happens over the G minor7 to C7, are called guide tones (taken together, sometimes called a guide tone line). Guide tone lines usually move by step. Each note of the guide tone line is of the same rhythmic value as the chord change they occur over. Guide tone lines, when played against the roots of the chord, imply the chord qualities of the progression. Or, in other words, when you hear the 7th of the G-7 move to the 3rd of the C7 above the bass notes of these chords, your ear supplies the harmony of the rest of the chord: we hear the inner voices that aren't present and recognize that a ii-V is being played even though notes are missing. We'll talk more about guide tone lines and voice-leading later, but the important thing to understand now is that a progression of C7sus4 to a C7 is functionally the same as a G-7 to C7.

Since the dominant7 sus4 chord is new to us, we should mention that this chord has some unusual available tensions. The most common tensions are natural 9 and natural 13, but the 10th (or the 3rd) functions as a tension on this chord as well, usually placed above the 4th of the chord in the voicing. Less common tensions are the b9, b13 and b3rd. On sus4 chords we find either the natural tensions or the flatted tensions, but not combinations of both, so essentially these are two different types of sus4 chords: dominant7 sus4 natural 9, natural 13 and dominant7 sus4 b9 b13. When you see the chord symbol: C7sus4, the natural tension version of this chord is implied. Usually, the flat tension version of the chord is written: C7sus4b9 (and occasionally as C Phrygian or DbMaj7/C).

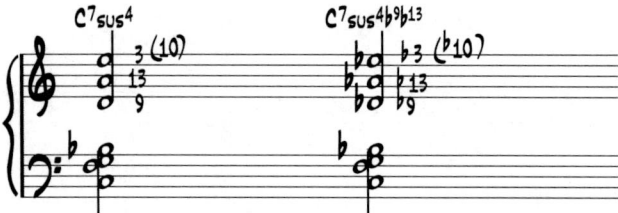

While we're on the subject of available tensions, I want to re-iterate a few things about dominant7th tensions. As we noted above, dominant7ths have more different available tensions than any other chord quality. These tensions come in two groups, the natural tensions, 9, #11 and 13, and the altered tensions b9, #9, #11 and b13. (Both groups contain the #11 since this is the only 11 available on dominant7th voicings, so technically, the #11 is both an altered tension and a natural one.). The altered tensions are more dissonant than the natural tensions. The more dissonant the dominant 7th tensions are, the more this chord wants to resolve up a fourth to the I chord. When we were talking about secondary dominant chords we noted that D minor7 to G7 had less forward motion feeling than D7 to G7. I can increase that forward motion feeling by playing D7b9b13 to G7. So the turnaround C major7 to A13b9, D7b9b13 to G7b9b13 has more of a feeling of forward motion than C, A minor, D minor, G7. (Note that the A7 above is a kind of mixed animal—a natural 13 with a b9.) We'll talk more about the scalar implications of certain combinations of tensions later, but you can always make choices about which tensions to use by ear. You should try out all the possibilities so that you get to know these sounds. As I said earlier, the use of tensions on dominant7 chords is one of the defining features of the jazz harmonic language. In the case discussed above, the dominant area of a tune, with a repeating ii minor7 to V7, or V7sus4 to V7, you probably won't want to use altered tensions on the dominant until you get the last dominant7, the one that resolves up a fourth to the I chord. So in the C7sus4 to C7 turnaround above (at the bottom of page 42), it's more likely that the last dominant 7 in bar four will have altered tensions than the ones that come before it in bars 1 through 3.

Many songs are constructed with the elements that we've discussed so far: Turnarounds, ii-V sections, secondary dominants and their related ii-7 chords, particularly secondary dominants leading to vi minor, IV major or ii minor. These basic elements (and these alone) account for literally tens of thousands of standard chord progressions.

CHAPTER 5 – THE FOURTH CIRCLE: PASSING CHORDS

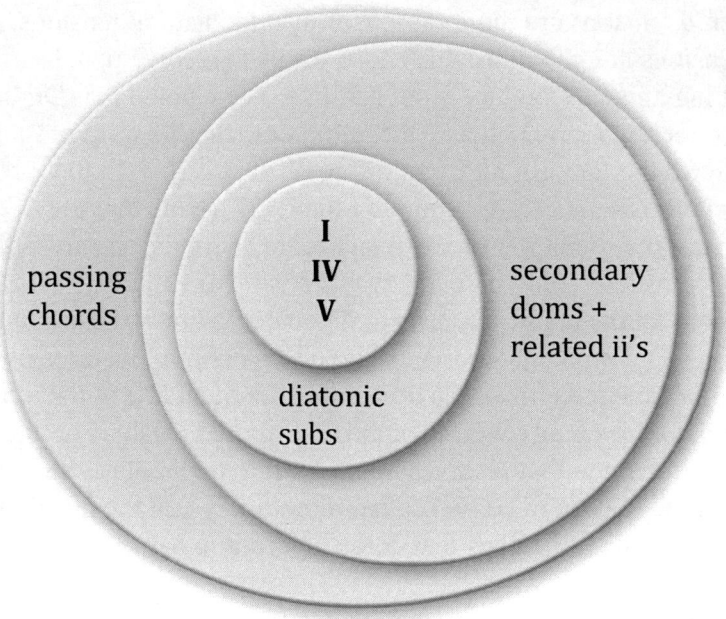

For our purposes, I'm defining passing chords as chords either a half step or a whole step away from some other chord that they are leading to. The chords that passing chords pass to are called target chords and these chords are the standard chords of the tune. You can get a chord progression for a song: 1) by working through the tonic, subdominant and dominant relationships suggested by the melody, 2) by diatonic substitution and adding secondary dominants and their related ii-7 chords, 3) by transcribing multiple versions of the song to determine what the most commonly played changes are, or 4) just by reading a lead sheet of the tune from a fake book. However you get your set of changes, passing chords can be added to them, connecting two chords by adding a third chord between them.

Half-step passing chords are far and away the most common. I can precede any target chord by a passing chord that is either a half-step above or a half-step below the target chord. Here I've added passing chords to the first four bars of "All the Things You Are".

(CD TRACK 12)

I can also add diatonic passing chords, (sometimes in combination with half-step passing chords)

(CD TRACK 13)

Here's another, somewhat simpler example of diatonic passing chords in the standard "When Lights are Low".

(CD TRACK 14)

(Incidentally, the above diatonic passing chords offer another variation on a turnaround progression, walking up and down the major scale.)

Let's return to half-step passing chords since those are the most often used. Passing chords that are a half step above the target chord are most often dominants (with natural tensions.) This is the default option for these passing chords. Passing chords that are a half step below the target chord are most often diminished7ths.

When I say that these are the most common choices, that doesn't mean that they are boring choices, or that you should look for more colorful chord choices instead of these common ones. The reason that dominant 7ths are used so often as passing chords is that they PASS, meaning, they have a lot of forward momentum and we hear their function quickly and identify them as leading chords. Other chord qualities can work well too, and so we have this very simple rule for finding passing chords—try every chord either a half step above or below the target chord that works with the melody of the song. If you try all the possibilities, you can let your ears determine which work best for you. Having said that there are no hard and fast rules here, one of the most common student re-harmonization "mistakes" is choosing overly complicated chords as passing chords. Chords that are extremely complex take longer to register on the ear. Some chords, chords that usually have a different function than what I am expecting, don't lead well to other chords—they steal the focus like a hammy actor in an amateur play. Minor 7 b5 chords are good examples of these. They are complex chord sounds and tend to take a moment for us to digest them—they usually occur as related ii chords in ii-Vs leading to minor keys and in another context, here as passing chords, they are often not effective and a bit confusing sounding. (I say that they are **often** not effective, but not **always**—again, let your ears be the judge.) They slow the harmony down when I am looking for something that moves, something that directs my ears to the target chord that's coming next. In a similar way, b9 or other heavily altered chords often don't make the best passing chords. Keep in mind that altering a dominant chord tends to make it want to push for a resolution up a fourth. Also, the b9 of the dominant 7th, that particular tension, or voice if you like, usually craves resolution itself, by moving down a half-step to the 5th of the target I chord. A lot of students will use a dominant7 b9 in a situation in which the target chord is a half-step down and where the b9 note itself doesn't move (it turns into the natural 9 on the target chord.) Again, I don't wish to say that that's always wrong, but it feels wrong to me often enough that I encourage you to listen to your passing chords carefully to be sure they really are passing to the next chord, not lingering.

Let's return to "All the Things You Are". In the first example, I added only passing chords a half step above the target chords and they were all dominant7s with natural tensions. As I mentioned above, these are often good choices because they give a feeling of passing to the next chord change and they don't steal the focus from the target chord harmony. However, I had a number of other options.

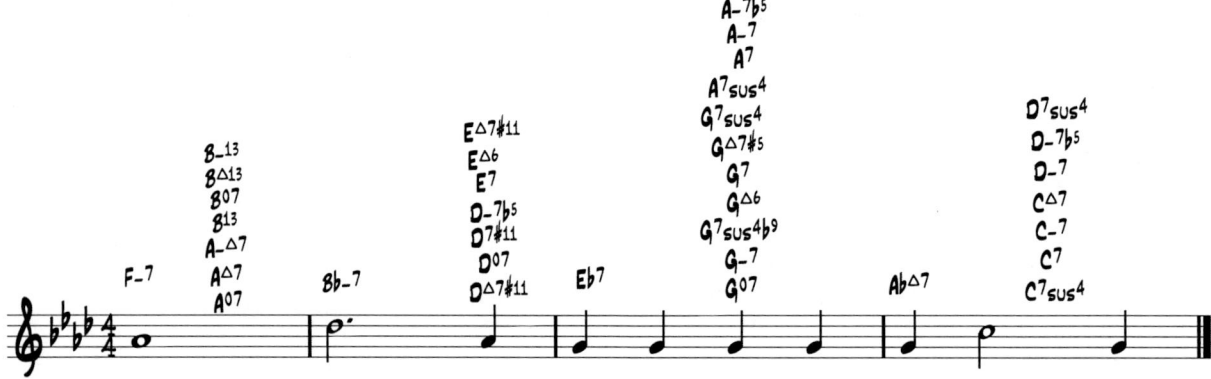

As you can see, there are a lot of possibilities for passing chords a half-step away from the target chord. Many of these won't be good choices, but again, rather than make rules for what sounds good and what doesn't, I'd suggest that you check out the possible chords and see which ones sound good to you. The process of finding possible chords is a pretty simple one—For example, in the first bar, there's a place for a passing chord on beat 3 leading to the Bb-7. I have two possible bass notes, A and B. The Ab/G# in the melody becomes a major 7th in relation to the A root, so I need to choose a chord quality that has an A in the root and a G# in the melody. Any chord that has a major 7th in it is a candidate for a passing chord in this spot, so A major7, A min major7 (We haven't encountered this chord before—it's a minor triad with a major 7th added to it., A minor6 (doesn't contain a major 7 as a chord tone, but is consonant with it), A major6, and A diminished7 are all possibilities. (Remember: the possible tensions on a diminished7 include

THE FOURTH CIRCLE: PASSING CHORDS

CHAPTER 5

all notes a whole step up from the chord tones, so the major 7th is available as a tension on diminished 7th chords.) Turning now to the B root—our other choice for the bass note of a passing chord in this spot—the Ab/G# in the melody is the 6th or 13th so any chord that has the 6th as a chord tone or is consonant with a 13th is available to me. Those would be: B13, a dominant 7th with the 13th (specified not just as available, but in this case, present in the chord), B minor6, B major6, B minor7 (or more accurately, B minor 13, for the same reason as the B13 above), B7sus4 (or B13sus4), B major7 (or B major13) and B dim7 (the 6th equals the double flatted 7th of a diminished chord.)

This skill, picking a bass note, assessing the relationship of the melody to that root and being able to find all the possible chord qualities that will work in that spot quickly, is a very important skill for re-harmonizing.

Re-harmonizing with passing chords can have a subtle effect because the basic chords, the expected chords (or target chords) are all in place and their function doesn't change. This is an important concept. Most novice re-harmonizers find it much easier to make large changes, changes in the harmony that wipe out the original functions of the chords, than it is to make small ones. Making small changes, subtly re-framing the harmony of the tune, creating harmonic nuance, usually requires a more complex understanding of harmonic colors. The plain fact is that, in the end, you can change any chord you want into any other chord, create large dissonances and use unusual chord qualities, "unavailable tensions" or non-chord tones, wherever you like. Often, students bring in re-harmonizations that employ these kind of harmonic weapons of mass destruction in severe ways, and when I suggest that they need to be able to find the harmonic connections to the original harmony of the song using subtler types of re-harmonization, they may feel that they have lost an outlet for their creativity, and that to become a good jazz musician, one has to play by the rules in an uncreative way.

Nothing could be further from the truth. I am not an advocate for any particular harmonic approach and I always encourage students to write their most radical re-harmonizations based entirely on their ears and ideas, alongside the exercises they are doing that are more rule-driven. However, it always comes down to this: What music moves you? Are you interested in the harmonic vocabularies of Bill Evans, McCoy Tyner, Oscar Peterson, Hank Jones, Mulgrew Miller, Herbie Hancock and Thelonious Monk? (to name a few of the many, many pianists who speak the mainstream jazz harmonic language with subtlety and an individual personal voice.) If you are, then it's necessary to learn to be able to "paint with a small brush" harmonically. This reminds me of something I heard attributed to the great blues/jazz organist Jack McDuff. He was one of the last road warrior jazz musicians, playing local venues all over the country, driving a van with his band and his Hammond B-3 organ in the back. Playing with Jack's band was one of the gigs that used to be available to younger musicians because established, older musicians would have balked at the working conditions and pay. Working with these younger college-educated players, he would complain that they would play outside of the chord changes because they didn't know enough music that was inside the chord changes. When I hear a player like Jack McDuff, or Stanley Turrentine, or countless other great blues players including John Coltrane, Lee Morgan, Wynton Kelly and Wes Montgomery, I am often struck by how much mileage and freshness they can get out of blues sounds and harmonic ideas that are very well known. Coming up as a young jazz player, I worked hard, trying to play that music with the same sense of authenticity and blues feeling that these great players do. In the end, no matter how harmonically adventurous one is, one still has to try to derive new combinations from old harmonic concepts. There isn't a whole lot that's completely new out there, except the particular way that you have of putting it all together.

Having said all that, I am always looking for new ideas of things to try. Of course, these experiments are (part of) what this book is about.

So to return to passing chords, they are among the potentially more subtle changes that one can make to a chord progression. As I mentioned earlier, to employ these chords with subtlety you have to be attuned to how fast they want to pass on to the next chord. In the above list of possibilities listed for "All the Things You Are," the A minor major chord (in the first measure) is probably not one that I would pick. That's because this is a complex chord and my ear really needs a moment to take this chord in. If I play this voicing on beat three of the measure I feel a slowing down harmonically as I try to come to terms with the dissonance of this chord quality. This slowing down feeling keeps me from hearing the Bb minor7 as the destination of this passing chord. I'm more likely to feel focused on the passing chord—with a 'what just happened?' kind of feeling.

One of the problems composers and arrangers have to deal with is the difference in time scale between the process of writing music (often very slow, especially if you are working at the piano and your piano skills are weak) and the process of hearing what you've written played back (very fast, a passing chord that gets two beats lasts for about a second if the song is played at a medium tempo). The tempo has a lot to do with how the harmony resonates: there are possibilities on a slow ballad harmonically that aren't available to you on a medium tempo tune. (I don't mean because technically you can play more on a ballad, I mean because your ear takes time to sort out complex harmony and with ballads, you have that time.) If you are always hearing your harmonic choices played at a very slow tempo, you have to try to imagine how the tune will sound when played at a normal tempo. In my first classical composition class in college, I fell victim to this problem. I was working on an octet and I spent hours and hours at the piano pouring over 8 bars and other small sections of the piece. When I assembled a group for a performance, I was shocked to find that I had been unconsciously changing the tempo every three or four bars.

THE FOURTH CIRCLE: PASSING CHORDS   CHAPTER 5

Let's see more passing chords in action. Here are the first few bars of Body and Soul.

(CD TRACK 15)

Now I am going to add passing chords.

(CD TRACK 16)

This version of the song would probably be played at a fairly slow tempo, quarter note = 60, say. Even though there an awful lot of chords on the page, the passing chord harmony is mostly smooth and doesn't call a lot of attention to itself. On beat four in the first bar the E major7 is an example of a half step above passing chord that is not a dominant7th. Beat four in bar 2 has a dominant7th b13 that passes well to the next chord in spite of its altered tension. The G7 with altered tensions in bar 3 is a nice effect because the melody goes from being very consonant notes (Ab and Bb, 5 and 6) on the Db major7th chord to extremely colorful notes (b9 and #9) on the G7. (Again, the motion in these melody notes helps us here.) I chose not to add a passing chord on beat four in the 4th bar where the harmony is already moving to the next chord by half-step.

CHAPTER 5

THE FOURTH CIRCLE: PASSING CHORDS

Or how about "Silent Night" again, this time with passing chords:

(CD TRACK 17)

THE FOURTH CIRCLE: PASSING CHORDS

CHAPTER 5

These re-harmonizations are stuffed with passing chords and this might be more than I would use in a performance situation, but the point is that I am not in a performance situation—I am trying to get as much experience applying this technique as I can. In general, if you are too concerned with being tasteful or careful, you don't force yourself to find passing chords in unusual places and you don't really see the full possibilities of this technique. Try to find passing chords leading to every chord change and then eliminate some if the result feels like too much. Passing chords are a very easy technique to apply and the results are often quite effective. There are some bars where the passing chord doesn't effect the overall feeling much. In the above example, bars 2 and 8 the passing chords are diatonic 7ths and the effect is subtle. Bar 11 has a slightly different use of the passing chord—in this bar the passing chord surprisingly takes the place of the target chord on beat 1 resolving to the target chord on beat 3. (Some might argue that this isn't exactly a passing chord, but again, I keep things simple to avoid quibbling—in my definition, the passing chord is a chord that leads to the target chord either by half-step or whole step, and this chord does that.) Bar 21 has two passing chords (a passing chord leading to another passing chord leading to the target chord) and Bar 23 repeats the technique of having the passing chord occur on the downbeat, where we are expecting the target chord, before resolving in the last bar to the I chord.

Some of these harmonic moves can be understood in other ways, as modal interchange chords, tritone substitutes or diatonic passing chords at the same time as being half-step passing chords. That doesn't change the fact that these chords are half-step passing chords. A chord can have more than one function. Again, I like simple rules. Chords added to existing chord changes a half-step away from the target chord are half-step passing chords, however else they can be understood.

The discussion of passing chords opens the door to diminished chord harmony. This is a very big topic, one that we will have to tackle in a chapter of its own later, but let's sketch some of the basic outlines of how diminished chords work.

Diminished chords are very unusual chords. For one thing, they are symmetrical, meaning they are made up of one interval only, minor thirds. This means that every inversion of a diminished 7 is another diminished 7: Bbdim7 = Dbdim7 = Edim7 = Gdim7. Because of this there are really only 3 diminished 7ths: Bbdim7, Bdim7 and C dim7, the rest are inversions. (Pick any three diminished7ths moving up or down in half-steps and the rest are inversions of them.) Also, the tensions of a diminished chord are a second diminished chord up a whole step. These two chords taken together make an octatonic (8 note) scale that is also symmetrical, constructed of alternating whole steps and half steps. I can make a second diminished scale (it's a mode of the first scale) by starting on the second degree of the scale and continuing in alternating half steps and whole steps. This second scale is used when playing over dominant 7th, b9, #9 natural 13 chords. It's easy to think of this function of the diminished if we put a diminished 7th chord over a root a minor 7 below—if I take Bbdim7 and put it a C root below it, I have b7, b9, 3 and 5, all of the chord tones except the root (the C) of a C7b9 chord. In fact, to make a diminished chord into a dominant 7, you just have to flat one chord tone. (Take Bb, Db, E, G and lower the Bb to an A and you have an A7, lower the Db to a C and you have an C7, lower the E to an Eb and you have an Eb7, lower the G to Gb and you have a Gb7). It also follows that the Bbdim7 is a dominant 7th b9 chord (minus the root) for **all** of these 7ths, C, Eb, Gb and A. Diminished7ths are like an 8 of clubs in a trick deck of cards that keeps re-appearing and then hiding itself in myriad ways. What's that in your ear? A diminished7th chord!

CHAPTER 5

THE FOURTH CIRCLE: PASSING CHORDS

So, what are the common functions of a diminished 7th? The most common is as a passing chord. The diminished 7th a half step below a target chord functions a lot like a secondary dominant. (The most common targets for a diminished7th are the ii minor7, iii minor7 and vi minor7; the I chord with the fifth in the bass is a common target for a #iv diminished chord in a blues turnaround following the IV chord—but any chord can be a target of a diminished chord.) In the progression Bbmajor7 to G7 (V/ii) C-7 F7, a Bdim7 often substitutes for the G7. Place a G root under a B diminished7th and it becomes a G7b9. In any context where you find a passing diminished chord, you can substitute a dominant7b9 and whenever you find a dominant 13 b9 chord, you can substitute a diminished 7th.

Here's an example from the standard "It Could Happen to You". This tune is often played with passing diminished chords in the first four bars.

(CD TRACK 18)

However, it works just as well with secondary dominants and their related two chords.

(CD TRACK 19)

Both of the above versions of this tune are often played. If I am playing with a bassist and we aren't using a lead sheet (which I very much prefer when playing standards), we have to pay attention to each other and make the decision together as to which set of chord changes we will use. Because of the close relationship of these two sets of changes, it's not always crucial for both of us to be playing them the same way at the same time.

There are many standards that are often harmonized with either diminished passing chords or dominant7ths. These include: "Softly, as in a Morning Sunrise" (bridge), "Body and Soul" (bridge), and "Slow Boat to China", but I could make a list of thousands of standards that present a choice between dominant7th chords and diminished chords—pretty much all of them since secondary dominants are present in almost every standard tune.

Getting back to the other functions of a diminished7th chord, we've already discussed the next function, as an upper structure of a dominant7 b9. This has many applications that we will look at later when we explore diminished harmony in more depth.

A third function of the diminished chord is a color chord replacement for a I chord. This is a sound that I associate with Bill Evans, but of course, many other instrumentalists use this technique. Two famous places for this re-harmonization are as the first chord of "Misty"

(CD TRACK 20)

and the last bar of the bridge of Stella By Starlight:

(CD TRACK 21)

Very often when you see this last function of the diminished 7th chord, it comes in a slightly different form, as a dim major7th. This chord is essentially a diminished 7th chord with one of the tensions of the diminished (a whole step above the double flatted 7th) replacing the 7th of the diminished chord. It has a more modern sound and a very strong voice-leading relationship to a major 7th chord (the middle two voices move up a half step to change a dim major7th into a major 7th.) We will explore this voice-leading relationship in much greater depth later when we look at diminished chords in detail.

CHAPTER 5

These diminished major7th chords are often used as a way to delay the final resolution of a tune, slowing things down as the second last chord of a song. Jazz players often don't simply land on a I chord at the end of a song and call it a day. An extra chord, or chords are needed to soften the impact of the ending chord, to signal that we are moving toward the final resolution (that sounds kind of ominous—I just mean the last chord of the tune, nothing deeper than that.) Bill Evans was fond of the diminished major7 as the penultimate chord on a song, often ending tunes that way.

One last function of the diminished chord is as a passing chord a half-step **above** the target chord. Songs like "The Song Is You", "Smoke Gets in Your Eyes", "Embraceable You" and "How Long Has This Been Going On?" all contain diminished 7th chords that work this way. Most often, this chord is a biii diminished7 leading to a ii-7 chord.

(CD TRACK 22)

Diminished chords that resolve down a half step are far less common than diminished chords that resolve up a half step.

So now you can add passing chords to your repertoire of re-harmonization techniques. As I always say about this point in the chapter, go out and find many places to employ them, so this concept becomes internalized in your thinking and available in your writing, arranging and/or improvising.

I would include melodies and tunes for you to harmonize at this point, with chord changes for you to add passing chords to, but copyright issues prevent me from doing so. Fortunately, you can go to any fake book and start working on this with tunes of your own choosing.

Chapter 6 – The Fifth Circle: Modal Interchange chords

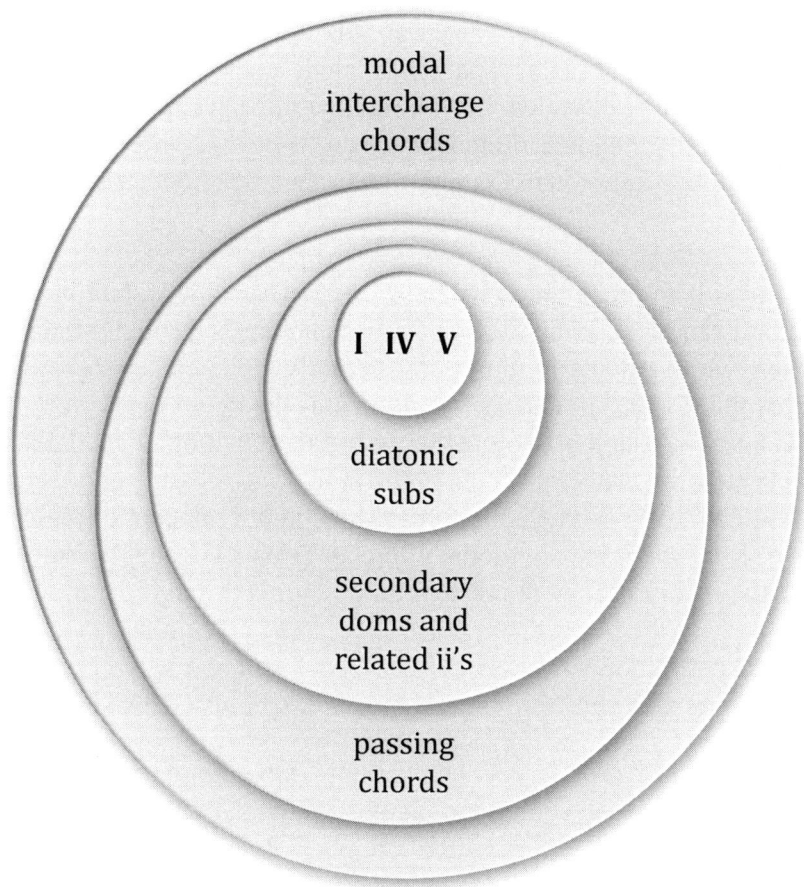

A quick review: we started with the first circle that contained I, IV and V chords, the basic elemental chords that give us the concept of tonic, subdominant and dominant function. The second circle of harmony added the rest of the chords built from the major scale, chords that had different harmonic colors, but still behaved in tonic, subdominant and dominant ways. We added a little more nuance here by adding seventh chord harmony, inversions and even more harmonic color by adding the available tensions to the chord tones of these chords. The third circle gave us secondary dominants and their related ii-7 chords, chords that function as dominants and sub-dominants leading to different diatonic chords and create cadences that resolve to chords other than the I chord.

Still, these chords have a clear harmonic function, targeting (or "tonicizing" as it is sometimes called) various diatonic 7ths. The fourth circle, passing chords, gave us a larger palette of leading chords, chords that resolve to target chords (which now can include any chords of the tune, not just diatonic 7ths) by half step or whole step. Some of these passing chords are diatonic, but they needn't be, and we also saw some new harmony in the form of passing diminished 7ths, but all of these chords have clear functions: either leading to a target chord (somewhat in the manner of a secondary dominant although by half step instead of by fourth) or acting as a delaying chord that resolves to the I chord (in the case of the color chord use of the I diminished chord.) The important thing to remember is that we are charting rules for how chords behave and each new group of chords acts in ways that make functional sense.

The fifth circle is devoted to modal interchange chords. Modal interchange chords are chords that are borrowed from a parallel scale. A parallel scale is a scale that starts on the same root, so G minor and G major are parallel scales. I can build diatonic sevenths out of a G minor scale, or any scale, just as I did on the major scale in chapter one—by stacking the scale in thirds to build 4 note chords. If I build these chords in G minor, I can then borrow these chords to use in the parallel major key of G.

That's the theoretical side of modal interchange. The practical side is that there are so many scales out there, that I can make an awful lot of different chords through modal interchange and not all of these chords are particularly important. Actually, I can make ANY chord by constructing a parallel scale (and if I can't find a scale that creates the chord that I want, I can simply make up a scale that will do the job). So the theoretical explanation of modal interchange doesn't really tell the whole story—what's important is the modal interchange chords that get used *all the time*, the chords that have become common features in our concept of major key tonal songs. These chords have clear functions. So, modal interchange as a concept is really about history and practice as well as the theory of how to create a lot of chords through parallel scales.

Finding modal interchange chords is relatively easy. As I said above, you just make diatonic sevenths using a scale that is different from the major scale, such as C dorian:

An incomplete list of all the parallel scales would include all the modes of the major scale, the harmonic minor, the 5th mode of the harmonic minor, and the melodic minor scale and all of its modes. These are the possible chords that come from these scales: I major 7, i minor 7, i minor major 7, I7, i-7b5, bII major7, bII minor major7, bII dim7, bII maj7#5, II7, ii-7, ii-**7** b5, bIII major7, biii-7, biii minor major7, bIIImajor7#5, and so on.

However, as I said above, simply making a list of every chord that you can construct from common parallel scales doesn't really get us closer to the practical application of modal interchange chords in songs. bII minor major7 may be a modal interchange chord but bells don't ring for me when I see that chord, because it doesn't have a clearly defined function in a key. Similarly, the IV7 above is a chord that does have a function in a key, but as for the V-7 next to it, not so much. So the modal interchange concept is most useful to me when I focus on the most often used modal interchange chords.

Think of the set of common modal interchange chords as a group of chords, a little like a bunch of your relatives. They aren't the relatives you see the **most** often (like your mother or your sister, they would probably be dominant or subdominants depending on their personalities, and of

THE FIFTH CIRCLE: MODAL INTERCHANGE CHORDS   CHAPTER 6

course you get to be the I chord, you egomaniac), but still some of them turn up quite a lot, often enough so that you have a pretty good idea of how they're going to behave. If you've been to the same sorts of Thanksgiving dinners that I have you already know that these folks are a predictable lot.

And, just like this motley group of relatives, I am a lot less interested in where they come from than what they are going to do when they get to my house. So, I think it's possible to dispense with building chord changes from parallel scales and just focus on the key modal interchange chords to understand how those chords work.

The most important modal interchange chords are (in ascending order up the scale) I7, bII major7, II7, ii-7b5, bIII major7, IV7, iv-7, iv-6, #iv-7b5, bVI major7 and bVII7. Here they are in the key of C:

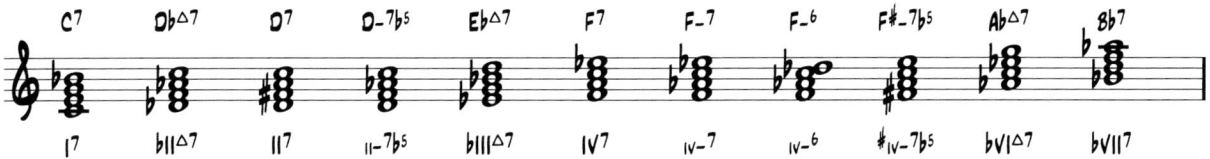

Of these, II7, ii-7b5, iv-7 (or iv-6), #iv-7b5, bVII7 are the most important and most often used so let's tackle them first.

The II7 Chord

How do these important modal interchange chords work in tunes? Our first modal interchange chord, II7, (D7 in the key of C) looks a lot like a secondary dominant, V7/V. However there is a functional difference between a II7 and a V7/V. A secondary dominant of V7 has the function of leading to the V7 chord. It often has altered tensions (to suggest that we are heading to a resolution up a fourth). It is often preceded by its related ii-7 chord. A II7 is a different animal. It tends not to be preceded by its relative ii-7 chord but rather by the I chord. It has natural tensions and it just sits there, without much desire to move on to the next chord. Examples of tunes that feature a II7 include "Take the A Train"

(CD TRACK 23)

CHAPTER 6

and "The Girl from Ipanema"

(CD TRACK 24)

In each of these tunes when we get to the II7 chord we just kind of sit there, without an urgent need to move on—and take in this chord color before resolving. The above examples are particularly exposed examples of the II7 chord change, but it most often appears toward the end of an A section. I can often substitute the II7 chord change in situations where I have a vi-7 to V7/V. Cherokee provides a good example of how that would work. Usually this part of the tune (bars 11~12 of the A section) is played with a II7 chord

(CD TRACK 25)

But vi-7 to V7/V also works.

(CD TRACK 26)

In the above examples, the effect of the ii-V softens this part of the tune. The II7 is a little more abrupt on the downbeat and then it feels kind of relaxed, not pushing forward, just a-sittin' and a-rockin', so to speak. All this is extremely subjective, but to me the II7 feels like another "place" in a tune, in the same way that waiting on the I chord feels like **being** in a certain place. The ii-V above feels like **going** to a place but the II7 chord feels like being somewhere.

Often the parts of tunes that use a II7 are somewhat contested—meaning, I might like a II7 but someone else might prefer a vi-7 to V7/V. Two such tunes (to my never-ending disappointment) are bars 25~28 of "Triste" and bars 28~30 of "How Deep is the Ocean."

"Triste" is often played as

(CD TRACK 27)

but I prefer

(CD TRACK 28)

Interestingly, one of my Brazilian students pointed out that the original changes of Jobim's are D-7 (iii-7) instead of the Bb Major7, and where I use the II7, Jobim uses a biii dim7th (C# dim7) to lead to the ii-7 chord.

CHAPTER 6   THE FIFTH CIRCLE: MODAL INTERCHANGE CHORDS

(CD TRACK 29)

I've come to like this change as well, although I haven't entirely abandoned my II7 chord on this tune. Even more important, though, is how this illustrates the way a II7 functions as a ii-7 preparatory chord, just as biii dim7 functions as a ii-7 preparatory chord. We end up with three functionally equivalent options for the third and fourth bars of the excerpt above: I maj7 to II7, a ii-V starting on the vi-7, and iii-7 to biii dim7th. Since every standard I can think of has a ii-7 in it, these three substitutes are extremely easy to employ in harmonizations of standards.

"How Deep is the Ocean' is a similar case, often played as

(CD TRACK 30)

but I usually prefer

(CD TRACK 31)

In both of the above examples, the use of the I maj7 going to the II7 gives me a little more breathing room in the chord progression and so is an especially nice option on up tempo songs. The II7 feels like an older style of chord change to me, but also in giving me one less ii-V7 to play over, I get a different feeling—a variation from the more prevalent ii-V7s in the tune. As with any harmonic variation that you feel connected to, when you have a nice spot that you like using a particular harmony, to lose that to another ii-V7 feels a little less special—it makes the tune feel more generic. So to any bass players out there—Get your head out of the fake book and listen up! It may seem like a small difference, but an awareness of these kind of details and the ears to hear them are what makes a pianist pick one bassist over another for a gig (among a lot of other things, of course).

The ii-7b5 chord

The next modal interchange chord on our list is the ii-7b5. So far, the only minor7b5 chords we've seen are the vii-7b5, the diatonic 7th of a major key, and the related ii-7 chords of V7/ii, V7/iii, V7/vi and V7/vii. When the ii-7b5 occurs as a modal interchange chord it's a kind of a subdominant chord and replaces the ii-7. Since ii-7b5 is the subdominant chord of minor key cadences, its appearance in a major key implies that we're going to resolve to a I minor chord (even though we aren't going to.) Because this is such a strong color change the ii-7b5 has a lot of power. Functionally, it is exactly the same as a ii-7 chord, it's a subdominant chord and acts like it, but it has a blast of minor-ness that makes it feel significantly different from a ii-7 chord.

Many, many tunes exploit the ii-7b5 chord. Two of the most famous are "I Love You" (which uses it repeatedly)

(CD TRACK 32)

and "Night and Day"

(CD TRACK 33)

A couple things are worth pointing out in the above examples. One is that both of these tunes extend the feeling of minor borrowing in the melody by going to the b3rd of the key: in "I Love You" the b3 occurs at the downbeat of the 3rd complete bar, as a kind of suspension over the I chord (here I harmonized it with some passing diminished notes, which we'll get into a bit later) and in "Night and Day" the b3rd comes on beat 4 of the second complete bar, leading to the major 3rd on beat 1 of the next bar. This is pretty slick of Cole Porter, who wrote both of these tunes. The effect of the minor ii-Vs above is to signal that we are heading to a minor key, then—surprise—it's major instead. Cole Porter plays with our expectations a bit here, poking around on the minor 3rd before landing on the major 3rd. Another thing to point out is the stuffed voicing on the F-7b5 in the "Night and Day" example. Here I've chosen to add the natural 9, which is a very colorful note on the minor7b5 chord because it's the same note as the major 3rd in the key. If I want a minor7b5 chord to more strongly suggest minor, I'll leave that note out of the voicing. That would be a reasonable choice here, because the more strongly the minor7b5 suggests minor, the more of a surprise the I major7 is in bar 3 of the song. However, for voicing considerations, and just to help get you more acquainted with this chord, I used the natural 9 above. It gives the minor7b5 a more brilliant, brighter sound. Try playing this chord with the 9th and without and see which one you like better.

(We can dispense with another modal interchange chord here because the bVImajor7th often substitutes for the ii-7b5 in "Night and Day". This is a very common use of the bVImaj7. It functions as a subdominant, leading to the V7 of the key from a half-step above.)

(CD TRACK 34)

Another tune that uses this element of "surprise—it's a major I chord", is Stella by Starlight. This tune has a lot of minor7b5 chords in it and they have a few different functions, but when we hear the ii-7b5 in the last four bars of the tune, we might think that the tune will end in i minor, but—surprise!—it doesn't. (Although right about now the feeling of surprise might be wearing off for you a bit.)

(CD TRACK 35)

Of course, you can try the ii minor7b5 chord wherever it doesn't conflict with the melody, but you have to really want this minor-sounding color to use this chord effectively. There is a very big difference between a minor 7 (smooth, moves quickly and without dissonance to a V chord) and a minor7b5 (more complex with tragic overtones— it tends to make me want to linger over it and meditate about death but then, watching the TV show "Friends" has the same effect on me, so I may not be typical).

The iv-7 and iv-6 chords

Our next modal interchange chord is the iv-6 or iv-7 chord. I can use these chords somewhat interchangeably but the IV-6 if anything gives me a clearer statement of this chord's function. It is an inversion of the ii-7b5 and it functions in the same way—it's a subdominant chord. For me, this is a deeply nostalgic chord that brings a romantic minor feeling to a cadence. It also has an "old chord" harmony feeling to it. The place I always think of this chord is in the last phrase of "Embraceable You":

(CD TRACK 36)

Compare this to the often played more neutral sounding cadence

CHAPTER 6

(CD TRACK 37)

In this case, the diatonic passing chords help emphasize the important position of the Ab-6. This is a good example of where using a more colorful chord choice adds drama and emotion. Sometimes, I'll have a piano student prepare a rubato version of a ballad for me. If he or she plays the same standard chord changes as the "Real Book" version of the tune I wonder: 'What are you trying to say in your personal statement of the tune? Why not try and use harmonic substitution to let the listener feel what you think about this tune—to tell a story and to create drama and emotion.' This is something great jazz pianists do. If the mood is right and I play "Embraceable You" really well with a strong connection to the emotion of this romantic ballad, this IV-6 chord sends a chill through me, and I hope people listening in the audience can feel the same thing.

By the way, you don't have to agree with me here. You might prefer to play what I am calling the more neutral sounding version of the last four bars of this tune. We all get to like different things—I just want you to be aware of the differences.

The #iv-7b5 chord

Moving on, our next modal interchange chord is the #iv-7b5. This might be the most used modal interchange chord. Common examples include: "Night and Day"

(CD TRACK 38)

and "Stella by Starlight"

THE FIFTH CIRCLE: MODAL INTERCHANGE CHORDS CHAPTER 6

(CD TRACK 39)

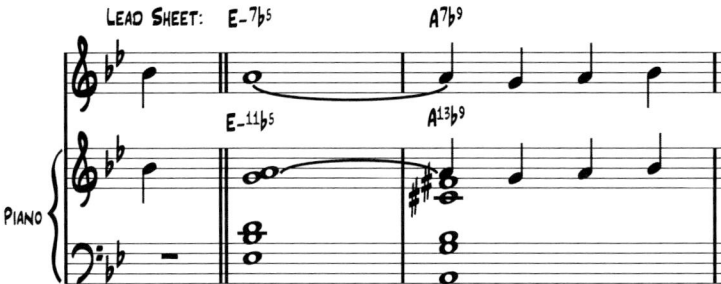

Here's the #iv-7b5 used as a replacement for the first chord of "Somewhere Over the Rainbow". First a neutral common harmonization of the tune:

(CD TRACK 40)

and then the fairly common re-harmonization which substitutes the #iv-7b5 chord:

(CD TRACK 41)

"I Thought About You" is another tune that often is re-harmonized (usually at the start of the second A section of the tune) with a #iv-7b5 replacing the first I chord.

CHAPTER 6

THE FIFTH CIRCLE: MODAL INTERCHANGE CHORDS

(CD TRACK 42)

This same tune has a #iv-7b5 toward the end of the tune that is used in another common way. In this case, the bass walks down from the I chord to the #iv-7b5 diatonically. This device often appears when we are working our way toward a final cadence. Here are bars 27 and 28 of this tune:

(CD TRACK 43)

This modal interchange chord looks a lot like a related ii chord of a V7/iii and is almost always is followed by the V7/iii, so why give it special status as a modal interchange chord? This is another case of multiple-functioning chords. True, we can't really separate this chord from its related ii status, but as Lucy said once to Charlie Brown, 'of all the Charlie Browns out there, you are the Charlie Brown-iest' and perhaps of all of the related ii chords out there, this one is also the Charlie Brown-iest. Or the related ii-iest. In any case, it is a chord that has such a strong signature and harmonic personality that we really need to consider it as a special case.

Functionally, it is usually a kind of tonic chord, replacing in a surprising way an expected I chord at the top of a chorus, the top of a section, or at the end of a phrase (leading to an extension of that phrase.) Often it is followed by the V7/iii which leads to a turnaround iii-7 V7/ii / ii-7 V7 (or some other turnaround variation.) Since it's a chord that leads to iii (or a tonic chord at the beginning of a turnaround) it can also sometimes replace a ii-7 chord (leading to a V to set up a tonic). This happens in some re-harmonizations of "I Should Care", a song that starts on a ii-7 chord. Wherever it occurs, this chord tends to feel like a surprise when you hear it, a very colorful substitute.

THE FIFTH CIRCLE: MODAL INTERCHANGE CHORDS   CHAPTER 6

It occurs in so many tunes, either as a re-harmonization or a standard feature of the harmony, that there isn't any point in listing more examples but I will anyway: "Stardust", "I've Grown Accustomed to Her Face", "I Remember You", "That's All", "Just One of Those Things", "There Will Never Be Another You," "I Could Have Told You", "In Love in Vain", "I Should Care", and a gazillion others. It is a favorite technique of both Keith Jarrett and Bill Evans, among many other pianists.

This chord with the turnaround that often follows it is one of the most common (improvised) endings to a standard tune, and this ending is written into the progressions of "Night and Day" and "That's All". Many songs that go to the IV chord (followed by either iv-7, bVII7 or #iv diminished7) and then have a turnaround back to the original key such as rhythm changes, "The Masquerade is Over", "All the Things You Are", "All of Me" among thousands of others, will work with a #iv-7b5 as a substitute for the IV chord. This is from the last A of "All the Things You Are". First the normal changes

(CD TRACK 44)

Here's the same section with the #iv-7b5 taking the place of the IV maj7:

(CD TRACK 45)

This is such a beautiful chord. It takes a very often-played tune like "All the Things You Are" and gives it a fresh sound. In your own re-harmonizations, try these various uses of the #iv-7b5, to replace a IV chord that leads to a iv-7 before a turnaround back to the top or to replace a I chord, especially one that leads to a iii chord or a turnaround. As always, you have to make sure that the melody works with your substitution.

CHAPTER 6

THE FIFTH CIRCLE: MODAL INTERCHANGE CHORDS

The bVII7 chord

The next modal interchange chord is the bVII7 chord. This chord has a bluesy sound and usually leads to the I chord. It feels something like a plagal cadence (IV to I, the Amen cadence) and is found in blues related tunes such as "Killer Joe"

(CD TRACK 46)

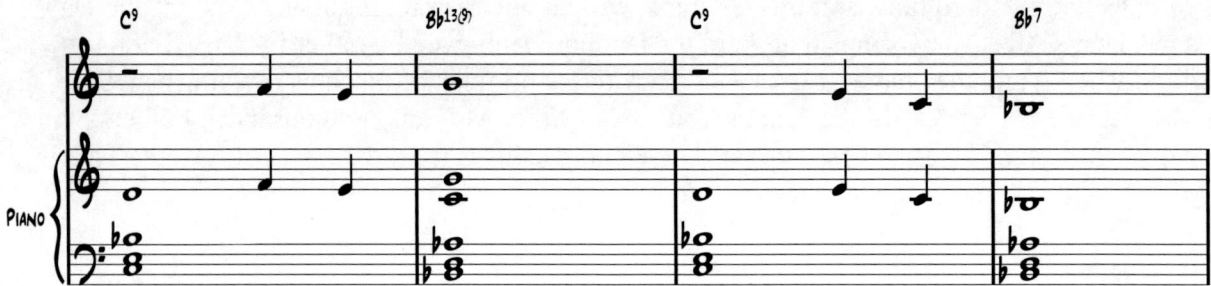

Charles Mingus's "Nostalgia in Times Square"

(CD TRACK 47)

"On Broadway" is another blues-oriented tune that features the bVII7 chord change.

We also find this chord in more traditional standards like "Old Devil Moon."

(CD TRACK 48)

64

These I, bVII7, I tunes show that the bVII7 is another way to lead back to one. This can be used as a substitute in a ii-V, so that the progression ii-7 bVII7 (with or without the related ii-7 chord of the bVII7) replaces the V chord and leads back to I. This is a less forceful way of going back to I than using a dominant that resolves up a fourth. This kind of resolution feels a little duller to me, kind of blunt and a little slower, with a slightly bluesy natural tension dominant feeling. An example of this type of chord can be found in bar 10 of "It Could Happen to You".

(CD TRACK 49)

The bVII7 occurs in "Stella By Starlight" several times.

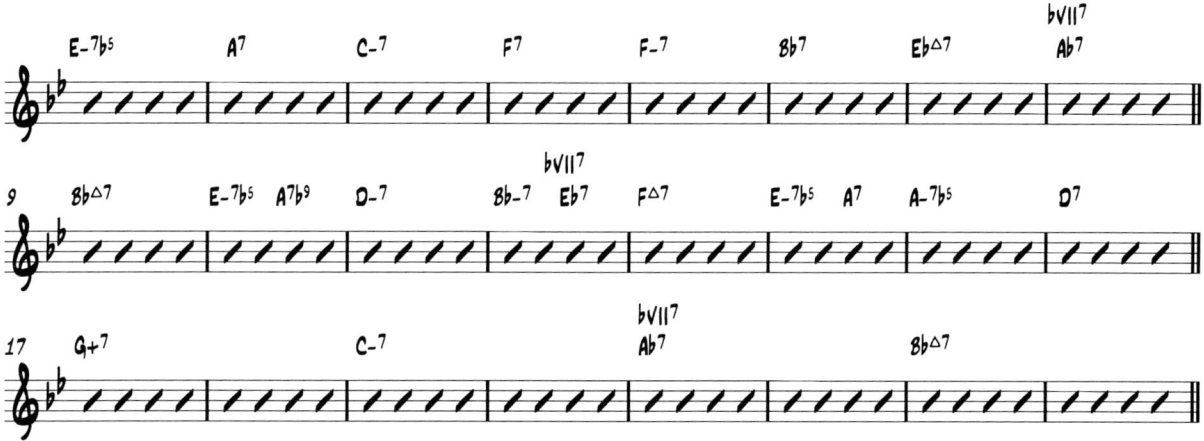

Bars 8, 12 and 21 all feature bVII7 chords resolving up a whole step to I. Please note that G-7 C7 is often played in bar 12 to lead to the F major7 chord in bar 13. Bb minor7 to Eb7 are "up a minor third" substitutes for the ii-V. One of my students calls this ii-V substitute a "back-door ii-V" because it leads to the I chord through an unexpected route.

So much for the most common modal interchange chords. These are the uncles and aunts of the modal interchange family. Going back to our list above, we can now quickly run down the roles played by the remaining family members. These are the second cousins and divorced folks who used to be related by marriage but show up to most of the larger weddings.

I7: A substitute for the I chord. I dominant 7th is a chord that comes to us from blues and like the I7 chord of a blues, tends to take natural tensions. Standards using this device include, "Honeysuckle Rose", "Sweet and Lovely", "Lover Man" and "Willow Weep for Me".

bII major7: a delaying chord that precedes the I major7th at the end of a form or phrase. Generally speaking this chord substitutes for the I before resolving to the I. Functionally similar to a I dim major7. This chord is found in "Lush Life" and "Spring Can Really Hang You Up the Most".

bIII major7, usually takes the place of the second tonic chord in a turnaround (so Cmajor7 to Aminor7 would become Cmajor7 to Ebmajor7). "Ladybird" features this turnaround.

IV7: a bluesy dominant 7 substitute for a IV chord. "Lover Man", "Willow Weep for Me," "Sweet and Lovely" and "Honeysuckle Rose" all contain IV7 chords.

bVImajor7: a substitute for a ii-7b5 chord and thereby a substitute for a ii chord. Also commonly used in a turnaround of I bIIImajor7 bVImajor7 bII major7). As mentioned above, this chord is used in "Night and Day". It can also be found in the turaround at the end of "Ladybird".

And that pretty much does it for the modal interchange family. The better you know these chords, the more you will notice the way they change the harmonic landscape of common standards. By employing these colorful and subtle chords, you will make your renditions of standards a lot more personal and less generic. So, again we are in the part of the chapter where I suggest that you go out and try these modal interchange options on many, many standards in your repertoire. Look through tunes in fake books and see if you can find examples of the various types of Modal Interchange chords in action. As I mentioned once or twice before, using these devices on many tunes (as well as analyzing tunes to look for these devices being employed) is the way to get a feeling for the effect these chord variations have.

CHAPTER 7 – THE LAST CIRCLE: TRITONE SUBSTITUTES

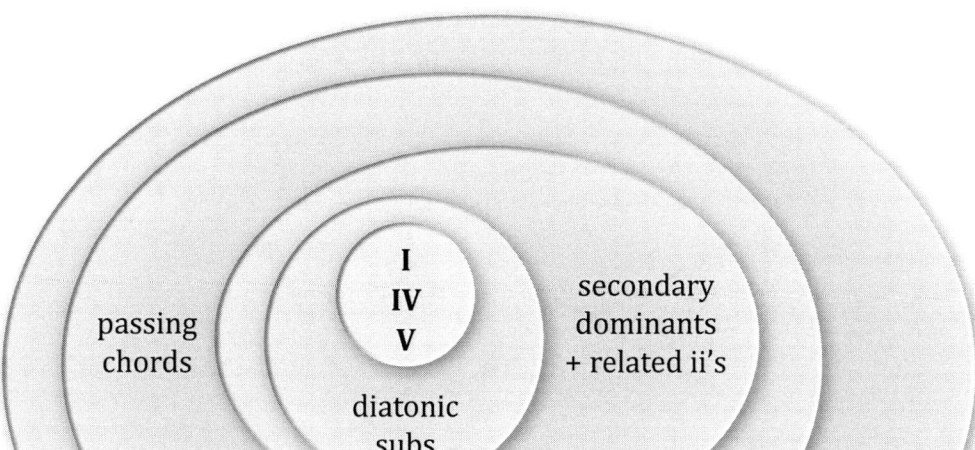

We're almost to the end of our concentric circle harmonic universe. The last circle concerns tritone substitutes. Perhaps more than many of the harmonic devices used by jazz players, this is the one that students think they understand. However, as I've been saying regarding all of the techniques we've been studying, there's more to this one than meets the eye, and you can use tritone substitutes in many subtle ways, even in situations where it you might think that tritone substitutes are unavailable.

When I was a young pianist coming up in Cleveland I used to work with a great older bassist named Lamar Gaines. Lamar had played with many jazz greats, including Wynton Kelly and was one of those local heroes that can be found in every urban area with a jazz community, particularly industrial centers like Cleveland, Pittsburgh and Detroit. Lamar had started on piano I believe, but had also played organ before coming to the bass. As an organist, he was used to controlling things harmonically, since organ players generally play the bass as well as chord changes and frequently re-harmonize on the spot, since there is never a problem of chord agreement between the bass note (organist's left hand) and chord (organist's right hand). This background gave Lamar a lot of license to go wherever he wanted harmonically on a standard and whenever I played with him, I always got a real workout, trying to hear the changes that he was playing since they differed from what I knew, and sometimes differed chorus to chorus. Of course, he used all of the re-harmonization techniques we've been discussing (all the circles) but I still remember that feeling of fourths and tritones flying around, bass lines that sounded good to me, but weren't the changes as I knew them.

Chapter 7

The Last Circle: Tritone Substitutes

Another association that I have with tritone substitution comes from the first day of the great alto saxist Bob Mover's ensemble in Berklee College. He had played with many great players as well, including Charles Mingus, George Adams and Albert Dailey (the night I heard Bob and Albert Dailey play together was probably the night I decided to become a full-time jazz musician, but that's another story). Bob came into the classroom and wrote this diagram on the blackboard:

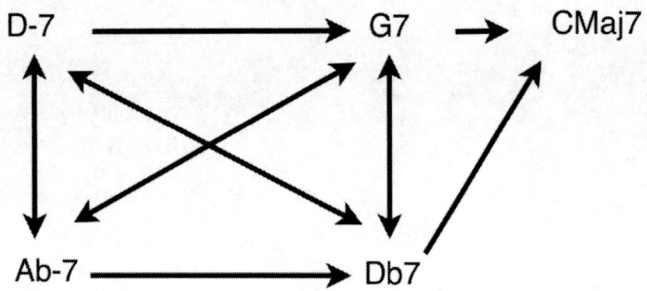

Bob told us that this was a key piece of theory that we needed to solo over chord changes. It meant that every ii-V has a "light side" (the D-7 G7 side of the ii-V, playing dorian on the ii-7 chord and mixolydian or Lydian b7 on the dominant) and a dark side a tritone away. A lot of jazz line vocabulary involves seeing a G7 and thinking Db7 (or seeing a G7 and thinking Ab-7 Db7.) This is because these two dominant chords have a lot in common. First of all, they share the same tritone, meaning the 3rd and 7th of both chords are the same notes. (In other words, the notes B and F are both the 3rd and 7th of the G7 chord and the 7th and 3rd of the Db7 chord). Play a dominant 7th scale with no altered tensions (1, 2, 3, #4, 5, 6, b7 or a lydian b7 scale) and then play a scale a tritone away with ALL altered tensions (1, b9, #9, 3 #11, b13 b7, or an altered scale) and you'll see that these two scales have the exact same notes in them.

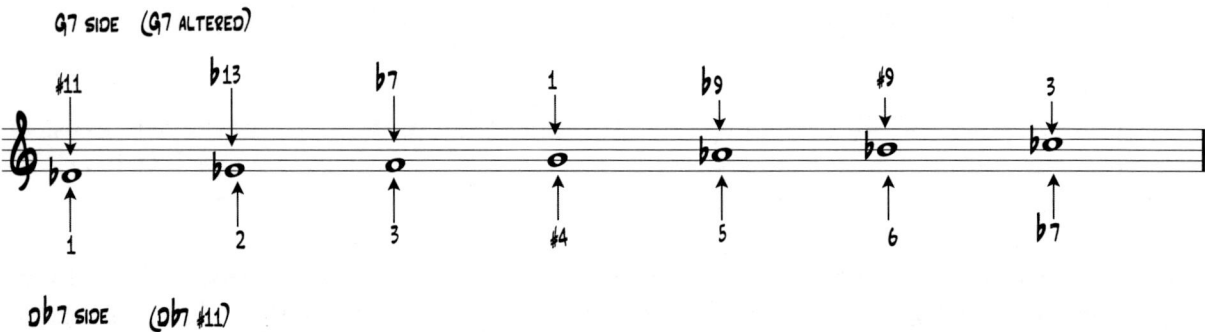

So you can see from above that the G7altered scale = the Db7 #11 scale. And of course, the opposite is also true, the Db7altered scale = the G7 #11 scale.

THE LAST CIRCLE: TRITONE SUBSTITUTES — CHAPTER 7

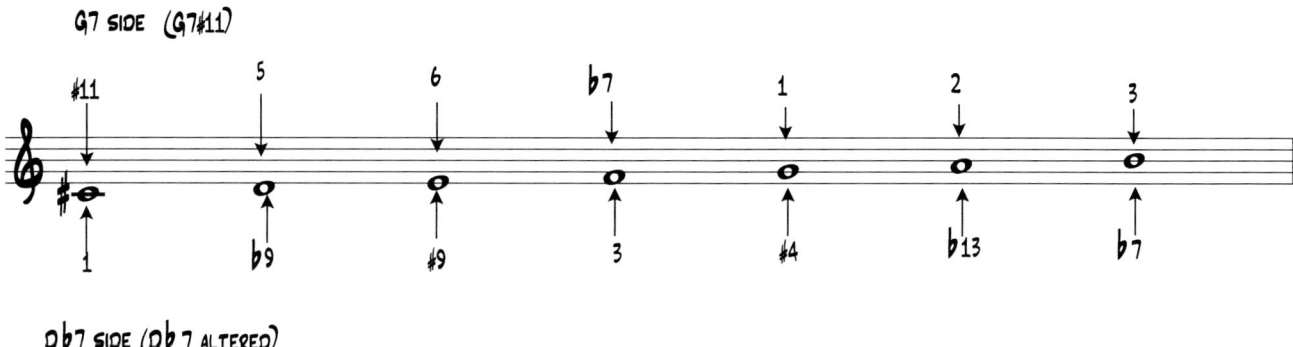

The altered scale is a darker scale that (pretty much as you would expect by now) implies resolution up a fourth to some target chord. I can get there either by thinking: D-7 to G7 altered or D-7 to Db7#11 (Lydian b7). Sometimes students use a tritone substitute and then to make it sound even hipper they alter the tensions on it. Altering tensions on the dominant7th a tritone away is possible (as long as it doesn't clash with the melody) but often defeats the purpose of the tritone substitute because altering the Db7 makes it more like the G7 with natural tensions. Of course, that's allowable, but it doesn't increase the tension in the chord sound—it does the opposite. A tritone substitute often gets natural tensions (because we've essentially modulated to a sound a tritone away and natural tensions enhance that feeling of modulation.) Or to state it more simply, natural tensions on a dominant a tritone away are the same as altered tensions on the original dominant. Using a natural tension dominant a tritone away is like going from the original dominant to its altered form, which is the way dominant tensions usually go. Natural 9, for example, leads well to b9 which leads to the 5th of the chord the dominant resolves to. Natural 13 leads well to b13 which resolves to a natural 9 on the target chord.

No doubt many of you will already know this about tritone substitutes. Again, the issue is 'knowing' versus 'using'. Let's look at tritone substitutes in context. Usually when students hear the term tritone substitute, they think of changing the ii-V to a ii-7, bII7 (sometimes called the sub-V7). This is one of the possibilities of tritone substitution (and it is an important one) but it is usually the least dramatic transformation of the normal ii-V.

When you find the right place for a tritone substitute, especially when it's possible (with the melody) to use the whole ii-V a tritone away, it can be a very surprising and dramatic change to the harmony, but it's a change that preserves the function of the ii-V. One famous example of this is in "All the Things You Are". First the regular changes for the first four bars:

CHAPTER 7

THE LAST CIRCLE: TRITONE SUBSTITUTES

(CD TRACK 50)

And then the common tri-tone substitute in bar 3:

(CD TRACK 51)

In this example, the normal chord change in bar three is Eb7. If you add the related ii-7 chord to the Eb7, Bb-7, you can see that the above substitution is a ii-V a tritone away or E-7 to A7.

I've always liked this tritone substitute in the second half of the A section in "My Romance". Again, first the normal changes

(CD TRACK 52)

THE LAST CIRCLE: TRITONE SUBSTITUTES — CHAPTER 7

and then the substitute

(CD TRACK 53)

In the fourth bar above, the usual chords are F-7 to Bb7, a ii-V that leads to the IV chord at the beginning of the B section. I've replaced the whole ii-V, both the ii-7 chord and the V7 chord, with a ii-V a tritone away. That's what makes these tritone substitutes dramatic: there's a momentary feeling of modulation, or of a pleasantly wrong chord change that still makes harmonic sense.

But we can dig a little deeper into the process of using tritone substitutes. When I am re-harmonizing a tune I want to examine all of the possibilities of moving between the two "sides" of the ii-V:

> Ab-7 Db7 Cmaj7
> D-7 Ab-7 Db7 Cmaj7
> Ab-7 D-7 G7 Cmaj7
> Ab-7 Db7 D-7 G7 Cmaj7
> D-7 G7 Ab-7 Db7 Cmaj7
> D-7 Ab-7 G7 Db7 Cmaj7, etc.

Of course, these transformations will only be effective if they support the melody of the tune. Let's look at some ii-V passages from "Here's that Rainy Day". In this case bar 2 and 3:

71

CHAPTER 7

CD TRACK 54)

We are working with the F-7 to Bb7 bar for now. The tritone substitute for this ii-V is B-7 to E7. I'd like to substitute the whole ii-V like we did above in "All the Things You Are", but that's not possible because the melody won't allow it.

(CD TRACK 55)

Sometimes students will try this substitution anyway, changing the above B-7 to a B-7b5 to accommodate the F natural in the melody. But as I've said before, a minor7b5 is a very different chord from minor7. Tritone substitution works best for major ii-Vs, working with the ii-V and a second ii-V a tritone away. So simply flatting the fifth and on the ii-7 usually isn't a great choice since it doesn't preserve the special relationship between F-7 Bb7 and B-7 E7.

The easiest tritone substitute I can use above is to keep the F-7 and replace the Bb7 with an E7. As I mentioned above, this is the most common tritone substitute and it's useful, but in this case not particularly dramatic or interesting.

THE LAST CIRCLE: TRITONE SUBSTITUTES — CHAPTER 7

(CD TRACK 56)

If I analyze the melody, I find that the first note, D, is a 13 on the F-7, a third on the B-7, a 7th on the E7 and a 3rd on the Bb7. The second note, F, is a root on the F-7, unavailable on the B-7, a b9 on the E7 and a 5th on the Bb7. The third note Bb is an 11th on F-7, unavailable on the B-7, a #11th on the E7 and a root on the Bb7. The fourth note is a D again. Now I can harmonize each note with a chord that fits it. I also am thinking that I probably want to end the bar with a dominant 7th rather than a minor 7th since I want a chord that will lead more strongly to the Ebmajor7. Here are some of the choices available to me.

(CD TRACK 57)

(CD TRACK 58)

Chapter 7

The Last Circle: Tritone Substitutes

(CD TRACK 59)

Of these, the last is probably the strongest. I like it because it starts on the B-7 and has the whole tritone ii-V in there. I can also combine tritone substitutes with secondary dominants and/or sus4 chords to good effect.

(CD TRACK 60)

(CD TRACK 61)

The important thing about all of these examples is that on first glance the ii-V was incompatible with tritone substitution because the F natural clashes with the B-7 chord change, but upon closer examination, there are a lot of interesting tritone possibilities if I keep searching.

Let's look at another excerpt from this tune, this time bars 6,7 and 8.

(CD TRACK 62)

I've added a few tensions, but the basic structure here is D7 for a bar, G major7 for a bar and then a ii-V to the IV chord, so D minor7 G7.

First of all, if I want to, I can treat the D7 as a ii-V7 (although I may not want to, because the bar before had an A-7 in it and so A-7 here may feel redundant.)

The tritone substitute for A-7 D7 would be Eb-7 to Ab7. Next I analyze the melody. The first note, D, is an 11th on the A-7, the root of the D7, unavailable on the Eb-7 and the #11 of the Ab7, the second note F# is the 13th of the A-7, the 3rd of the D7, the 3rd of the Eb-7 and the 7th of the Ab7. The third note, A, is the root of the A-7, not available on the Eb-7, the b9 on the Ab7 and the 5th of the D7 and the last note, C, is the 3rd of the A-7, the 13th of the Eb-7, the 7th of the D7 and the 3rd of the Ab7. This analysis tells me that I can probably only use the Eb-7 (and this is the chord that I might want to try to find a spot for, because using the related ii-7 of the tritone substitute makes the substitution more dramatic feeling) on the second beat of the measure. It's also available on the last beat of the measure, but I probably want a dominant there. Here are some options:

CHAPTER 7

THE LAST CIRCLE: TRITONE SUBSTITUTES

(CD TRACK 63)

(CD TRACK 64)

(CD TRACK 65)

None of these changes are quite as dramatic as the first tritone substitutes in the second bar of this song, but that's how it goes. These harmonic options just give you choices and ideas of places you might take the harmony. When you plug them in and try them you can evaluate which ones really transform the song and which ones don't work for you. However, I do like the Eb-11 chord in there, leading the way to the D7 or Ab7. That changes the feeling, albeit in a somewhat subtle way. As I mentioned above, having subtle harmonic alterations available is very important in re-harmonizing situations because sometimes you want some sort of small harmonic movement to occur. You need a change in the harmony, but you don't want it to stick out.

One last point about these options—sometimes I want to keep the original dominant to get the full effect of altered tensions above the root, not going to the root a tritone away. It's all a matter of personal taste and context.

Again, if I add secondary dominants I have more possibilities.

(CD Track 66)

(CD Track 67)

And of course, passing chords are also available.

CHAPTER 7 — THE LAST CIRCLE: TRITONE SUBSTITUTES

(CD Track 68)

(CD Track 69)

Still, I am not convinced about the advantage of these changes in this bar, the way I was in bar 2. Sometimes the original changes are better than what you come up with. Or in the words of Lamar Gaines, "you're killing and killing but ain't nobody dying."

But there's more I can look at in this passage. The phrase ends on a Gmajor7 that is followed by a D-7 G7 in the eighth bar of the song (leading to a C-7 in bar 9 of the song.) I can replace the G7 with a Db7.

(CD Track 70)

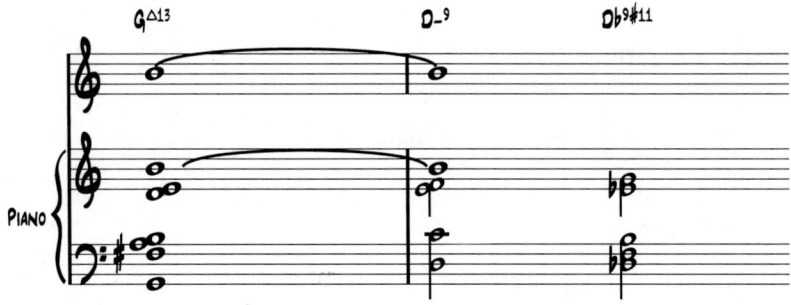

Or since the melody is a B natural (the 3rd of the Ab-7) I can replace the whole ii-7 V7

(CD Track 71)

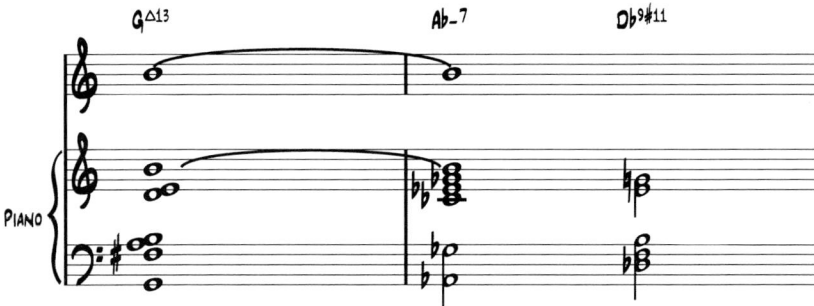

I can also use a modal interchange substitution to change the Gmaj7 to a I7 and add it's related ii-7 (the melody is the 13 so this works fine).

(CD Track 72)

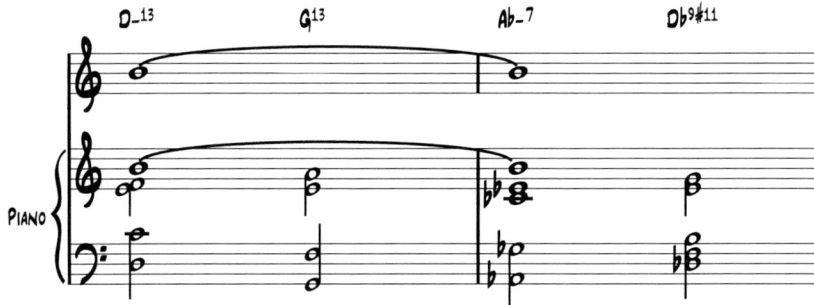

Now I could re-arrange these four chords however I like, since they all are consonant with the melody. Perhaps my favorite is to keep only the tritone substitutes, since this creates the most surprise.

(CD Track 73)

As you can see from the examples above, tritone substitutes can give you a wealth of possibilities and variations in chord progressions. These variations are all expressions of the fundamental harmony of this song, its harmonic structure at the deepest level. This probably requires a little bit of explanation although this idea has been in the background of all of the harmonic moves that we've been studying from the very beginning of this book.

What is the underlying harmony of a song? If all of the chords are negotiable (subject to the harmonic manipulations of the six circles that we've been exploring) then what are the actual, or "right" chords of a song? Some people would answer that the proper changes of the tune are what the composer wrote. And that's true in a sense, particularly if you want to develop a historical understanding of where the harmony of a tune comes from. You can check out the harmonic details that George Gershwin wrote on "I Got Rhythm" (for example) and you'll certainly learn something interesting about the harmony of the tune and about the way functional harmony was employed in 1930 when that song was written. But since these songs are tonal, meaning that their harmonic structures are determined by the rules of functional harmony, we can't say that what the composer wrote is the basic harmonic structure of the tune and that's the end of the story. When a composer writes a tune he decides whether there are passing chords, related ii-7 chords to accompany dominants, tritone substitutes, modal interchange chords, secondary dominants, diatonic substitutes and the like. But since these devices are somewhat interchangeable subject to the whim of the arranger, the composer's version of the harmony is really just one way of speaking this harmonic language to accompany a particular melody.

So for "Here's that Rainy Day" the changes for the first 8 bars of the song are often given as the following.

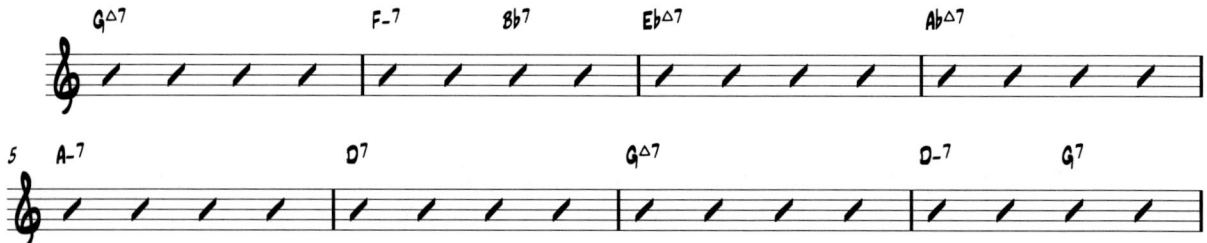

But this is just one of many variations (including, of course, all of the ii-V variations discussed earlier in the chapter) of possible chord changes for this tune.

If I want to think of a "deep structure" to the harmony of the tune, I have to think more in terms of the important harmonic areas that this song visits. This analysis will be a little closer to the first circle harmony we looked at on Christmas carols. Maybe this gets a little closer to it:

THE LAST CIRCLE: TRITONE SUBSTITUTES — CHAPTER 7

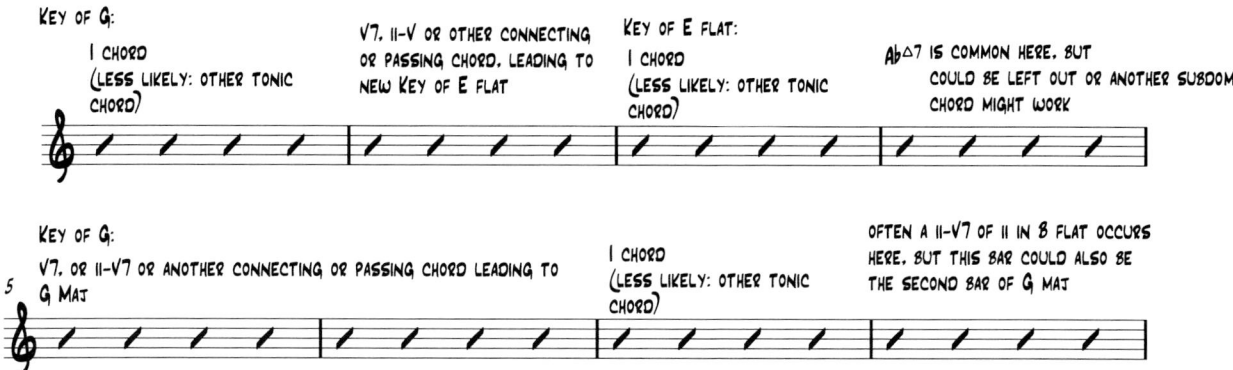

The deep structure is always somewhat vague or negotiable, meaning that there are some main points, such as that "Here's that Rainy Day" begins on the I chord in G and modulates to Eb in the third bar (or to speak out of any particular key, the song begins on a I major chord and then modulates to the key of bVI major). The deep structure is something like our first circle harmonizations, but now that we are looking at songs that are more complex than Christmas carols, the deep structure is a little more varied and often contains modulations to other keys. We'll be discussing this deep structure idea a bit more later, when we try to figure out what the "right" changes for a standard are, but for now, I just want to point out that all of the harmonic steps, the concentric circles that suggest how to harmonize a song, are a kind of language. If I have an idea I want to impart such as: "I am confused." I can say: "I have no idea what's going on." Or I can say: "What the?!!!" or "Are you out of your mind?!!!" or " I am paralyzed by an overwhelming sense of chaos and confusion." Or "I am at a loss…" or "I don't get it." Or "the depths of my confusion fill me with a sense of dread…" or "erp….uh…hmm…uh…" All of these are expressions of my confusion. In the same way, when I want to play a standard, I can add or subtract chords; add, subtract or alter tensions, use tritone substitutes, diatonic substitutes and passing chords; but finally I am trying to express "These Foolish Things" (or whatever standard I am playing) in that particular moment, with that particular harmony. Listening to younger players playing these tunes from the Real Book with all the harmony as given is a bit like living in a world of robots or pod people where everyone expresses thoughts using the same words. So let's all stop doing that.

I need to say one more thing about tritone substitution before moving on and that is that it's probably time to update our turnaround vocabulary. When we looked at the turnaround possibilities in Chapter 3 we didn't have access to passing chord, tritone substitute or modal interchange harmony, so let's add some more common turnarounds that utilize these approaches. Remember we were in F major, contemplating a part of a tune that either sits on the I major chord or cycles through turnarounds. Here are some more possibilities:

Using diatonic passing chords.

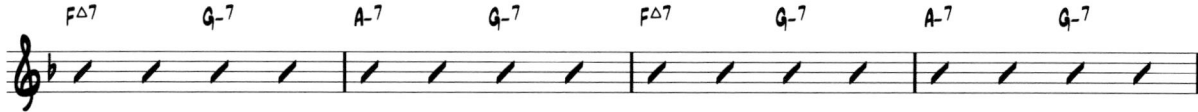

CHAPTER 7

Using diminished passing chords

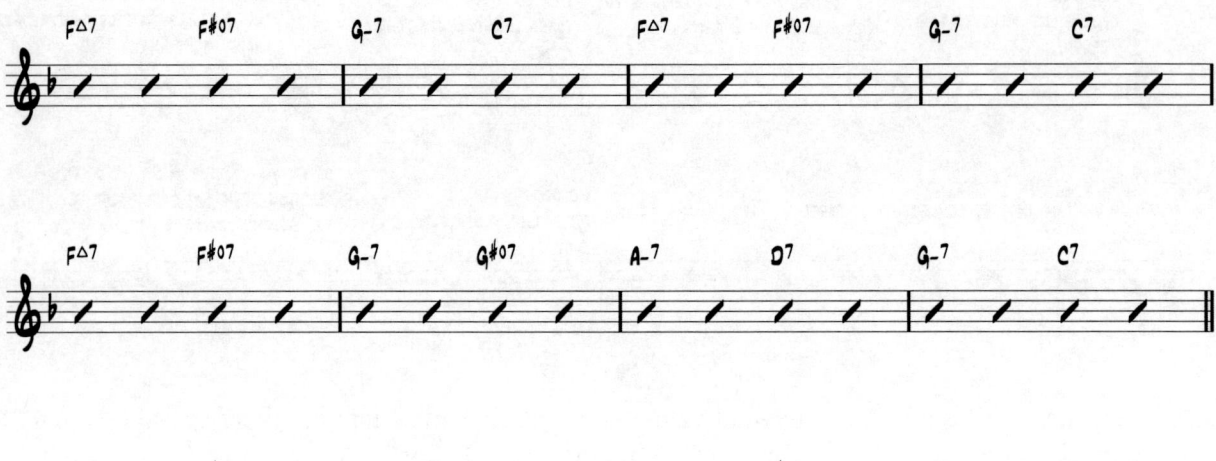

Using other passing chords and/or modal interchange chords

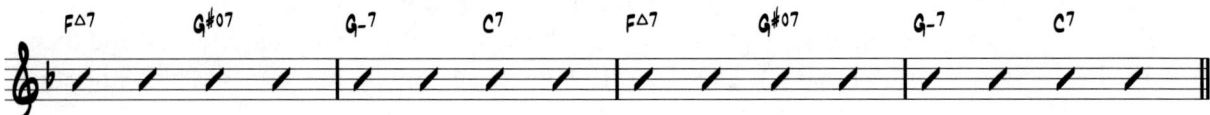

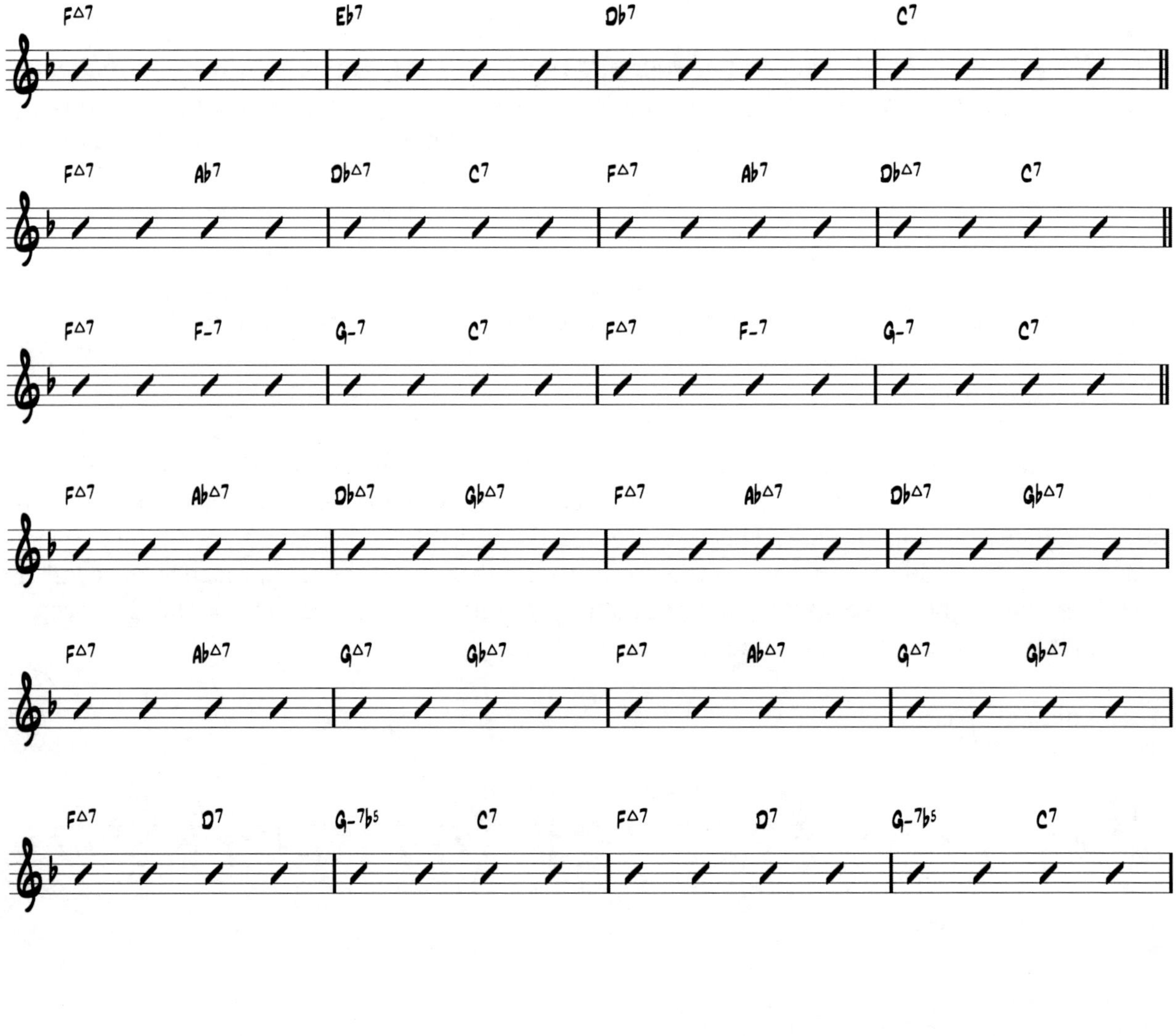

THE LAST CIRCLE: TRITONE SUBSTITUTES   CHAPTER 7

Using tritone substitutes and/or passing chords and/or modal interchange chords.

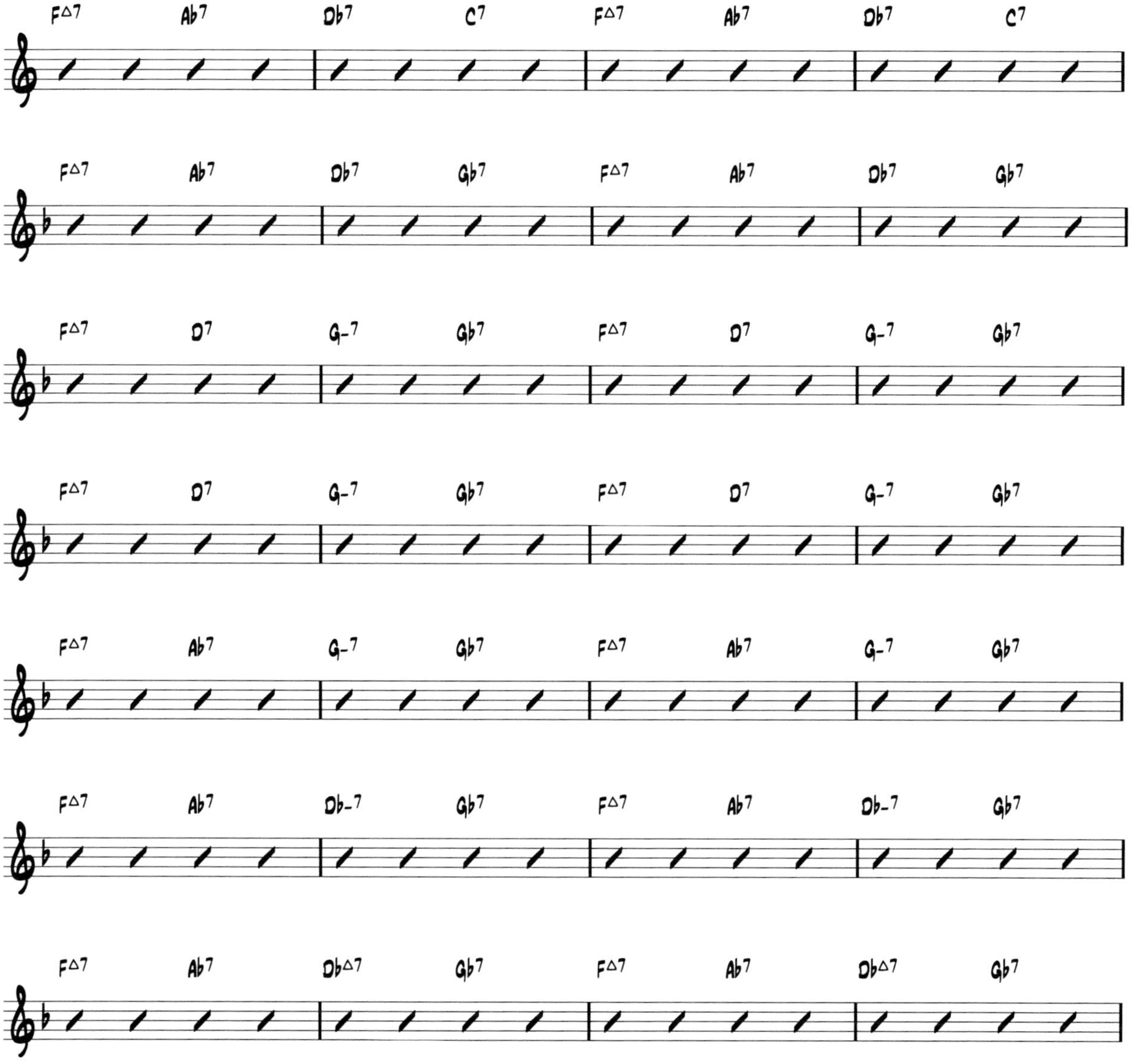

You can make many more combinations from the above tools, (Fmajor7 D7 Dbmaj7 C7; A-7 Ab-7 G-7 Gb7; A-7 D7 Db-7 Gb7 and on and on) but this is a start. Some of the above turn-arounds are in common use and are seen often and others are more unusual. With such a wealth of possibilities to pick from, how come beginning pianists so often play Imaj7 vi-7 ii-7 V7 as an intro to every tune when working with a singer?

Chapter 8 – The Harmony of Minor tunes

The more observant among you may have noticed that all of the songs and most of the cadences we've been using are major. And yet, minor tunes are quite common. Most of the relationships in minor tunes, however, end up being simpler than in major tune harmony for a few reasons:

1. Most of the harmonic approaches we've been discussing (the concentric circles) are available in minor tunes, although the application (particularly relating to tritone substitution and modal interchange) is much more limited.
2. Minor tunes tend to go to fewer places harmonically than major tunes.
3. Minor tunes often have passages of relative major harmony or modulations to other major keys, and these utilize all the major harmonic approaches covered.
4. Dominant 7th chords in minor cadences tend to employ a more limited palette of possible tensions.

If we approached minor tunes the same way that we approached major ones, our first step would be to make diatonic seventh chords from the minor scale. Classical harmony offers three minor scale options: the natural minor scale, the harmonic minor scale and the melodic minor (ascending) so which minor scale do we use? There isn't one simple answer to this question. If we use the natural minor (the Aeolian mode of the major scale) which is the one implied by the key signature (C minor has 3 flats in its key signature—this key is built on the C natural minor scale) to make diatonic sevenths, then our V chord would also be a minor7 and yet we really need a dominant 7th built on the fifth degree of the scale because all minor standards at some point have a V7 resolving to the i- chord. If I use the harmonic minor scale to construct diatonic sevenths, then V7 is available, but my only option for a i chord is I minor major7, a fairly intense chord that won't always feel like a resolved tonic sound. (It can be considered a tonic chord in minor, but I will probably need something simpler available as well such as a i minor6 which isn't available to me in harmonic minor.) If I use melodic minor, then i minor6 is available, but the diatonic iv chord in this scale is a dominant7. Since iv- is a very common chord in minor tunes I can't derive all the chords I need from the melodic minor scale alone..

The answer is to this problem is that I use chords derived from all three minor scales to make functional harmony and cadences in minor keys. Just as we saw when we were discussing modal interchange chords, where many, many chords are available as theoretical possibilities but there was a much smaller group of commonly used chords, the same goes for chords derived from these three minor scales. The most common of these minor chords are: i minor6, i minor major7, i minor7, ii-7b5, bIIImajor7, IV-7, V7(b9b13), bVImaj7, bVI7, vi-7b5, bVIImaj7, bVII7, vii diminished7. (Interestingly, the vii chord of the harmonic minor is a diminished7, which would allow us to consider all of the uses of diminished passing chords discussed in Chapter 3 as modal interchange chords borrowed from this scale.)

These minor chords then, are the family of chords from which we derive the functional relationships of minor chords in a key. We can now group them in tonic, subdominant and dominant categories. However, due to the complexity of the scales from which these chords are derived, the placement of some of these chords is a bit less cut and dried than in major key harmony.

THE HARMONY OF MINOR TUNES

CHAPTER 8

Tonic chords: i minor6, i minor7, i minor major7, vi-7b5, bIII major7
Subdominant: iv-7, ii-7b5, bVIImaj7, bVI7, bVI major7, bVII7
Dominant: V7, vii dim7

The most common cadence in minor is ii-7b5 to V7b9 to i minor of some sort, sometimes followed by the vi-7b5. Deceptive cadences, meaning cadences that resolve to a different tonic chord than i are much rarer than in major tunes. An interesting exception to this is the deceptive resolution to the parallel major, which is a kind of modal interchange chord that replaces the i- in songs like, "Alone Together and "What is This Thing Called Love.

Turnarounds can occur in minor tunes the same way they occur in major tunes, with diatonic substitutes, secondary dominants and tritone substitutes. Here are some common minor turnarounds.

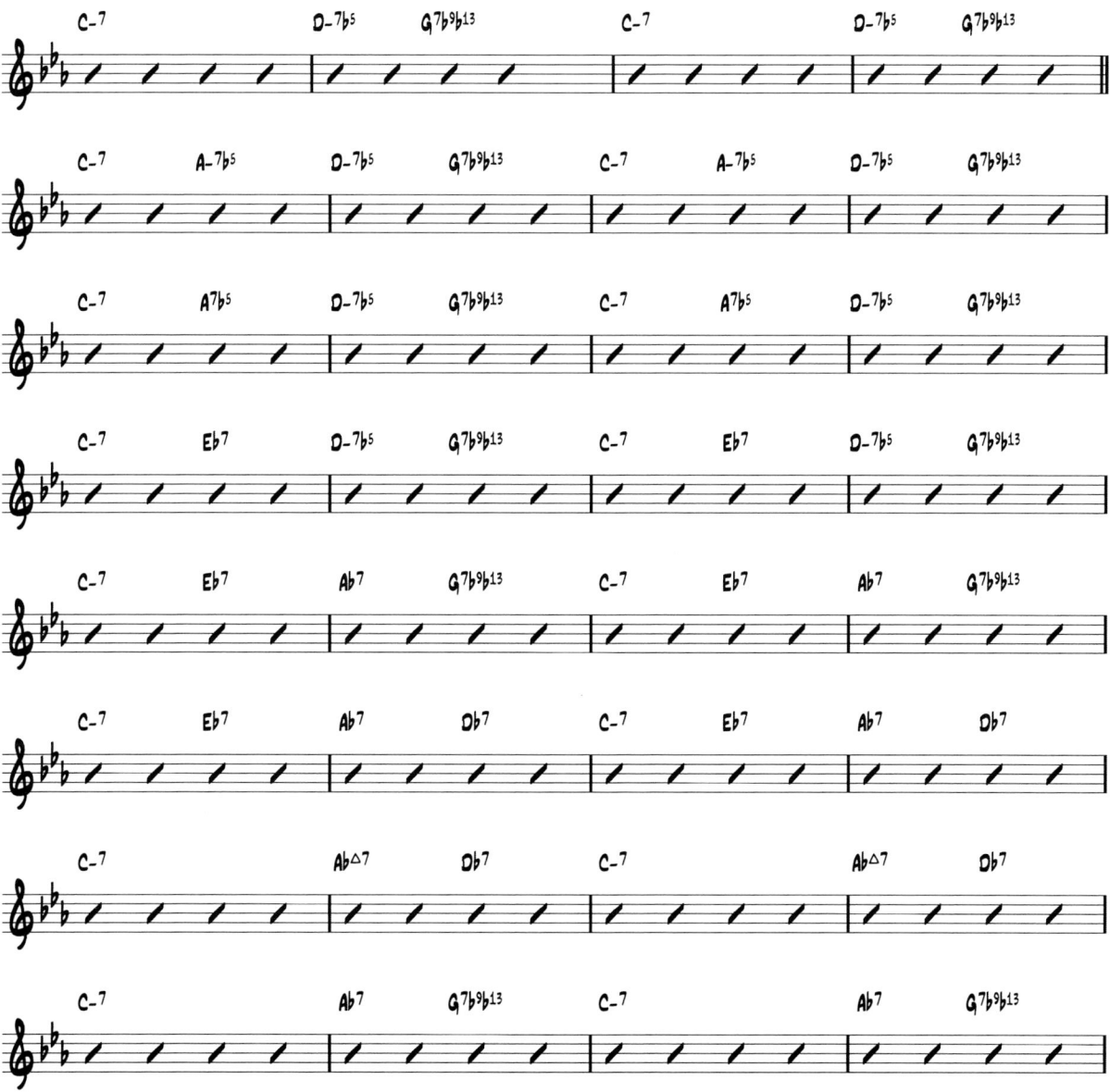

CHAPTER 8

THE HARMONY OF MINOR TUNES

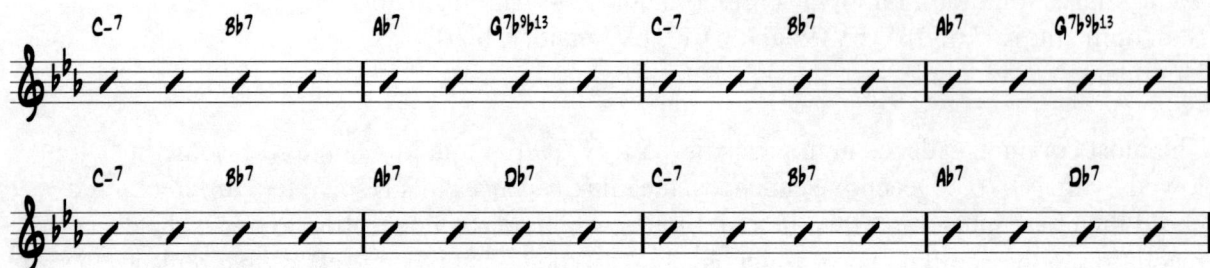

Just as we saw above regarding major turnarounds, you can create more variations using passing chords, secondary dominants and tritone substitutes of dominant sevenths. Diminished passing chords are somewhat rarer in these turnarounds, although the vii diminished 7 sometimes replaces the V7.

Minor tunes (at least, in standards) tend to look pretty similar harmonically. Common harmonic movement in minor tunes include: the use of turnarounds such as those listed above, modulation to the relative major (bIII major) modulation to the bVI major, modulation to the iv minor.

Let's look at a few of these chord progressions in action. Perhaps the most famous minor tune is George Gershwin's "Summertime." (Q: How many singers does it take to sing Summertime? A: Apparently all of them.) Here is fairly standard version of the chord progression.

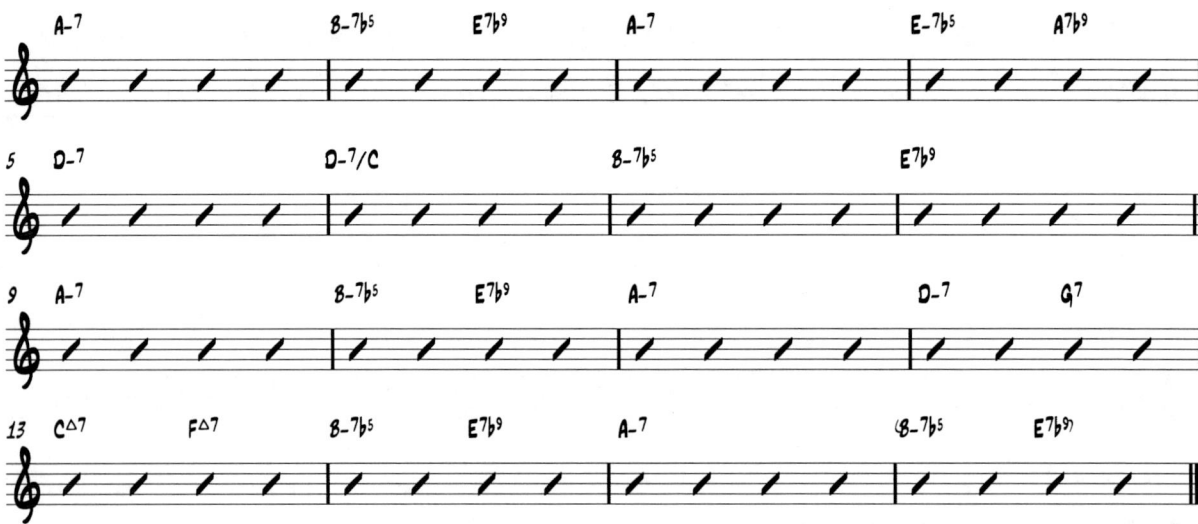

This tune has many of the common features of minor tunes that we've been discussing. The first 3 bars are a standard cadence (i-, ii-7b5, V7, i-) in A-, followed by a secondary dominant with its related ii chord that resolves to iv- in bar 5. Bar 6 is iv-/7 which is just a passing bass note to lead to the ii-7b5 V7 b9 which brings us back to A-. Bars 9 – 11 are the same as bars 1 – 3. Bar 12 is a ii-V to bIII major7, the relative major then IV major of the major key, or bVI major of the minor key—this is a dual function chord that bridges the major and minor sections of the tune, then ii-7b5 V7b9 and resolution to i minor.

86

THE HARMONY OF MINOR TUNES   CHAPTER 8

Black Orpheus, another very familiar minor tune, has almost all of the same features:

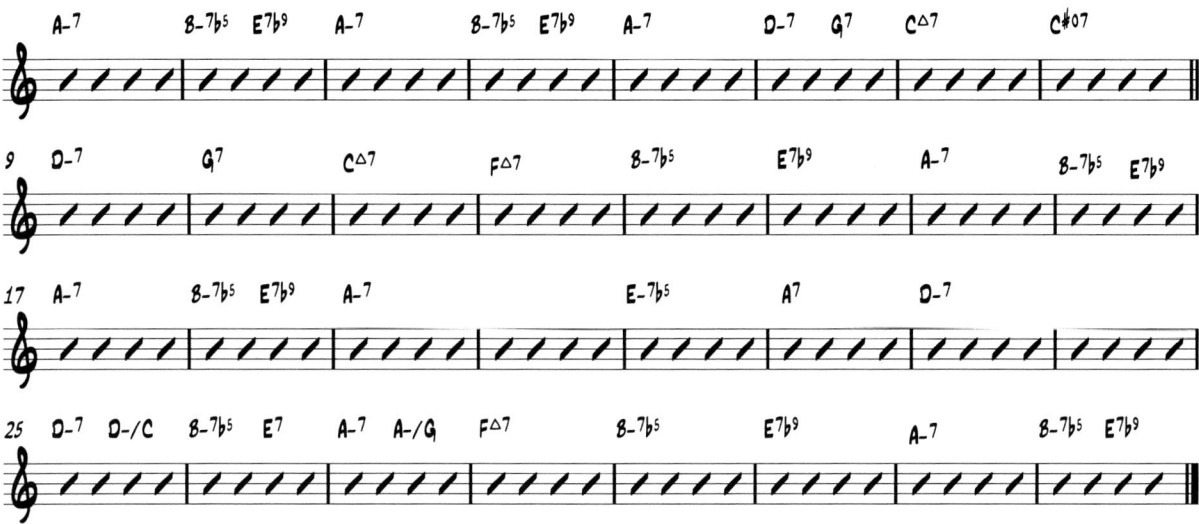

Again, after setting up the tune in the minor key we get a ii-V7 to the relative major where we turnaround and then go back through the ii-7b5 V7b9 to the i minor. In the second half of the tune, secondary dominants lead us to the iv- chord, back to the i-, again through the iv- to iv-/7. The IV major again is a pivot between major and minor tonalities.

Let's do one final tune before leaving the world of minor songs. (After all, we don't want to spend too much time here because these songs are kind of sad, right?) "If I Should Lose You" is a more complex tune but sure enough does a number of the things we've already seen.

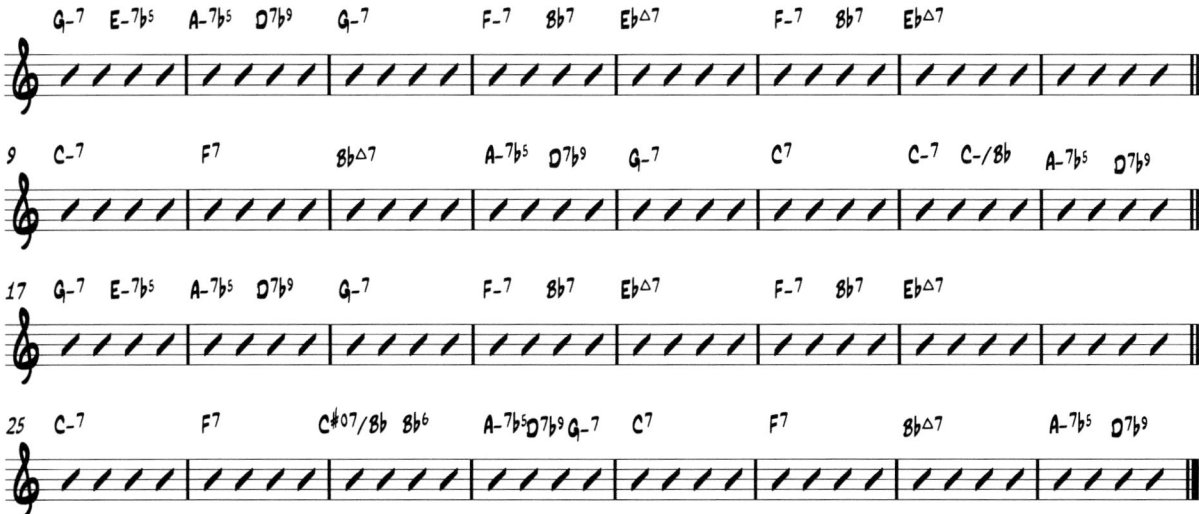

There's a little more going on in this song. First of all, in bar 4 we modulate to the bVImaj7. This is the third most common place to modulate to in a minor tune, after bIIImaj7 and iv- (and it makes sense that it ought to be this way, because if you modulate to the bVImaj7 which is a kind of subdominant in minor, it's going to be very easy to get back to the i minor area through the V7 a half step away.) After that, as expected we head to bIII major7 (aka the relative major) of G-, Bb. In bar 12 we modulate back to G minor, but when I hear the C7 in bar 14 I'm uncertain whether to analyze this as a IV7 (in G minor, a somewhat uncommon chord) or as the more common V7/V in Bb. One way of looking at bars 13 ~ 15 is to say that for these bars, the song is really in both keys, the relative major and the i minor at the same time since it is analyzable in both keys and you can hear it either way. I hear the C7 in bar 14 as a V7/V in Bb major, but bar 15, strongly suggests that we're in G minor as do bars 16 and 17. Another neat section of this tune is in the last 8 bars where we get this same key confusion. We have a quick cadence to Bb (actually, the diminished chord makes it sound a bit like we might be going to D-, but the Bb bass note is clear. We'll look at this sort of diminished activity in the next chapter) and then another fast cadence to G-. The tune ends in major as many other standards do—"My Funny Valentine" and "In A Sentimental Mood" are two famous examples of this. (Do I have to mention that now would be a good time to analyze all of the minor tunes you know or to look at examples of minor tunes that follow these patterns, or perhaps break them in interesting ways? Probably not, but it never hurts to remind you. For your convenience, here's a list of minor tunes for you to look over and analyze: "You Don't Know What Love is", "Gentle Rain", "How Insensitive", "O Grande Amor", "Just One of Those Things", "Softly as in a Morning Sunrise", "Beautiful Love", "Autumn Leaves" (although this one is equally in the relative major key), "Four on Six", "Cheesecake", "What Are You Doing the Rest of Your Life", "Simone".)

Chapter 9 – Another approach to jazz harmony using diminished chords

Every time I teach Jazz Harmony, something new strikes me and often it's in an area that I thought I understood pretty thoroughly. Maybe it's a transcription, or an observation of a student or just my own struggle to explain something more clearly, but usually something will lead me to re-examine some aspect of harmony that I hadn't thought of in a while and I make a discovery that transforms my own sense of the jazz harmonic landscape. A few years ago, it was diminished passing chords.

This chapter offers a different approach to jazz harmony than what we have studied so far and it gets a little complicated. If you find this material difficult you can skip this chapter and continue on (and I won't think any less of you.) However, if you are able to slog through it, this is important material that is often overlooked by younger jazz musicians, particularly non-pianists.

As you'll remember, we've already seen passing diminished chords in the chapter on passing chords. Passing diminished chords usually are found a half step below the chord they are leading to (the target chord). They tend to function like dominants. This makes a lot of sense because (structurally) they are very similar to dominant 7th b9 chords.

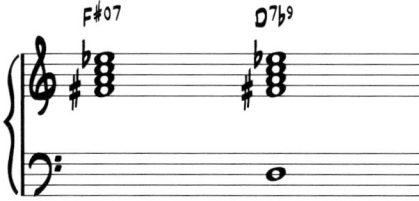

However, older pianists also have a long tradition of using passing diminished harmony that is a little more involved than what we've covered up to now. To explain why this approach is so radically different from the approaches we've been discussing, and to see how we can use this approach to explore both old and new harmonic ideas, I have to backtrack a little bit.

As I mentioned earlier when we were discussing tensions on chords, jazz harmony—the harmony that is taught in schools like Berklee College and North Texas State University—is based on an idea about seventh chords, which is that they are built up from the root in stacked thirds. Seventh chords have a root, 3, 5, 7, 9, 11 and 13. Also, as discussed earlier, the tensions on the chords are chosen so as to minimize dissonance between non-root chord tones, avoiding b9 intervals in particular.

The result of this kind of thinking is a chord scale associated with each chord. (Actually, I'm simplifying a bit here—as a soloist I have many, or at least several, chord scale options for each type of chord, but when I'm stacking notes in thirds to find tensions to use in voicings my choices are limited by the pesky b9 intervals.) For each chord I see on a lead sheet, these seven notes (1, 3, 5, 7, 9, 11 and 13) are available for me to use. I say "chord scale" but I prefer to think of these as a set of notes that are available for me to harmonize any particular melody note. The word scale conjures images of linear (horizontal) movement, and I am thinking of a set of notes that I can dip into, using any of the members of this set at my discretion. (For dominant chords

Chapter 9: Another Approach to Jazz Harmony Using Diminished Chords

I may have more than 7 available notes—I can use b9, natural 9, #9, #11, b13 and natural 13 in addition to the four chord tones of a dominant 7th—but in actual practice, I still frequently end up with seven notes because dominant sevenths come in different flavors and I don't get to use all of the available tensions and chord tones together simultaneously on a particular chord. (For example, natural 9ths and b9ths rarely occur in the same dominant 7th voicing.) There are some exceptions to the stacked third approach (namely dominant7sus4 chords) and sometimes I end up with 8 available notes (when harmonizing with a diminished scale) or 6 (whole tone scale), some of these notes are a little harder to use (so called "avoid notes") but these are slight deviations in our system of harmony and don't change the fundamental point—the standard view of these chords as collections of available notes—tensions and chord tones, usually containing four chord tones and three tensions.

The strength of what I am calling the "stacked thirds" approach, is that it gives us a way of describing any note in relation to the root (even a weird one that we don't normally use, like a b9 or a b13 on a major7th.) It also gives us a set of notes that work on each chord and are used in most common situations: the set of chord tones (fundamental sounds on the chord) and tensions (coloristic notes that create color variations on the fundamental chord sound.) What this system doesn't tell us is **how these notes want to move**. A 9 on a C-9 is a static sound that has no inclination to resolve up or down. Of course, we develop a sense of where some of these tensions might want to go by working with them, but there's nothing written into the theory that tells us anything about this—**tensions are discrete colors that don't want to do anything in particular except bring that color to the chord voicing.**

The big idea with the diminished harmony that I am going to describe in this chapter, is that there are **chord tones** (1, 3, 5 and 6) and **diminished 7th neighboring chord tones** (2, 4, #5 and 7) that go along with them. The diminished notes "want" to resolve to the chord tones much as a suspension does in classical harmony. It's these 8 notes, not the 7 stacked thirds (1, 3, 5, 7, 9, 11, 13) that determine the vertical harmony of a chord voicing in this alternative system of **Sixth/Diminished 7th pairs**.

Okay, so that's the big picture of what I hope to explain in this chapter. ("Thank you, and goodnight!") Now let's go step-by-step to explain the details of how to get there.

One of the main proponents of this concept and its centrality in jazz harmony is the great jazz pianist, Barry Harris. Barry is one of an amazing number of brilliant jazz players to emerge from Detroit (along with Tommy Flanagan, Roland Hanna, Kirk Lightsey, Thad, Hank, and Elvin Jones, Paul Chambers and many others). When I moved to New York in the mid 1980s, he was teaching a weekly workshop in a cultural center on 28th street. A lot of this material comes from his approach I believe (but I studied this all so long ago, I don't actually remember where all of it comes from. Also, as everyone does with harmony, I have put my own spin on this material so there are, no doubt, big differences between my approach and Mr. Harris's.)

The first thing to notice is that diminished sevenths are diatonic 7th chords when we use a particular scale. That scale is the major bebop scale.

CHAPTER 9
ANOTHER APPROACH TO JAZZ HARMONY USING DIMINISHED CHORDS

A major bebop scale is an 8-note scale, a traditional major scale with one added note, the #5.

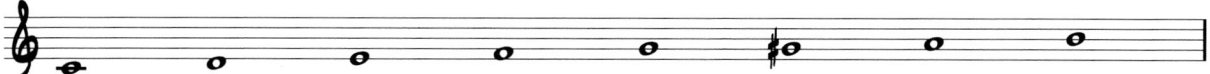

This is a very useful scale, as most jazz improvisers know. By adding a half step to the major scale, a pattern of accents is created (when the scale is played as 8th notes) that helps spell out the chord change that is associated with this scale, in this case C major 6th. That's because notes that occur on the downbeats of a bar of 4/4 tend to be accented harder than notes that come on the upbeats, especially in swing rhythm which has a slight elongation of 8th notes that occur on the beat. In a regular seven-note major scale, the pattern of accents is random, in a major **bebop** scale, the pattern of accented note outlines the chord tones of a major 6 chord.

This is an important feature of major bebop scales. However, there's another feature of these scales that's less obvious. If I make 4-note diatonic chords out of this scale by starting on each scale degree and then stacking every other note of the scale above the root (as we did earlier with the major scale) something surprising happens. Starting on the root of the scale and alternating scale degrees, the first chord is 1, 3, 5, and 6 (6 not 7, because of the half-step between 5 and 6). Starting on the second degree of the scale, the second chord is 2, 4, #5 and 7, a diminished 7th. The third chord is 3, 5, 6, and 1, or a I major 6th in first inversion. The fourth chord is 4, #5, 7 and 2, or an F diminished 7th (Since diminished 7 chords minor thirds apart are all inversions of each other we can either call this chord an F diminished 7th or a D diminished 7th in first inversion.) Whatever we call these chords, the important thing to notice is that these four note diatonic chords are all inversions of the first two chords. Instead of seven different chords (as I get in when I make diatonic 4 note chords out almost any other scale I can think of) I get only two different chords, and all of their inversions. You can see the pattern below. When we make 4-note diatonic chords from this scale, every chord is either a I major 6th (in C: C, E, G, and A) or a ii dim7 (in C: D, F, Ab and B).

(CD TRACK 74)

Okay, so far so good. Let's make these chords sound a little more pianistic by taking them out of root position. I am going to use a voicing called drop 2. To make a drop 2 voicing, start with a close position voicing (by which I mean, a voicing where all the notes are within an octave, like

CHAPTER 9 — ANOTHER APPROACH TO JAZZ HARMONY USING DIMINISHED CHORDS

the voicings above.) Then drop the second voice of the chord (the alto) down an octave. If I do that to the above close position voicings and then arrange these voicings going up the scale I get the following.

(CD Track 75)

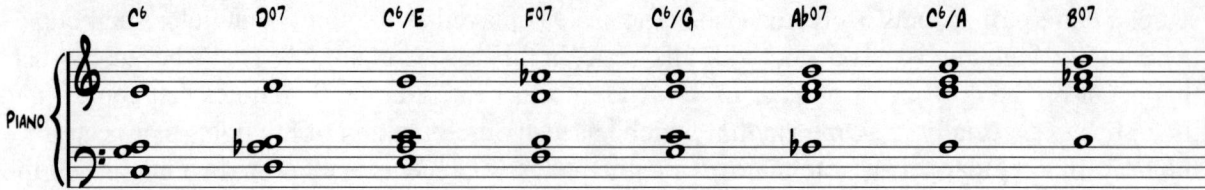

This is a pretty, somewhat old-fashioned sound, alternating diminished 7th chords and major 6th chords. It has very nice voice-leading with the half-steps that result from the addition of #5 to the major scale.

So now I'll play the ascending diatonic chords again, but this time I'll play the first major 6 chord for the three lower voices, but I'll "borrow" the top note from the diminished chord that's coming next—the next chord up the scale—for the top note of the voicing. My first voicing will be (from bottom up) C, G, A and **F**. While still holding the bottom 3 notes of the chord, I'll resolve the F to an E, the third that "belongs" on the C6 chord. Now I'm ready to play the next chord moving up the scale. Again, I'm going to play the bottom 3 notes of this voicing, in this case, the D, Ab and B of the D diminished 7th with the top note **G** borrowed from the next chord up the scale, the C6/E. While the bottom voices sustain, the top note resolves down a step to the F, the note that belongs on the D diminished 7th. You can see the pattern below. It's a lot easier to see at the piano or to read in music notation that to describe in words (fortunately!) We get a pattern of chords with a dissonance created by the borrowed tone—a suspension—that resolves to a chord tone.

(CD Track 76)

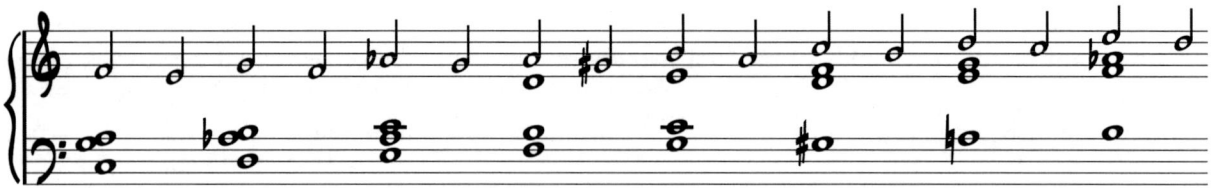

One interesting thing about borrowing tones, is that this process creates extremely unusual and dissonant voicings before they resolve. In the above example (and this is perhaps the simplest application of the idea of borrowing tones—borrowing the top voice from the next chord that's coming up) we generate the following chords (before resolution):

(CD TRACK 77)

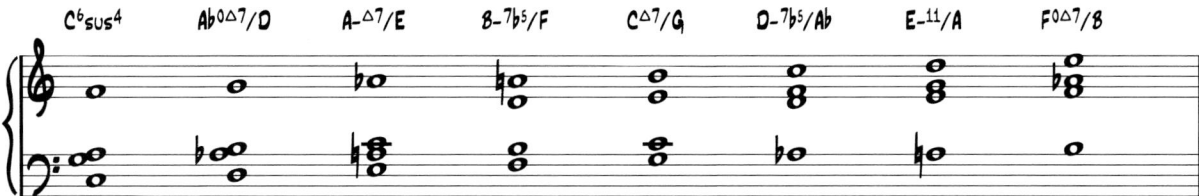

I've labeled the above chords, not because I think you need to memorize these new chord qualities (you don't), but just to show how strange these chords are. They are unusual additions to my voicing vocabulary, and of course that's not all. I can use any combination of borrowed notes and chord tones. So let's do something a bit more complicated. Let's borrow notes for the middle two voices (so for the first voicing, C6, we borrow Ab and B from the upcoming diminished chord before resolving to G and A. For the second voicing, D diminished7, A and C are borrowed from the C6 chord before resolving to the Ab and so on.) This generates the following pattern.

(CD TRACK 78)

Please notice that (so far) whatever notes we borrow, we give back, so after each resolution, we have the same diatonic voicings for the scale that we started with: Cmaj6, D diminished7, C6/E, F diminished7, C6/G, Ab diminished7, C6/A and B diminished7. However, as above, before we resolve the borrowed notes in these chords, there are some pretty unusual voicings created. Cmaj7#5, F min major7, G9 (no3), Ab minor major7#5, A minor major7#5, B-7b6. Again, I want to think of these chords not as strange new chord qualities but rather as interesting combinations of the diminished neighboring chord and the major 6th chord. The Sixth/diminished 7th pair approach to these chords makes for a certain kind of fluidity. Chords are the intersection of movement between these two groups of notes, and they flow into one another, as we shall see.

All of the combinations we've examined so far come only from borrowing the top voice and the middle two voices. You can now look at borrowing the bottom voice, the two bottom voices, the top and bottom voices, the two top voices, the top three voices, the bottom three voices, and so forth. As the saying goes, 'do the math', but even without doing it I know it's a huge number of combinations. I suggest that you spend some time working on many different combinations of borrowings to see how these voices moving between these two 4-note groups (the major 6th notes and the diminished notes) sound. Practicing some of these patterns every day in different keys will help you familiarize yourself with a lot of interesting sounds and unusual combinations, as well as getting better at visualizing these two sets of notes and their relationships.

Again: so far, so good. We can also use this passing diminished concept with a second chord scale, the melodic minor bebop scale. This is the same scale as the bebop major scale except that we flat the 3rd.

CHAPTER 9
ANOTHER APPROACH TO JAZZ HARMONY USING DIMINISHED CHORDS

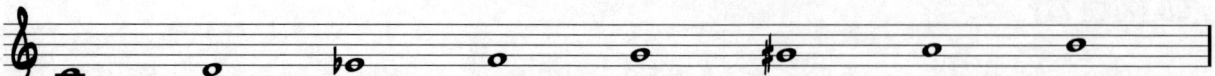

This scale generates the same diminished passing chords, but instead of the inversions of the C major 6th chord we get inversions of a C minor 6th chord.

(CD Track 79)

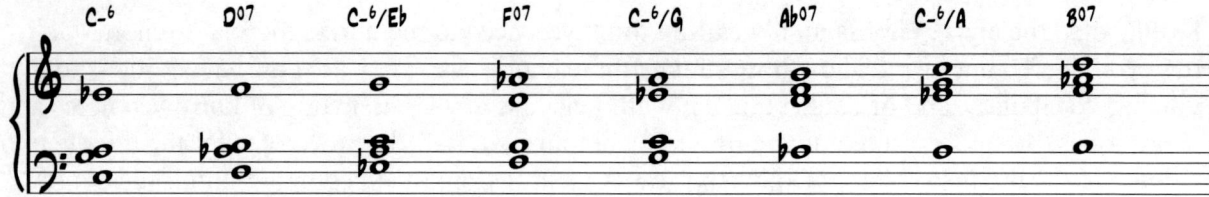

Now we can revisit our borrowing patterns using this scale. First, borrowing the top note only.

(CD Track 80)

Now we can try borrowing using the two internal notes.

(CD Track 81)

Once again, many interesting combinations occur with this kind of borrowing. Again, you would do well to check out many of these possibilities in different keys, going through different borrowing combinations as you are doing with the C major bebop scale above. (At least, I hope you are working on those borrowing patterns. I'll suggest again that you do so now.)

Let me just stop here and tell you that, in my own playing and writing, this was where I was with all of this kind of material a few years ago. I understood these patterns—how they worked and what some of them looked like, had practiced some of them in all keys, but not rigorously. Like many pianists and arrangers, I used diminished voicings in comping and arrangements all the time. But I tended to use the same diminished chords, or more accurately, I used these voicings in a kind of intuitive way. Of course, being intuitive is fine (it's essential) but I hadn't gotten serious enough about working on this material to keep developing new combinations, or to really see

ANOTHER APPROACH TO JAZZ HARMONY USING DIMINISHED CHORDS — CHAPTER 9

the power of this approach. I'd say my approach to working on Sixth/Diminished 7th pairs was hit or miss. Now I have a much more thorough approach to working on these sounds to harmonize songs, but before we get to that, first—a story.

Years ago, a good friend of mine was attending New England Conservatory at a time when Miroslav Vitous, a wonderful modern jazz bassist, best known for his work with the first version of Weather Report and Chick Corea's trio with Roy Haynes, was the head of the jazz program there. My friend felt that the school lacked an appreciation of traditional jazz players and arranged to have Barry Harris brought in to do a workshop. The workshop began, and at one point, Miroslav Vitous, a large imposing guy, walked into the room, grabbed a stool and sat down about 3 feet away from the piano at which Barry Harris was seated. It appeared that they didn't know each other. Barry looked up from the piano before continuing on. In the course of his presentation, a few moments later, Barry said, "Creativity in jazz consists completely in knowing how to use passing diminished 7th chords". Miroslav got up in a huff and walked out of the room. At the time, I thought he had a point. Obviously there's more to creativity than knowing how to use diminished chords. (…or is there?) The deeper I get into this method, the more I realize what Barry was talking about.

So how do we use this approach to harmonize melodies? Let's take the first four bars of "If I Should Lose You." The song is in G minor so I will use the G minor melodic bebop scale to harmonize it, meaning that I'll be using the notes from G-6 and its neighboring diminished 7th chord (I tend to think of the half step below diminished chord, the F# diminished 7th, but you can think of any of the four diminished chords diatonic to this scale since they all have the same notes in them.) Now, reasonable people will say that I can't harmonize the first four bars with this scale alone because the song has a lot of chords other than G-6 in it.

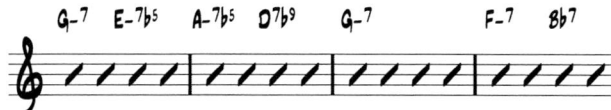

Leaving out the fourth bar, which is a modulation to Eb and really does have to be harmonized differently, the first 3 bars are turnarounds in G-. Using the G- scale with its neighboring diminished seventh (alternatingly) creates a kind of i- to V7 to i- sound that takes the place of the turnaround. (Keep in mind that the F#dim7 is a lot like a D7b9 or V7 of G-, as we noted above.) Suffice it to say, that in the above chord progression, harmonizing the melody of the first three bars with only G-6 and F# diminished 7ths creates a very similar feeling to turnarounds in the key of G-, so I can think of the first three bars above more simply, as all G-6/F# diminished 7th.

To get started, I will analyze the melody and determine whether a particular melody note is in the minor 6th note set (G, Bb, D and E) or the diminished 7th note set (F#, A, C and Eb). Melody notes in the G-6 note set get treated as the top note of a G-6, melody notes in the F# diminished7 note set get treated as the top note of an F# diminished7. There are no decisions to be made here, this is a mechanical application of a rule.

95

CHAPTER 9

ANOTHER APPROACH TO JAZZ HARMONY USING DIMINISHED CHORDS

(CD Track 82)

If I put the above voicings into their drop 2 form, it starts to sound a little more pianistic.

(CD Track 83)

The above harmonization is clear and effective and as I said above, entirely mechanical in that I have no choice what harmony to put under each melody note: melody notes in the G-6 note set get G-6 chords under them, and notes in the F# diminished7 note set get diminished7ths under them. However, if I apply the concept of borrowing notes, I have many more options: I can use notes of the G-6 chord underneath a melody note from the G-6 note set, I can use notes of the F# diminished7 chord under a melody note from the G-6 note set or combinations of the two . The same thing applies for a melody note that is from the F# diminished7 note set: I can harmonize it with G-6 notes, F# diminished7 notes or combinations of the two. Traditionally, whatever notes are borrowed are treated as suspensions which resolve to the notes that belong with the melody note, as we did above when we were borrowing notes on the voicings moving up the major and melodic minor bebop scales. An example will make this a lot clearer.

(CD Track 84)

In the example above, the pickup bar of "If I Should Lose You," the first melody note is a D, a member of the G-6 note set and is harmonized with a G-6 chord. The second melody note is also a D, and is harmonized with Bb (the lowest voice), which is also a member of the G-6 note set, but the middle two voices, the Eb and F# are borrowed from the F# diminished7 note set. These notes are held for the next beat while the top and bottom notes move from Bb and D to A and C, the remaining two voices of the F# diminished 7th. So the chord on beat two is a G-6, the chord on beat three is a mixture of these two sets of notes, and the chord on beat four is an F# diminished 7th. (To be completely accurate, the Eb and F# on beat two aren't really the borrowed notes, here, it's the Bb and D which are borrowed, because those are the notes that resolve, but that's a minor point. As I said above, moving between these sets of notes is fluid; they resolve into one another as I wish.) Of course, these weren't my only options. I borrowed two notes, but I could have borrowed more or less.

(CD TRACK 85)

In this example, the chord on beat 3 has three G-6 notes in it . It resolves smoothly to the F# diminished7 on beat 4. Here's another option:

(CD TRACK 86)

This time, the second chord is harmonized with three notes from the G-6 (from the bottom up) Bb (G-6) Eb (F# diminished 7th) G (G-6) and D (G-6) . Also, on beat 4 instead having the pure F# diminished7 sound, I've borrowed the G from the G-6 chord, and then resolved it to the F#.

Here's another example.

(CD TRACK 87)

This time, the second chord has a different diminished note (the A) which resolves to the G.

CHAPTER 9
ANOTHER APPROACH TO JAZZ HARMONY USING DIMINISHED CHORDS

So you can see from the above examples that once we start using this concept of borrowing tones between the 6th chords and their neighboring diminished 7ths, we have many, many options. I tend to think of the 6th chord and its neighbor diminished tones together, so if I see, say, an Eb major 6th, the first chord of a song that starts in Eb major, I think of any combination of Eb, G, Bb, C and D, F, Ab, B, with the second set of notes (the diminished notes) prone to resolving into the first set. I say, "prone" to resolving, because there's another option we haven't considered yet. I can resolve the tones completely, or if I like the sound of it, I can rest on the suspended sound without resolving it.

With that idea in mind, here's the first bar of "If I Should Lose You" (the bar after the pickup bar we've been looking at). In this example, the borrowed notes don't resolve, they just hang there, contributing their dissonant color to the voicing.

On beat 1 above, the Bb and D are borrowed notes since the melody note and lowest voice belong to the F# diminished7 group of notes. The D resolves to an Eb on beat 2 but the Bb doesn't, it sustains through this chord change. On Beat 3 the chord changes to a G-6, but the 6th, the E natural, moves to a borrowed note on beat 4, the F#. This way of thinking gives me a lot of freedom, since I can resolve the notes I borrow or not resolve them. I can say that, generally speaking, borrowed notes often resolve but they aren't required to.

This is why this Sixth/diminished 7th chord approach has so many interesting applications. If I resolve the borrowed tones completely, I will have a certain (somewhat more traditional) kind of harmony. If I let the suspensions hang there, I can use this same concept to create a more modern almost 20th century classical kind of sound.

It should also be noted that it's not always possible to say which note is borrowed and which chord is harmonizing a given melody note, since the melody note can be treated as either borrowed from one set of notes or a member of the other set. Or stated more simply, on beat 1 above is the chord an F# diminished7 with a borrowed D and Bb, or a G-6 with a borrowed A and F#? I don't really need an answer to that—the point of these explorations is to use these suspended sounds in ways that are pleasing to my ear. I tend to think of the two four-note sets available to me as the available notes for harmonizing a G-6 with A in the melody and leave it at that. When I am thinking in this way, this chord would have an implied bass, G, which I can play or not as best serves the arrangement.

No doubt some of you, when looking at these borrowed notes in the above example, probably thought, 'the A and F# aren't borrowed notes on the G-6 chord, they're just the 9th and the major 7th of G-, making this chord a G-maj9.' That's both true and not true. It's true that we can refer to these notes in this way, but that's using our old system of stacked third thinking. I was once at a workshop where a student asked Barry Harris something about a 9th or a #11 and he responded, "there's no such thing as a 9th. There's nothing bigger than an octave." Within the context of this system there really is no major7th on a G- chord. There's just a G-6 with a borrowed diminished note (F#) awaiting a possible resolution in the E natural. This may seem limiting, but in fact, it's the strength of this system. By giving this F# a potential to move somewhere, we hear the energy of this note and the chord: G, Bb, D and F# becomes something like a snapshot of harmonic movement, frozen for a moment before the suspension resolves. If we choose to keep the unresolved suspension there, then we can hear the potential movement that we are preventing from occurring.

This issue (is it a 9th and a major 7th or is it a sixth/diminished pair?) is what makes using the 6th chord/diminished 7th method somewhat tricky. That is, we already understand harmony using our pre-existing system of stacked third thinking. I am so used to seeing these chords as 9ths, major 7ths and so on, that at first it was difficult for me to visualize chords entirely as major or minor 6ths and their neighboring diminished chords. The first time I went to a Barry Harris clinic, after an hour or two of trying to rename the chords I knew as combinations of 6ths and diminished 7ths, I had a headache and gave up on it for a few years. But recently, I've come to see that the benefits of this approach outweigh the difficulties of converting chord nomenclature. When I have renamed a voicing in terms of 6th chords and diminished notes, I have a whole family of voicings that spring up alongside it, voicings that are related to one another by one or more voices moving up and a down a second—some of which I have already encountered in my third based system (such as a major7th that resolves to the 6th) some of which are completely new to me (like the unusual chord qualities that resulted from the borrowing that we saw in the examples above.)

So with this system, I am forced to think about chords in a new way. I have to become adept at converting the chords that I already know into pairs of 6ths and their neighbor diminished7ths. If I want to harmonize a B melody note with a C major7, I can use a C6 with a borrowed diminished note (B) replacing the 6th of the chord (A). Harmonizing a D with a C major6 is a similar process—the 9th is a borrowed note from the B diminished 7th. Harmonizing an F# with a C6 chord is a little trickier—I need to think of another 6th chord because the note sets of C6 and its neighbor Bdim7th don't have an F# in them. In this case, I can use an A-6—which has an F# as a chord tone—or a G6 which has the F# as one of the diminished neighbor tones. If I put a C bass note below these voicings, then I'll hear them as C chords.

So this is my first step in the conversion process—finding appropriate 6th chords and their diminished neighbors—for any chord quality.

Here are some of the main 6th chord conversions for different chord types. There are probably possibilities I haven't considered, but these are among the most commonly used choices. I'm going to put everything in C to make things easier, but of course you should learn these in all keys.

C major possibilites = C6/B dim7th, G6/F# dim7th (over C) and A-6/B diminished (over C)
Cmin6 = Cmin6/B dim7th (this is the most often used way to harmonize a i minor sound.)
C-7=Eb6/D diminished 7th (over C) (Minor sevenths are the same as major sixths in 3rd inversion. This chord sometimes occurs as a tonic i-7 chord.)

CHAPTER 9 — ANOTHER APPROACH TO JAZZ HARMONY USING DIMINISHED CHORDS

C-7b5=Ebmin6/D dim7th (over C) (Minor seventh b5 chords are the same as minor sixths in 3rd inversion.)

Cdim7=Cdim7/Bdim7 (A diminished chord can't be understood as a 6th/diminished 7th pair so this actually is an exception to our rule. However, we can make a pair for the diminished 7th chord by using a neighboring diminished 7th to it. These two diminished chords together make a diminished scale. Not to complicate things even further, but this does raise another possibility—you can harmonize passing diminished 7th chords, even the chords that are paired with a sixth chord, with a neighbor diminished chord if you wish. That one might take a bit of pondering on your part, but I invite those that are into working with this harmony to try that out.)

That leaves us dominant sevenths to consider. Once again, the dominant seventh chords are the most complicated, because we have to provide for all of the different combinations of available tensions. So we really need to look at three different types of dominant 7ths—natural tensions dominants, fully altered dominants and 13b9#9 dominants.

C7 natural 9 #11 = G-6/F#dim7th (over C)
C7 b9, #9 #11 b13 (C7altered)=Db-6/Cdim7th (over C)
C7b9 #9 natural 13=Bbdim7/Adim7 (from C, this is a half/whole diminished scale.)

There you have it. Now you can use any of these 6th chord/diminished 7th combinations in the place of the chords that you normally think of on a particular tune, giving you lots of voice-leading and interesting harmonic movement.

Wow, that was a mouthful. I know these harmonic options seem abstract when stated in this fashion so we need to get to some real musical examples so you can see how this works in action. Let's return to the first four bars of "If I Should Lose You", but before we do, here's a quick review of the rules for utilizing these 6th/diminished 7th chords.

1. Figure out what 6th/dim 7th chord pairs you are going to use to harmonize a passage. To do this you must convert the lead sheet chord symbols to sixth/diminished7 pairs. Remember, sometimes a single pair can take the place of a I chord and turnaround.
2. Borrow notes as you wish. Resolve them as you see fit.
3. Use the **roots** from the lead sheet chord names for increased clarity of the progression if you wish.
4. Dominant seventh chords should be analyzed to determine which 6 chord/dim 7th pair (or dim 7th chord pair in the case of the dominant 7th 13b9 chord) provides the appropriate tensions.
5. Diminished chords can be treated either as neighbor chords of 6th chords or as dim 7ths with their own neighboring dim 7th chords and can be harmonized with available tensions.

Now let's return to "I Should Lose You" as promised. We spent a lot of time looking at possibilities that utilized borrowing techniques for the pickup bar of the song. Here's an example of the first four bars of the tune using borrowing techniques. I also included the sixth/diminished 7th pairs below the staff. See if you can figure out which notes are borrowed.

ANOTHER APPROACH TO JAZZ HARMONY USING DIMINISHED CHORDS

CHAPTER 9

(CD TRACK 88)

Can you follow these harmonic moves? Here's the explanation. We've already talked about the pickup bar and the next bar. Continuing with the second full bar, beat three is a G-7 with one borrowed diminished note. Here I'm using G-7 instead of G-6 (Don't forget when I am using a G-7 as another tonic chord option, I am still using a sixth chord because G-7 = Bb6, F# dim 7th = A dim 7th.) On beat 4 of this bar, the top two voices resolve to F# dim 7th, with one note of the G-7 sustaining (the Bb). In the third full bar, I stay with the G-7 with one borrowed dim 7th note, the A. Beat 2 has Bb and F (E#) from G-7/Bb6 and F# and C from the dim 7th. Beat 3 of bar 3 is a G-6 with a borrowed dim 7th note (F#) which resolves to E on the fourth beat. Bar 4 is a pickup bar to the next phrase modulating to Eb6, so for this bar I am using the Eb6/D dim 7th pair. Beat 2 of bar 5 is Ab, D and F from the D dim 7th and Bb from the Eb 6th. Beat 3 is G, Bb and Eb from the Eb 6th and D from the D dim 7th. Bar 4 is F, D and Ab from the D dim 7th and C borrowed from the Eb 6th resolving to a B an eight note later.

Let's walk through this process once more, using something more complicated (with more sixth chord/diminished pairs, anyway) than "If I Should Lose You."

Here are the first four bars of "Body and Soul". This song is more typical in that most of the lead sheet chord changes will have its own sixth/diminished 7th pair.

My first step is to figure out what the appropriate sixth/diminished 7th pairs are. To do this, I am going to follow the suggested conversions above. I do have some choices here, for example the Db major 7th chord in the third bar could be harmonized with either the Db6/C diminished 7th pair or the Ab6/G diminished 7th pair. I'm going to pick whichever sound I like better.

101

CHAPTER 9

ANOTHER APPROACH TO JAZZ HARMONY USING DIMINISHED CHORDS

The Eb-7/D diminished 7th pair works for the first two chord changes. The D diminished 7th chord is functionally the same as the Bb7b9 chord. The Ab7 in bar 2 needs an Eb-6/D dim 7th pair because that is the pair available for natural tension dominants. (Eb-7/D dim doesn't work because of the note Db, the natural 11.) On the Db maj7 chord, I had a couple of options: either F-7/E dim7 (Ab6/G dim7) or Db6/C dim7 (Bb-7/A dim). I chose the first. On the Gb7, again the natural tension dom 7th option. On the E dim7, the double diminished pair.

Next, I am going to harmonize the melody using 6th chords (I've been giving you both names, but personally find it easier to keep the chords labeled as minor 7ths when these occur in the lead sheet, since minor 7ths are inversions of 6th chords—it's a little less converting.) I'm harmonizing completely mechanically here so I have no choices: melody notes that are part of the 6th chord get harmonized with a close position 6th chord, melody notes that are part of the diminished 7th chord get harmonized with a close position diminished 7th chord.

(CD Track 89)

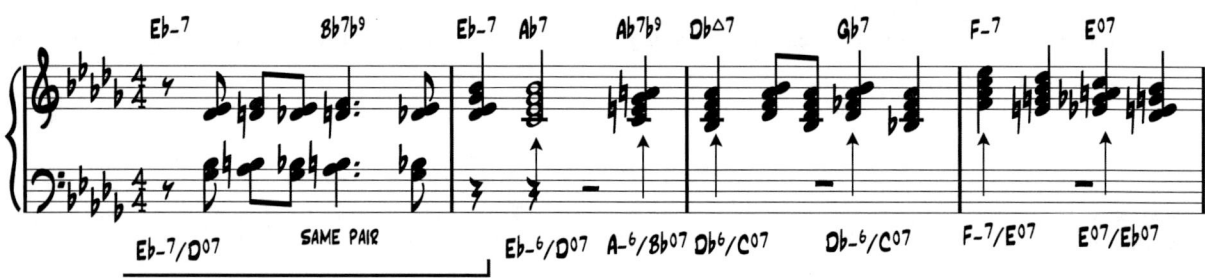

Next, I'll put these chords into "drop 2" form to make it sound a little fuller and more pianistic. To do this, I am simply taking the second voice from the top (the alto) and dropping it an octave.

(CD Track 90)

102

Before I continue, I want to point out that this is a completely acceptable harmonization of this passage, it's clear and has nice voice-leading. Harmonizing in this way is very useful and in many contexts is completely appropriate. For this reason, it's a valuable skill to master for pianists wishing to improve their comping and melody playing.

Now let's add some borrowed notes. Suddenly, I have lots of choices available to me. Here's one possible version of the thousands available to you. Also, if you wish to add the occasional bass note beneath your drop 2 voicing for more harmonic clarity, you can do so now.

(CD Track 91)

Now, using the same step-by-step process, you can harmonize the rest of the A section with Sixth/diminished 7th pairs. First, figure out what pairs are available to you. Next, harmonize mechanically in close position. Put the close position voicings into drop 2 form. Finally, start looking for notes to borrow between the pairs of chords to create richer harmony and resolution through voice-leading.

I hope these examples give you some insight into how to use the diminished 7th/6th pairs approach. Let me reiterate that this system is not so easy to explain because it isn't entirely compatible with the way most jazz players talk about chords. It's a stretch for most players to think of an Ebmaj7 as an Eb6 with one borrowed diminished note, and that Ab and B might belong to this voicing as much as D does. But doing so opens a door to a lot of possibilities. A B natural added to this chord might resolve down to a Bb. An F added to this chord might resolve (or not) and an Ab might pass by on its way to resolving to the 3rd. Viewing an Ebmaj7 as an Eb6 with one borrowed diminished note allows me to see a whole family of chords and voicings that are available to me as possible directions for me to explore.

The other way of looking at the Ebmaj7, the system of available tensions, gives you 1, 3, 5, 7, 9, #11, and 13 as possible note choices. You can play them or not (and the #11 tension in particular is one that you want to be careful about because it implies a non-tonic harmonic function) but they don't go anywhere—they don't want to resolve or move by voice leading. Good voice leading is a value of course, but it's separate from the harmony. There's no counterpoint written into the theory.

So, in spite of the difficulty of conceiving of this approach, I hope I've managed to convey a little bit of how it works and some of its potential power and beauty.

CHAPTER 9 ANOTHER APPROACH TO JAZZ HARMONY USING DIMINISHED CHORDS

Of course, I don't want you to pick sides here. I don't want you to abandon the world of stacked third chords. However, exploring the world of diminished 7ths and 6th chords can improve your sense of counterpoint, give you more and richer harmonic options and fill in gaps in your playing and writing. But it takes a little practice jumping back and forth from these conceptually somewhat different approaches.

Before we leave this chapter I wanted to give you a few excerpts from various tunes exploring these diminished options. The first example below is the first four bars of "Polka Dots and Moonbeams". I've labeled the chord changes using traditional jazz harmony chord nomenclature. See if you can analyze the voicings to find where the borrowings are and whether or not each chord resolves. (These arrangements are a bit dense, but that's how you learn to use the technique, by trying to apply it everywhere. Once you become familiar with using Sixth/diminished pairs on every chord of the tune, you can be more judicious with how much you want to use them.)

(CD Track 92)

Okay, here's the analysis:

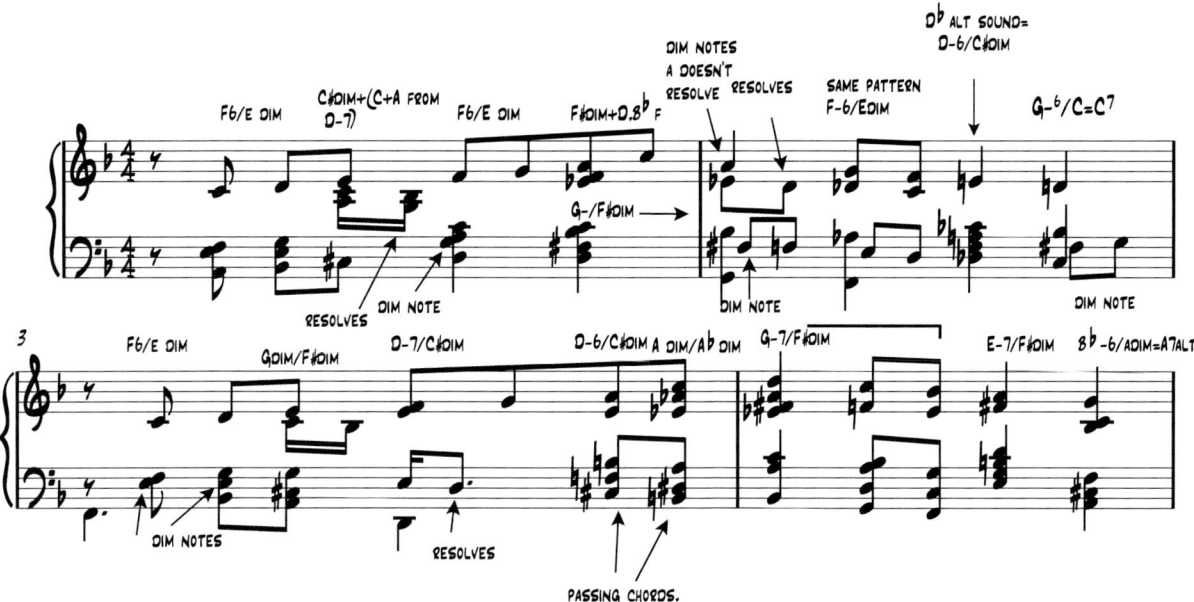

Here's one more, this time on a few bars from the middle of "The Days of Wine and Roses". Can you do the analysis yourself on this one?

(CD Track 93)

When I began re-organizing my thinking about 6th chords and diminished 7ths, I made many of these type of arrangements of standards, working slowly and writing down which 6th/dim 7th pairs I was going to use in different bars of the tune, trying many different possibilities of borrowed notes for inner voices. I still spend time taking tunes apart this way. Once I started studying this approach, I noticed how often this technique is employed by pianists—everyone from Art Tatum to Bud Powell, Hank Jones, Chick Corea, Keith Jarrett and many others. And you, of course, if you decide to work on it, which is what I suggest you do now.

One more quick story about the usefulness of this approach before we move on. I was playing last year with Tom Harrell's chamber ensemble, playing his arrangements of Ravel and Debussy music. In one of his tunes, I found this voicing:

CHAPTER 9   ANOTHER APPROACH TO JAZZ HARMONY USING DIMINISHED CHORDS

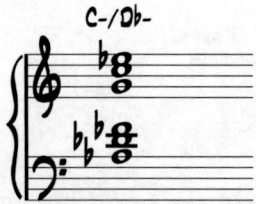

I loved the sound of this voicing and really didn't have a way of thinking about it very clearly. So I tried to break it down into its constituent 6th chord/dim 7th parts. See if you can do this yourself before you read the next paragraph.

(Did you figure it out? Go back and try before you read the next paragraph.)

(Come on…)

It can be understood as an Ab6/G dim7 pair. (Ab, C and Eb from the Ab6th chord, Db, E and G from the G dim7th). If I think of this chord in this way, then the chord is a suspension, the notes are going somewhere, toward the resolution of borrowed tones. This voicing becomes part of a family of chords that are defined by the interaction of these two sets of notes. However, this chord also exists as this beautiful suspension—two minor triads a half step apart, frozen in that moment before the voices resolve. Either way, it's a beautiful sound. Knowing that this chord can be a product of a sixth/diminished 7th pair has allowed me to find a lot more places to utilize this voicing. When I first encountered this chord it was a beautiful oddity, but now it's part of the family of voicings for Ab6, F-7—even Bb9—and part of my voicing repertoire.

CHAPTER 10 – DEEP STRUCTURE, THE RIGHT CHANGES AND RE-HARMONIZATIONS

So now we have a fairly complete picture of the world of tonal jazz harmony. There are a lot of other approaches out there and some players and jazz harmony teachers go into a lot more depth about the rules for what you can and can't do, all the possible places a dominant7th can resolve and so forth. I'm sure these approaches are valid and probably lead you in interesting directions, but for me, I like to have a harmonic system that explains what I need to know as simply as possible (believe it or not after that last chapter!) and then let my ears fill in the rest of the picture. When I was in college, I went to Berklee College of Music in Boston as an exchange student for one and a half semesters. I had been dabbling at playing jazz since I was 12 years old, but I had a lot of questions—for example I wondered why you see F#s on Cmaj7 chords when the C major scale has no sharps or flats in it. It's good to have a way of thinking that accounts for that mystery and I'll always be grateful to the Berklee folks for helping me develop a way of thinking about chords that's logical.

However, there is only so far a theoretical system can go. I've had academically oriented students that can talk theory with me until the cows come home, but can't play their way convincingly through a blues because they haven't developed their ears. I haven't seen the opposite—a student who doesn't know theory but has great ears and can't play. I **have** seen students who rely entirely on their ears and might benefit from giving their ears more to work with by examining theory more closely, so for me, theory does have a place. The role of theory is to open doors. You get to use your whole mind in your pursuit of music: your ears, your ideas, your brain, your spirituality, your mathematical skills if you have any, everything. Harmonic knowledge is a part of that.

Having said all that, you have to start listening for it to hear theory in action. At this point in my harmony class, students do a transcription. They transcribe a solo piano performance (or solo guitar, vibes or large ensemble arrangement) of a standard tune that contains a lot of the kind of re-harmonization that we've been discussing, usually from the mid-1960s or earlier.

But this raises a question: how do I know if something is re-harmonized? I mean, where do I find the right chord changes for the standard that I am listening to so that I can compare the harmonic innovations of a particular performance to the "regular" harmony of the tune?

Some people start with fake books. Fake books are books of lead sheets, meaning melody and chord symbols (so-called because you improvise or "fake" the arrangement of the tune from this simple melodic and harmonic sketch). Originally, these sorts of books were illegal because no royalties were paid to the composers and publishers of the songs. The Real Book, which came out of Berklee in the mid-70s was a real game-changer because it reached a much wider audience than previous fake books had. Nowadays, there are a lot of good ones out there (legal ones) that have fixed a lot of the problems and some of the mistakes and discrepancies of the earlier versions and reflect what a lot of the jazz community considers to be the (more or less) "correct" changes of the tune.

Fake books are a good resource, but they are limited. If I am playing with a younger player and he pulls out his iphone to read a tune from his iReal Book App (or whatever it's called), I usually suggest that he call a tune that he knows instead. That's because if you are reading through the

Chapter 10

chord changes as you play, you can't possibly be paying attention to whether or not I've changed one tonic chord for another, or added a passing chord or secondary dominant. The fact is, any lead sheet that gives you the chord changes for a tune is, by its nature, incomplete. So, with all due deference and respect to my publisher, Sher Music Company, who has created the gold standard of fake books (The New Real Books and others), I recommend that you don't make fake books your only source of information about any tune that you want to make a part of your repertoire.

Students today have abundant resources. There are many free internet music players that allow you to access songs, and listen repeatedly. It may be that in the future this free service will cost money, but if so, you should pay it. (And hopefully, when these sites charge, a reasonable rate will go to the artist, since that's an ongoing problem for all of us in this business.) At any rate, these sites allow you to search for a song and then get access to recordings of that song performed by a wide variety of artists. On a recent search for the standard "These Foolish Things", I found recordings by Lester Young, Stan Getz, Frank Sinatra, Ella Fitzgerald and Chet Baker among others. I found the two most common keys for the song favored by instrumentalists and I found out which are the common male and female vocal keys. (Male vocalists often choose keys close to the "original" key and female vocalists are often about a fourth away from the original, although there are many exceptions to this rule.)

Most importantly though, I got a sense of how this song is has been played by many different players. Whenever I do this kind of study, I try to check out some older players and vocalists: Billie Holliday, Frank Sinatra, Ella Fitzgerald and some mainstream jazz players like Stan Getz, Oscar Peterson or Chet Baker. Each performer will have certain harmonic tendencies and interests—for example, Oscar's harmony of standards can be fairly simple in the soloing sections but very ornate in intros and melody choruses. He will often use more church and blues harmony than you find in Frank Sinatra's recordings of the same song. I do notice all of these different harmonic approaches to the tune, but mainly I am trying to get at a sense of what the underlying deep structure of the song is, harmonically speaking. Actually, by hearing many different versions of the same song, I get a sense of what underlies **all** of the versions of the tune: the common thread. After I have figured out the chords for 5 or 6 different versions of the tune, I know it much better than if I had just read it out of the Real Book.

This is a kind of transcription. There are a lot of different ways to transcribe, or more exactly, I can transcribe on a lot of different levels. The deepest level, what I do when I want the transcription to become a part of me for the rest of my life, involves listening to a solo hundreds of times, singing it and learning it both away from my instrument and at my instrument, memorizing before writing it down, and so forth. (For more information on this mode of transcription, see my earlier book, "The Jazz Musicians' Guide to Creative Practicing", or Dave Liebman's excellent DVDs on this subject.) This is a deep and important kind of transcription, but sometimes I just want to know the answer to something: how does Stanley Turrentine find so many ways to play the blues? What's unique about Miles Davis' phrase lengths? What's Kenny Kirkland doing that makes his phrases seem to "turn around" rhythmically? How does Oscar Peterson use two note intervals (double stops) in his blues lines? These are specific questions that have specific answers and I can transcribe to get an answer to these questions. How does he do that? Transcribe, analyze and you'll know. (Or at least, you'll have a theory about it.)

CHAPTER 10

DEEP STRUCTURE, THE RIGHT CHANGES AND RE-HARMONIZATIONS

Transcribing the changes of several versions of a standard is like a research project. I am not going to kill myself laboring over every voicing. I pay a lot of attention to the bass and I want to know what the pianist, guitarist, bassist or arranger think the chord changes are. If there's a part that's extremely hard to hear because the recording is old and the quality is poor, or because there may be some harmonic confusion between the comper and the bass (it happens a lot, even on great recordings and 9 times out of 10 it doesn't really matter), I'll skip that part. But going through many versions relatively quickly I both learn the harmony and get better at hearing harmony. In the end I have a messy lead sheet that looks something like this:

©1936 by Boosey & Co., Ltd. Copyright renewed. This arrangement ©2013 by Boosey & Co., Ltd. All Rights for USA, Canada & Newfoundland assigned to Bourne Co., New York. All Rights Reserved. International Copyright Secured.

I'll explain a bit. In the first bar some people played Ebmaj7 to C-7 but one version added an F7 (V7/V or II7). That was interesting to me, because I'd never played this song that way. It's a surprising moment that lasts one beat but sets up the second bar with its ii-V a bit differently. Another version had an Eb pedal that lasted most of the first four bars, with an Eb7 on beat three

CHAPTER 10 — DEEP STRUCTURE, THE RIGHT CHANGES AND RE-HARMONIZATIONS

in the first bar. While most versions had a ii-V in bar 2, one version began with the other diatonic subdominant chord, the IV chord, Abmaj7 (instead of the ii chord) followed by a diatonic passing chord that led to the ii-V. (The Eb pedal version had Eb6 to D dim7/Eb.) Most versions returned to I followed by vi in bar 3, but one version went to another tonic chord, the G-7. Beat three of this measure was either a vi minor7, a II7, or a passing diminished over C leading to a C-7, or the biii dim7. One version added a V7/ii on beat 4. Bar 4 could be either a ii-V, or a iii-7 V7/ii, ii-7, V7. Another version used ii-Vs in half steps, a harmonically neat way of leading to the Bb-7 in bar 5, but a little bit insensitive to the melody.

Sensitivity to the melody is a big issue in what changes players use on standards. For example, the C falling on beat 3 of the 4th bar will clash with the B-7 chord change, but in the small group recording this was taken from, that wasn't really a problem. So singers interpreting the melody freely, or horn players playing the melody with a lot of ornamentation can sometimes deal with changes that don't exactly fit the melody. Besides, who is to say what the exact rhythm of a standard melody is? No one playing the melody above will play it mechanically as it's written, so performers in small groups have some latitude and can play changes that make harmonic sense but might clash with the melody here and there. If you are voicing this passage for horns, however, the clash will be significant. Similarly, a pianist would struggle to voice the melody using that particular harmony in that passage.

Bar 5 is some kind of preparation for the IV chord, either a Bb-7 Eb7, or an Eb7 for the whole bar, a tritone substitute for the Eb7 chord, or a modal interchange bVII7 with it's related ii-7 chord. Functionally all these choices are essentially the same and it illustrates some common variations in getting to the IV chord.

In bar 6 we arrive at the IV chord and then begin moving back toward the cadence that will lead us to the second A section. The most common version, arguably, is the one that has a V7/II on beat three leading to a II7 for the next bar but iv-6 or bVII7 (or IV7 of IV) are also equally common ways of leading away from the IV chord to a turnaround (and are often used in rhythm changes.) Gmin7b5 to C7 is a nice variation that leads to the II7 chord change. In the first ending we have a few choices as ways of leading to the V7 that we know will get us back to the top—II7 for the whole bar, V7/II7 with its related ii-7 chord leading to II7, with or without its related ii-7. The last bar is a ii-V to the top with an optional tritone substitute that has some clash potential but will no doubt fit some interpretations of the melody. The second ending has a ii-V to I—with an optional ii-7b5 (modal interchange chord). The second bar of the second ending has a possible delaying progression of bVII7, VII7 to I before the V7 chord that leads to the top of the bridge in G minor.

The first four bars of the bridge present some variations but largely there is agreement about the changes until the last four bars where there is a modulation to Bb major. Bar 5 of the bridge stays around the tonic (with several different ways of leading to the ii-V in bar 6. That ii-V leads back to a Bb6 in Bar 7. Then we get a lot of variations in the last two bars of the bridge. The simplest version would have a Bb6 in bar 7 of the bridge, going to a ii-V in the last bar. A second version treats these two bars as a sort of transition to Eb with dominant 7th chords moving down in whole steps to the tritone substitute for the V7. Another version treats these two bars as a turnaround in Eb: G-7 C7 (or Gb7) F-7 Bb7. Another version offers a more re-harmonized take on a ii-7 V7 for these bars with Bb7sus4 (think F-7/Bb here) to Edim7 (the diminished neighbor of F-7) to Bmaj7 to Emaj7 (modal interchange substitutes that we saw in turnarounds above.) The final version (Monk) offers a series of dominant 7#11 passing chords, moving down in half steps to a Bb7sus4 resolving to a Bb7 on beat 4.

And that's it—the sum of my not very exhaustive research into the chord progression of this song. I spent an hour or so listening to four or five different versions of the tune and jotting down chord changes. I may have listened to more versions—often after the first 4 or 5 different recordings, the variations are mostly accounted for and I am just listening to confirm that I am not going to find anything new. If I encounter a version with lots of re-harmonization, I might ignore that one—I am not looking for re-harmonization ideas here, really. I am just looking for a sense of what the jazz community thinks the chords to this tune are: what is the history of this song's chord progression?

Another perhaps obvious point is that in the above analysis of the harmonic possibilities of "These Foolish Things," most if not all of the variations were **variations in using the harmonic techniques we've been discussing.** Progressions vary as to whether or not modal interchange chords are used, whether or not secondary dominants are used, variations in turnarounds, tritone substitutes and diminished passing chords. In fact, in the above analysis, I think every technique that we've talked about came into play at one time or another. Not to belabor the point, but these harmonic techniques are the language of jazz chord progressions and the reason I began writing this book. Hearing them in action on recordings underscores the importance of understanding this language.

Another realization came when I went through this same process with the standard "Detour Ahead." In classes, I usually ask students to find all the harmonic possibilities and then come up with their own re-harmonization drawn from the concentric circles idea of harmonic possibilities. I immediately regretted choosing "Detour Ahead" because I thought, 'This will be a hard tune to re-harmonize. It's already filled with a lot of re-harmonization—that's the way it was written.' It was only after going through this process that I realized I didn't know the standard changes of this tune. I knew Bill Evans' re-harmonization of it. That's what is in the fake books that I've seen. Once I had listened to several versions, I found the simpler structure underneath Bill's re-harmonization and that allowed me to find interesting harmony of my own on this song. This brings us to a real musical truth. If you love Bill Evans (or Herbie Hancock or Keith Jarrett or Robert Glasper, or 'substitute your own favorite player here') and study only that person and never dig further back, you'll know what that person **played**, but you won't know what that person **knows** (or knew). To say that all of the versions of "Detour Ahead" that I had known were derived from Bill Evans and that was limiting me, doesn't mean I don't like Bill Evans. (After all, Everybody Digs Bill Evans. Look it up.) It shows how big his influence has been on jazz pianists, since his re-harmonization dominates most players' knowledge of this tune. But, I want to understand the tune beyond an individual's conception of it. This is what makes playing other musicians' tunes (Monk tunes, Bill Evans tunes, etc.) somewhat daunting. How do you play the tune without playing Monk's or Evans' conception of the tune? How do you find yourself on it?

Just for the heck of it, here are some of the harmonic possibilities on this tune "Detour Ahead" minus the melody to keep the publisher happy.

CHAPTER 10

DEEP STRUCTURE, THE RIGHT CHANGES AND RE-HARMONIZATIONS

Looking over the above changes, I think I was mostly concentrating on the A sections of the tune. I'm sure there are a lot more variations of changes for the coda, but I think you get the idea. You might want to research the melody if you are interested. A good fake book like The New Real Book series will give you that. Here's the re-harmonization that I did after this chord study of the tune:

CHAPTER 10

DEEP STRUCTURE, THE RIGHT CHANGES AND RE-HARMONIZATIONS

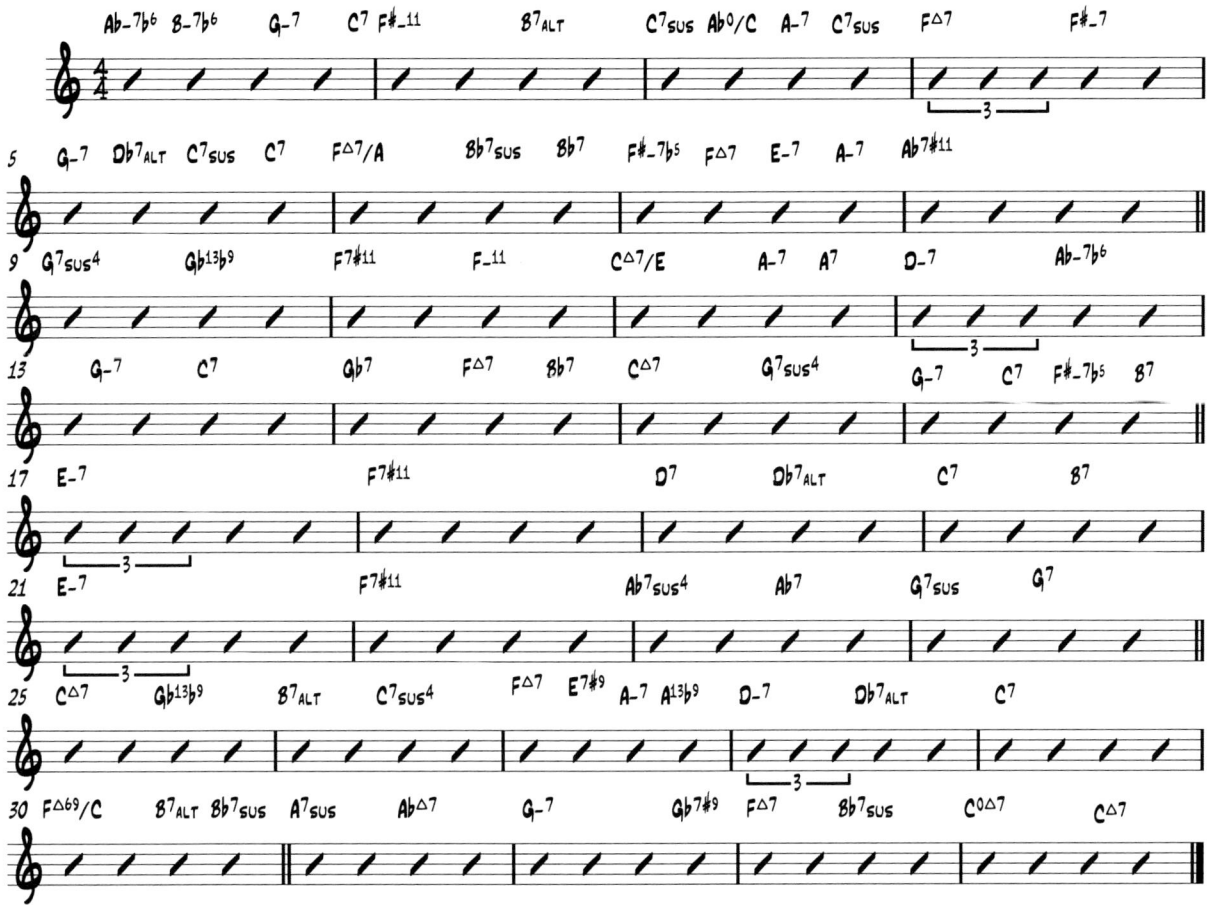

My point here is, learning the tune in its different harmonic guises allows you to glimpse the structure underneath and figure out what the deep harmonic structure of the tune is. I can often infer these things from a fake book, but if I am serious about studying a tune, especially a standard tune that has a lot of history connected to it, I'll usually want to go deeper.

So now that I understand some of what's been played on "These Foolish Things" I want to come up with my own re-harmonization of it. Here's one of mine.

Deep structure, the right changes and re-harmonizations — Chapter 10

CHAPTER 10   DEEP STRUCTURE, THE RIGHT CHANGES AND RE-HARMONIZATIONS

Again, this re-harmonization is a little on the over-stuffed side, to give you a sense of what you can do. I'd usually play a bit less in performance (or a lot less—sometimes I want simplicity, not ornate re-harmonization), although mood and tempo and a little use of space can make a rubato version with over-stuffed harmony sound very musical. You'll notice that I used every technique I've discussed in this book (until now) at some point in the piece. If you've come this far you should be able to follow all of the harmonic "moves" in this re-harmonization.

I didn't write out all of the piano voicings on this one. Perhaps by now you can come up with reasonable voicings of these chords on your own. If not, please refer to the CD recording of the tune. (This might help you construct voicings by ear.)

I suggest you go through this process yourself now. Find the possible chord changes on a standard—one of your own choosing—and then re-harmonize it. Repeat that process with any other standard tune that interests you.

Working through the possible chord choices for a standard and re-harmonizing standards with an eye toward the techniques we've talked about in this book are two ways to increase your harmonic sensitivity and improve your ears. Another way, as I mentioned above, is to transcribe pianists who are adept at using harmony and see the way they use these same principles. I always tell my students that if they are following my directions about how harmony works (or the ideas in a book or some other teacher's concepts) they don't really know if what I'm saying is true. After all, it's only my opinion about how harmony works. But if they transcribe a melody chorus of a solo performance by Bill Evans, Oscar Peterson, Hank Jones or Keith Jarrett, then they can see for themselves how the harmony functions and develop their own theories.

Usually, transcription confirms some things about how I think harmony works, although I am almost always surprised by some subtlety on the part of the pianist that I hadn't noticed before. Sometimes I encounter things I can't explain and sometimes I struggle to hear something that's hard. Both of those experiences are okay with me. I don't have to get it all at once, in terms of my theoretical understanding or my ability to hear every voicing perfectly.

Finally, you don't have to be a pianist to transcribe pianists. No matter what instrument you play, it will certainly help your harmonic understanding to do so. Among the best transcriptions of solo pianists I received last year (playing the melody choruses of re-harmonized standards), one was done by a guitarist, one was done by a trombonist and two were done by vocalists. If you are interested in composition and arranging, you should transcribe groups of horns or larger ensemble recordings. Keep in mind that you don't have to do all of it, and you don't have to do it perfectly. This is a very important point. Often students bring me their transcriptions wanting to know if they are right or not. While I do check them and re-transcribe parts of what they've done (and believe me, with 35 students in a class and a pretty busy playing schedule of my own, this is no mean feat) whether the voicing they've been struggling to hear has a 13th in it or not isn't really so much the point. The point is, that if you spend 30 minutes playing a voicing over and over trying to hear whether there's a 13 in it, you've probably developed a greater sensitivity to what a 13 sounds like in a voicing.

Sometime students tell me that they don't transcribe because they aren't very good at it, or they don't have that talent, and I often think of one of my most talented piano students who transcribed an entire 14 minute recording of the Miles Davis Quintet: piano, bass, drums, saxophone and trumpet—every note on the recording, hundreds of bars and many, many hours of work. While this is beyond the reach of most of us, the fact is that this student, even with a lot of musical gifts, spent hours and hours on this transcription. The students who tell me that they don't transcribe because they aren't good at it, have spent almost no time on it. This is often the way with talent—the obvious gifts of the talented person blind us to the incredible amount of effort that they put into their work. So if you aren't that good at transcribing, follow the method employed by prodigies and throw yourself into it as much as you are able to—by finding things that are easy, by passing over more difficult sections, but by continuously exercising this faculty.

So my suggestion is, with these ideas still fresh in your mind, transcribe something. Do your best to figure out what Bill Evans, Hank Jones, Oscar Peterson, Keith Jarrett or Art Tatum are thinking about when they play a melody chorus, complete with harmonic embellishment. I was going to put one of my student transcriptions here, but why should I cheat you of the process of doing this yourself? Go on…you know you want to…

Okay, let's include this student's transcription anyway. This is "In a Sentimental Mood" as played by Hank Jones, transcribed by a fine vocalist from one of my classes, Soi Shin.

CHAPTER 10

DEEP STRUCTURE, THE RIGHT CHANGES AND RE-HARMONIZATIONS

In A Sentimental Mood

By Duke Ellington

©1935 Sony/ATV Music Publishing LLC in the USA. All Rights Administered by Sony/ATV Music Publishing LLC, 8 Music Square West, Nashville, TN 37203. Rights for the world outside the USA Administered by EMI Mills Music Inc. (Publisher) and Alfred Music Publishing Co., Inc. (Print). This arrangement ©2013 Duke Ellington Music. International Copyright Secured. All Rights Reserved Including Public Performance. Reprinted by permission of Hal Leonard Corporation and Alfred Music Publishing Co., Inc.

Deep structure, the right changes and re-harmonizations — Chapter 10

119

Let's look at some of this in a little more detail. The first four bars of the song stay pretty close to the original harmony of the tune, but in the second half of the first A section, Hank uses a harmonic motive that he repeats every A section. Bar 6 of the tune is usually a D7 but he adds its related ii-7. Bar 7 and 8 are usually a simple ii-V-I, but he adds some secondary dominants with related ii- chords. Then he uses a ii-V a tritone away from these ii-Vs. (It's a little clearer if you think of the substitutions in stages, so the basic harmony could be viewed as G7 to C7 to F or V/V to V to I. Add the related ii-7 chords and you get D-7 to G7 to G-7 to C7 to Fmaj7. Now, use tritone substitutes for all of these chords. Ab-7 to Db7 and Db-7 to Gb7 to F major7. Voila!)

In the second A section of the tune, Hank begins with a substitute for the D minor chord, a B7#9. This is a secondary dominant that begins a chain of dominants, but it also has a little of the feeling of the #iv-7b5, modal interchange chord (thinking in the relative major, F) because when that chord is struck he is playing the notes of a B-7b5, but his left hand on beat two defines it as a B13#9. The chain of dominants ultimately brings us to the G root where the G- chord usually happens. A C-7 (a ii-7 of IV) follows, then more dominants, the V7/IV and finally IV7, a bluesy modal interchange chord. I do hear this as a sequence but also as a kind of turnaround because of the roots of the chords—in the second and third bars of the A section are (scale degrees) 3, 6, 2, 5.

Let's leave it there for now. Actually in this version of this tune, Hank uses mostly tritone substitutes, secondary dominant chords and chains of dominant chords. He also uses a few modal interchange chords and some diminished chord harmony. Still, a lot of what he does in the third A section of the tune isn't really functional. Even with pianists that we think of as fairly traditional there are often moments that we can't entirely account for with our functional harmonic theory. The concentric circle approach is a handy way to think about a lot of logical re-harmonizing techniques but we really need to move beyond them to think about the next realm of harmonic exploration. In this way, Hank Jones' version of "In A Sentimental Mood" serves as the perfect lead-in to the next section of the book because it begins using very functional harmony and then morphs into a world of parallel harmonic movement that isn't really so much concerned with the functional relationships of chords (coming from I, IV and V). This is what we will examine next—the world beyond the functional harmonic universe, where we look for ways to connect chord changes that are not based on tonal chord function.

PART 2
Beyond the Harmonic Universe: Some rules of non-functional harmony

CHAPTER 11 – ELEVEN ORGANIZING PRINCIPLES OF NON-FUNCTIONAL CHORD PROGRESSIONS

We've covered a lot of ground. In general, studying functional harmony is probably more essential for most students than studying non-functional approaches. I can always create chord progressions that have some non-logical or coloristic connection going from one harmony to the next, but I want to know that I've exhausted, or at least considered and understand the functional connections between chords before moving on to other approaches. Sometimes when I'm working with a student ensemble, they do very well at playing complicated original music, but struggle to play standards with the same level of competence. For those players, studying and practicing the harmonic options available on simpler jazz tunes and standards can improve their playing over these forms. If you haven't spent a lot of time on the many scale options available to you on standard cadences and turnarounds, you'll play fairly primitively on standards.

Having said that, I certainly want to keep exploring, and there are more harmonic approaches than what we've considered so far, as we saw in the Hank Jones example above. How can we understand the harmonic palette of players like Herbie Hancock and Richie Beirach not to mention composers such as Messiaen, Bartok and Hindemith?

When I was younger I was very interested in Chaos theory, a relatively new field in science. Chaos theory was developed in part through the use of computers to graph millions of points using mathematical formulas that generate random strings of numbers. Graphing these many bits of random data created images of white noise or chaos. Within these pictures of random data, islands of order emerged (things like bifurcations, meaning the appearance of 2, then 4, 8, 16, 32, 64 and then a return to randomness.) Some experiments found that even though the numbers seemed random, they were oscillating around a certain point, a "strange attractor." Sometimes beautiful "fractal" pictures emerged from the "noise" and if you have few minutes, go and search "Mandelbrot set" or "fractals" and you'll see what I mean.

All this is a rather grandiose way of introducing the idea that even when we are in a "chaotic" harmonic situation where we don't find traditional function (cadences, chords that act like tonics and so forth) we can still find patterns, and these patterns allow us to bring some ideas and logic into an area that is a lot more harmonically ambiguous than a traditional standard tune or Christmas carol.

I was having dinner with a fine classical cellist and arranger and he told me he didn't really understand why every modern jazz musician he heard was so stuck in 12-tone music since the classical world has largely moved on from that sort of thing. While there are jazz musicians who are interested in the 12-tone approach to improvisation or composition (from Bill Evans' "Twelve Tone Tunes" to much more thorough investigations of how to improvise using the manipulation of the tone rows one finds in dodecaphonic writing—see saxist John O'Gallagher's recent book on the subject), I think that, as a whole, jazz musicians **don't** employ a 12-tone approach to writing and playing. If anything, free jazz playing might tend toward a kind of pan-tonal approach where various keys are suggested simultaneously or in close proximity. However, many modern jazz players do lean toward a fairly tense harmonic framework. Players such as Herbie Hancock, Wayne Shorter, Danilo Perez, Steve Coleman, Vijay Iyer, Marc Copland, Bill Carrothers and Jason Moran, all employ a fairly complex mix of 20th-Century classical harmonic approaches in their playing and I think this is what the cellist was referring to. Sometimes, speaking imprecisely, I'll refer to a particular technique as being 12-tone, when what I really mean is that we are in a chromatic situation where rules of harmonic function (chord scales, in-a-key relationships and such) aren't in play. In that way, jazz harmony and contemporary classical harmony are not so far apart. Perhaps it would be better to call this kind of harmony "chromatic intervallic harmony" since what is really meant by this concept is that we are thinking more about interval relationships without regard to key.

Interestingly, one of the main differences between the way jazz players and classical players think about harmony isn't so much the types of chords we use, or the approach to dissonance and resolution (at least for writers of contemporary classical music and folks on the modern end of the jazz spectrum, harmonically). There's a lot of overlap between jazz and contemporary classical music in these areas. Classical composers are often more concerned with the long horizontal movement of their pieces, introducing a new note or voice-leading a particular chord, whereas jazz players as improvisers are necessarily more focused on the vertical—what chord am I on and what notes are available to play over it—and tend to view chords functionally from the bass, although again, it's hard to generalize when different musicians employ so many different techniques.

Since modern approaches vary so much player to player, I make no claim of completeness here. In fact, while I hope to examine some of the modern jazz/classical harmonic landscape, I am really concerned with picking up where the last chapter left off, to explain harmonic approaches used by a range of contemporary jazz musicians, from somewhat more traditional players like Hank Jones to modernists like Herbie Hancock when they are playing in mostly tonal contexts—even in tonal contexts, they make a lot of harmonic "moves" that aren't really functional. These non-functional approaches are used often enough to suggest a modern jazz vocabulary of ways to harmonize a melody and construct chord progressions. So, here are 11 techniques for non-functional re-harmonization. As in the concentric circle concept, sometimes these techniques will overlap each other, or overlap functional approaches, but that's not a bad thing. Different ways to think about the same chords will lead you to different places, I hope.

Eleven Organizing Principles of Non-Functional Chord Progressions — Chapter 11

1. Same root, different chord quality
2. Slash Chords
3. Harmonizing a bass line
4. Chords based on fourths
5. Giant steps
6. Color chords
7. Parallel chords
8. Pedals
9. Chord subtraction
10. Unavailable tensions
11. Incomplete chords

CHAPTER 12 – SAME ROOT, DIFFERENT CHORD QUALITY

The first approach is the simplest: for any chord on my lead sheet, I can keep the root and melody note and change the middle voices, changing the chord quality.

Like any harmonic approach, but particularly when I am using these non-functional approaches, it's very easy to overuse a particular idea. I could change every chord in the song, randomly applying whatever chord quality didn't clash with the melody note and the results would sound like—well, that I had randomly changed all of the chord qualities in the song. The goal of having ways to approach non-functional re-harmonization is greater freedom for the writer/player, but harmonic randomness isn't the kind of freedom I am looking for.

Regarding chord qualities that you might change a given chord to, there are some things to consider. First of all, I can change a chord to a relatively common modal interchange chord, like changing a I major7 chord to a I dominant7. This would be a functional change since we are using modal interchange chords whose function we recognize, in this case the I7 chord that we associate with blues (and so this is an area of overlap with functional harmony.) Next, I might consider variants on that relatively familiar (functional) modal interchange chord such as altered dominants (not usually what we are thinking of when we think of the first chord of a blues) or dominant sus4 chords. These are close relatives of the familiar modal interchange chord but with significantly different colors. I might add more extreme variants here, like the sus7b9 chord, which is the more unusual form of the sus4 chord, one derived from the Phrygian scale. Also, I might consider the original chord quality and pick a chord quality that is close to it, for example, substituting a dom7#9 for a minor7, since they both share the minor 3rd; or an altered dominant for a minor7 b5 chord because they share the minor 3rd and the b5/#11. Other near-relation chords might include diminished for minor7b5, minor major for major 7th and diminished with a major seventh for minor major or minor 6th.

I might also think about modal interchange chords that aren't common but come from common scales, like minor scales. Changing major chords to minor can sometimes be effective and is often done on the first chord of "Here's that Rainy Day" (at least that's what my old Real Book says.)

There are a couple of important points to think about when substituting chords in this fashion. One is that you have to be concerned with important notes in the harmony. For example, the minor third on a minor 7th chord is a very important note. So if I substitute a diminished major7 for the minor 7th chord, the minor 3rd is a kind of pivot or axis between those two chord changes. When you evaluate whether you want to substitute for a chord, there are always notes that act as pivot points between the original change and the substitute (in addition to the root and melody that we are keeping from the original harmony.) These pivot notes make a connection between the chord substitutes and the original harmony because when you substitute a chord on a standard, you are having a dialogue with the harmony (of it you like, the composer of the standard) and a listener (at least, a listener who is if familiar with these standard tunes) hears both the new chord and the original underlying harmony, buried in his or her memory of the song.

The second point is that usually, if I am going to change the original chord, I am looking for a chord that will have more intensity than the original chord change. I'm going in a non-functional direction to find more harmonic color. For this reason, I will tend not to substitute chords with strong functional harmonic implications. For example, substituting a major 6 or major 7th chord for a dominant is probably not going to be a terribly effective choice, because the major 7th chord has a strong implication of a certain harmonic function and that may conflict with the original harmony. The same issue arises with substituting minor7b5 chords. Again, that particular chord has a lot of functional implications as the ii chord in minor. It's probably harder to substitute dominant 7ths for minor major chords and the like. I don't want to make any hard-and-fast rules, since that would be unnecessarily limiting, but you really need to be sensitive to context when you are substituting chord qualities that have a lot of functional implications.

So, often in these non-functional moments in tunes, I will use a chord substitute that has a lot of color and is used less often in functional harmonic situations. Another way of saying this is that I probably will find myself substituting more dissonant chords that we associate with a modern jazz vocabulary. A friend of mine calls these "jazz power chords" (the phrase "power chords" comes from the world of rock guitar in which a voicing that doubles 5ths and roots leaving out the third is used for a triad because it sounds strong and heavy) because they often have an almost macho quality of dissonance and because in some less inspired compositions they are used whenever you want to make a strong and aggressive statement harmonically in a kind of superficial way. These chords can be personalized and integrated into your harmonic vocabulary in deep ways so that doesn't happen, but first you have to spend time with them.

In any case, these chords taken together give us another family of chords, much in the way the most common modal interchange chords are a kind of family of chords. (We encountered a lot of these chords when we were talking about borrowed notes in diminished/6th chord harmony, which means that we also have the option of working with these that way if we want to think about them more tonally.)

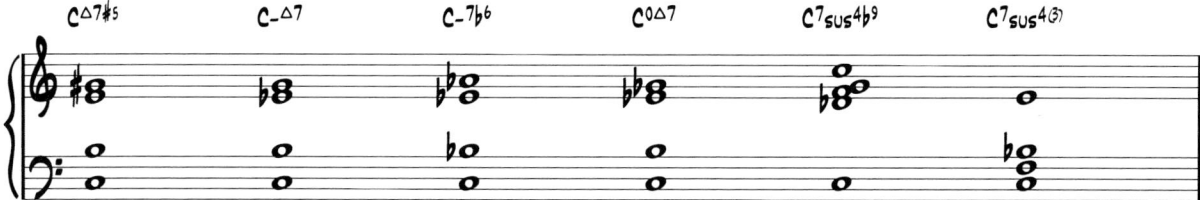

The first of these chord qualities is the major7#5 chord. In tonal contexts the #5 resolves up to the 6 or down to the 5. But it can also be treated as a static entity, one that comes from the 3rd mode of the melodic minor scale, which is a major 7, #11, #5 scale. I think some of the "voltage" of this chord comes from the internal augmented triad chord, an intense whole tone sound, topped off by the major7th which brings a different kind of dissonance and breaks up the symmetry of major thirds. However you want to imagine it, in contexts where this chord is used as a static sound, it has a lot of energetic dissonant feeling. In addition to the melodic minor mode, these chords are also diatonic to a 6-note symmetrical scale built of minor thirds and half steps sometimes referred to as the augmented scale.

The next chord quality is the minor major 7th. This chord is a functional chord, a tonic chord in minor, but it is a fairly dissonant choice and is often not used in tonic minor situations that require more resolution where a minor 6 is more commonly used. It's related to the major7#5 in that the minor major 9th chord contains a major7#5 chord starting at the 3rd (b3, 5, 7, 9) and so often functions as a non-root upper structure voicing for a min major 7th. It comes from both the melodic and harmonic minor scales.

The next chord, the minor7 b6 is another chord that we've seen before, but haven't focused on. In tonal situations the b6 can resolve down or up (think of the James Bond theme here). Again, in this non-functional context, it's stable and doesn't resolve. It comes from the Aeolian mode of the major scale so has a closer relationship to tonic function than a "regular" minor7th (which most often implies subdominant function because of the ubiquity of ii minor7s in ii-Vs.) It is also has the same notes as a major 7th with a third in the bass (Ab maj9/C = C-7b6). It's not a very dissonant chord so perhaps it doesn't fit the "jazz power chord" designation, but it does have a mournful modern quality that's not usually found in standard tunes (without resolution) and it has become a ubiquitous sound in contemporary jazz writing.

The next chord, the diminished major7 is really just a diminished7th chord with the 7th replaced by a tension a whole step up, but it stands alone so often that it really can be treated as a separate chord quality. It has the advantage over a dim7 in not having as clear a sense of harmonic function. By which I mean, a diminished7th chord without any tensions can be a little corny sounding in modern contexts. (Think of the suspenseful parts of silent films with piano accompaniment where the pianist plays diminished 7th chords in a tremolo moving up in minor thirds.) It's fairly common as a replacement for any type of minor chord in places where you want to increase the level of dissonance and harmonic tension.

As mentioned above, the next chord, the dominant sus4 b9 chord is derived from a Phrygian scale. It's a dark sounding chord and in tonal situations it functions like a ii-7b5 in a ii-V. It's often voiced with the b9 low in the voicing, like a maj7#11 over its 7th.

One last chord quality that I consider to be part of a modern jazz vocabulary is the sus4(3). This chord goes by a few names, including 11, which is what I tend to call it, although the first label is the clearest. It's a dominant7sus4 that has the major third as a tension, almost always voiced above the 4th. It is often voiced in fourths from the bottom up, with the top interval a tritone, so for an F11: F, Bb, Eb, A.

These six chord qualities often appear in modern sounding arrangements and using them will add a lot of color to your writing if you don't presently do so.

By the way, I mentioned certain chord scales above in association with these chords. Understanding the chord scale associated with the chord is helpful for soloing considerations. It also helps us when harmonizing passages of melodies because, usually, I am choosing a harmony that works with more than one note of the melody, often a scale fragment. Having some sense of the appropriate chord scale can help here as well. In addition to this, modern compers and arrangers often think of scalar harmony, instead of chords, harmonizing a melody with notes drawn from the scale, creating voicings by stacking interesting combinations of intervals.

Here's an excerpt of an arrangement of mine from a recording I did with the great trumpeter Scott Wendholt, called "Beyond Thursday." It's the last four bars of the bridge of "I'll Be Seeing You" (melody slightly altered) and it has three of the chord qualities we are talking about.

(CD TRACK 95)

Here's another example from an arrangement that I did for a recording with a singer last year. In this version of "Someone to Watch Over Me" the bass notes are the same as the original, but many of the chord qualities have been changed. The first chord B-7b6 has a very different feeling than the original B dim7th chord.

(CD TRACK 96)

With the above example as a guide, see if you can choose a few standards to work on and, while retaining the original bass notes of the chord progression, change the qualities of the chords to some of these jazz power chord qualities, as well as other chord qualities that appeal to you. One of the challenges of this sort of re-harmonization is coming up with a harmonic vocabulary of chords that makes sense together. The chords you choose need to be on speaking terms with each other, bringing harmonic color to the dramatic parts of the arrangement, but not making sounds that are too disjunct and disconnected to the more functional parts of the arrangement.

Chapter 13 – Slash Chords

A drummer friend of mine had a rehearsal with a pianist who was studying with Richie Beirach, a fine, modern, harmonically-complex pianist who uses a lot of slash chords (among many other harmonic techniques) in his compositions. My friend had played this woman's tunes many times and they were tense and fairly dissonant, with one chord in the right hand over an unusual bass note in the left hand, essentially two different harmonies that have a certain amount of clash in them when juxtaposed in that way. The pianist had recently hurt one of her hands, I forget which but I think it was her left hand. She decided to do the rehearsal anyway, one-handed. After the rehearsal, the drummer said, "all the tunes sounded like nursery rhymes." Without the clashing bitonal harmonies, everything had turned consonant.

This story illustrates how the sound of slash chords is derived from the fight between the root and the upper structure of the chord change. They often have an intense "power chord" kind of feeling to them. These chords work well together so are sometimes stitched into compositions or arrangements that have an angular, intense harmonic feeling to them. Also, they are easy for non-pianists to play. Here's a more or less typical version type of slash chord arrangement of "All the Things You Are".

(CD Track 97)

(Okay, this is a little off the subject, but I was listening to a radio show about Jerome Kern, the composer of "All the Things You Are", a few years back. Actually, the show was about the tune "All the Things You Are" which some poll had decided was the greatest American standard tune of all time—who decides that sort of thing and why?—but that's another issue. Anyway, apparently, all of his life Jerome Kern was frustrated and angry about the way jazz musicians used his song, changing the harmony, soloing chorus after chorus on the chord changes, and the fellow that was quoting him made him sound kind of huffy and irritated about it—why couldn't they just leave his tune alone or play it the way he intended it to be played? I remember thinking at the time, typical jazz musician that I am, "Tough luck, Pal. I'm sure I like the jazz versions of your tune better than the original Broadway arrangement, anyway." Every now and then I hear some Cabaret type berate Sarah Vaughan for adding too many additional syllables to words, or Betty Carter for not singing the melody clearly enough and I feel the same thing—these tunes are vehicles, not temples, at least that's how I see it, because for me, some (if not all) of the heaviest artistic statements on these songs were made by the likes of Miles Davis, Sonny Rollins and Charlie Parker (among countless others) working their magic on the song. Nonetheless, I felt a pang of guilt for the above re-harmonization. Poor Jerome, he would have hated it. Even **I'm** not

SLASH CHORDS — CHAPTER 13

too crazy about it.)

Anyway, harmonizing tunes using slash chords as above, is fairly easy and it is effective in its way, but if I want to get to more subtle uses of this harmony, I need to examine these kinds of chords more closely.

So what is a slash chord? A slash chord is any chord that is created by an upper structure over some lower structure and the name "slash chord" comes from the "/" line that separates the two parts of the chordal structure. The most common slash chords are major triads over bass notes but there can be other qualities over bass notes, or chords over chords (as we saw in the two minor triads at the end of chapter 9.) The major triad is a particularly effective upper structure sound because it is such a clear piece of chordal information. What I mean by that is, if I wish to put two sounds against each other, I need to have two pieces of harmonic information that are distinct and hearable—two elemental sounds that maintain their separateness so that I can hear the bi-tonal relationship between the two chords. Two very complex harmonic sounds will blend into a new combined sound—the sum of the parts. Two very simple sounds (like triads and bass notes) maintain their bi-tonal personality because the sounds are so simple we can hear them resonating, one against the other. For this reason, major triads make very clear upper structures and account for a lot of the slash chords one commonly finds in modern jazz compositions.

There are 12 possible combinations of major triads over a bass note: C/C, Db/C, D/C, Eb/C, E/C, F/C, F#/C, G/C, Ab/C, A/C, Bb/C, and B/C.

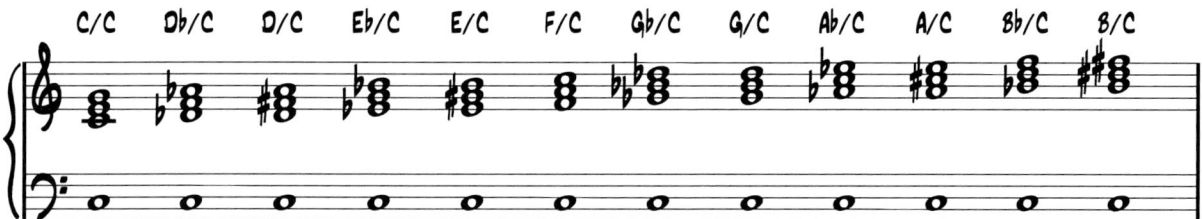

Of these, some are not particularly significant structures. C/C is just a triad over its own root. Eb/C is a C-7 and F/C is a triad in second inversion. That leaves the following chords: Db/C, D/C, E/C, F#/C, G/C, Ab/C A/C Bb/C and B/C which have harmonic usefulness. Let's look at these more closely.

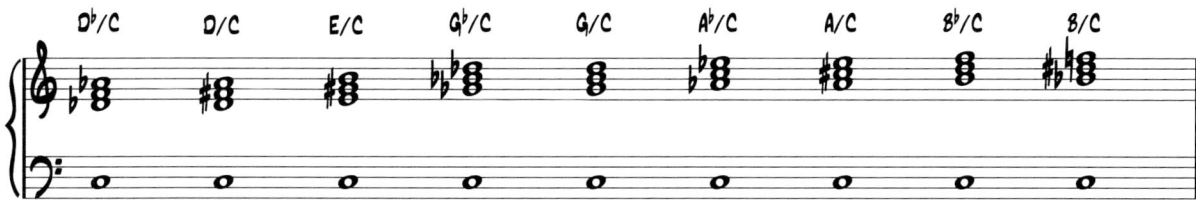

129

Chapter 13 — Slash Chords

In general, there are two ways to view a slash chord. Either I can treat it as a special-case chord, meaning that it truly is the particular triad sound over a bass note and when I comp this chord I use those notes and no others, or I can understand it as a particular voicing of a more complex chord with notes that are missing and the rest of this chord is available to me if I wish to add the missing notes. If I view the slash chord in the second way, it loses its special status and it becomes a particular voicing for a chord that could be named in a less specific way. Very often, both of these ways of looking at a slash chord are somewhat justified.

The Db/C is a variation of a C7susb9b13 that we looked at above. If I am thinking of it as a particular voicing for this chord it implies the Phrygian scale, but it's also compatible with the Locrian scale, the fifth mode of the harmonic minor and the augmented scale, since all of these scales contain Db, Ab, F and C. That's another important quality of slash chords: they are ambiguous. We'll talk more about this when we talk about incomplete chords, but for now when I see this slash chord, I want to figure out whether to understand it as a garden variety C7susb9b13 or whether I want to preserve its ambiguity. A more specifically Phrygian voicing of this chord has Dbmaj 7th b5/ C (or Db, F, G and C over C). Other variations of this chord include Dbmaj 7th #5/C (from the Bb melodic, Bb harmonic minor scale, or augmented scale. This last scale is a 6 note symmetrical scale built by alternating minor 3rds and half steps.) Knowing scales that these chords imply help me to understand these structures better, both for soloing and for developing a range of different voicings for them.

The D/C is a chord that one often hears in pop tunes, such as Barbra Streisand's old hit "Evergreen" (I might be dating myself here). In this case, the ambiguity comes from whether this chord is a major7#11 chord or a dominant7 #11 chord since there is no 7 in the voicing. It has a Lydian sound and without the 7th there is a sort of simplicity or purity to this chord . This chord almost always implies major, but another interesting possibility is to hear this voicing as a diminished7th sound since all of the notes can be found in a C diminished (whole step/half step) scale. Recently, I've been using this slash chord in this way and that's a very appealing sound to me, because it's such a deceptively open and simple voicing (albeit incomplete) for a diminished 7th chord. This chord can also be a D7 with the C in the bass in more tonal contexts, which makes it a kind of II7 when it occurs over a pedal on the first degree of the scale.

One other thing to recognize in these upper structures is that should I decide to treat this chord as a Cmaj7#11 or C7#11, preserving the upper structure while filling out the bottom half of the chord, it still retains some of the bi-tonal feeling of the slash chord. While I wouldn't really think of D/C7 as a slash chord—it's a C13 chord with all of the tensions present—voicing the upper structure as a triad gives the chord a special resonance. For that reason, let me say again that these slash chords (triads over bass notes) always have important near-relation chords that are functional. Upper structure triads tend to make very resonant and strong voicings and are particularly useful in arranging contexts (big band brass voicings, for example, often make use of these upper structure triads over complete seventh chords.) Dmaj7/C is a dissonant chord that is used more rarely in tense harmonic situations.

E/C is a voicing for a C maj7#5. This voicing with only chord tones present emphasizes the bi-tonal resonance of this chord. This chord can be derived from the C augmented scale, A melodic minor, C harmonic major and a number of other more obscure scales. (In tonal situations the #5 usually moves up to the 6 or down to the 5 or occurs with sixth/diminished borrowing. E major 7th/C is a more dissonant voicing that we'll encounter again when we talk about unavailable tensions. (Augmented scale, E harmonic major—this scale is the same as a harmonic minor scale with a major 3rd.)

F#/C, in addition to being the chord that's written on the side of a Polytone amplifier, can suggest C7altered or less commonly, C Locrian. The tritone clash is particularly jarring, giving this chord a lot of harmonic energy and dissonance. Gbmaj7/C is another locrian variation.

G/C is a chord that we'll come back to. Most commonly, it's treated differently than the other slash chords. What I mean by this is that common slash chords have clear bass notes in the low register (often in octaves) and triads with doubled notes in their upper structures. G/C often appears as a close position voicing with the bass note up an octave. It is usually used as an ambiguous version of a C major7 missing it's defining third. Its ambiguity allows for other scale options (or in other words, for this chord to function as an incomplete sound for minor major7ths, major 7th b13 and others.) Gmaj7/C is another ambiguous sounding (usually major) chord with a #11.

Ab/C can be a minor7b6 chord or an Abmaj7/C. This chord usually benefits from the addition of the G in the upper structure, since without it, it is a triad in 1st inversion and not really bi-tonal. Ab maj7b5, where the D replaces the Eb in this voicing is a more ambiguous variant. Ab is also a very common upper structure for a C7#9b13 or altered chord. Ab7sus4/C is another locrian or altered dominant sound.

A/C implies the half-step whole-step diminished scale. It's a common upper structure for a C13b9 chord. As a pure slash chord sound it's also a C6b9, an unusual chord that sometimes appears as the final chord in "The Theme" (Miles Davis' set closing tune in the 60s, sometimes called "Go-go") or in "Moment's Notice." I've been seeing it more and more in contemporary jazz writers. A near relative of this chord is the Cmaj7b9. Amaj 7th/C is a more dissonant variant also derived from the augmented scale and F harmonic minor scales.)

The next chord is Bb/C. This chord is almost always a voicing for a C7sus4 chord and as such isn't a particularly distinct slash chord kind of harmony, by which I mean, often there's no significant need to use this particular voicing over the more versatile C9sus4, C7sus4 or C13sus4. In general, if you don't specifically want the slash chord sound, or as is the case here, the slash chord sound doesn't have a particularly strong character, I'd encourage you to write the chord symbol name for the chord since it gives the comper more options. Many composers that don't have strong piano skills favor the slash chord form of the voicing simply because it's easy to find on the piano. Having said that, I don't want to make any hard and fast rules here. Sometimes when you are using a lot of slash chord harmony, the above voicing is useful because it maintains the consistency of the sound. As always, you need to give your ears the final say in the matter.

The last triad is a B/C or C dim major7th. This chord is a common variation of a diminished 7th (since the major 7th is simply an available tension on a diminished 7th.) It derives some of its strength from the bi-tonal feeling it gives.

Minor triads can be used over bass notes as well. However most minor triads over a bass note aren't significant chord structures and they are used far less frequently as slash chords. (For example, C-/C, D-/C (D-7 3rd inversion), Eb-/C (C-7b5), E-/C (Cmaj7), F-/C (2nd inversion triad), G-/C (sus4 chord variation), A-/C (1st inversion triad) don't have much utility as slash chords.) That leaves 5 chords: Db-/C, Gb-/C, Ab-/C, Bb-/C and B-/C that are worth considering.

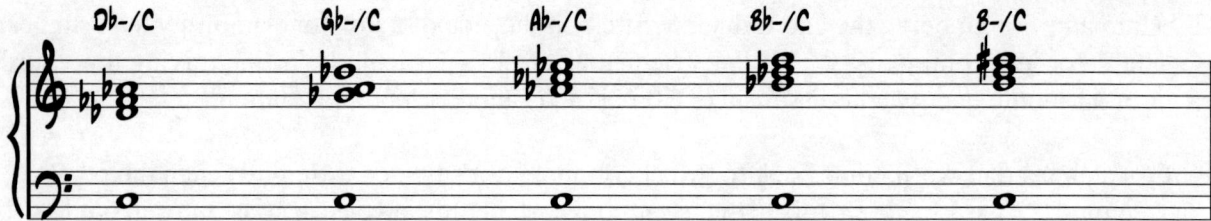

Db-/C is derived from the altered scale and Gb-/C comes from the half/whole diminished scale. Both chords have a lot of interesting colors (altered tensions) but without the seventh we associate with altered tensions, they are somewhat ambiguous. Ab-/C is derived from the C harmonic minor scale. Bb-/C is Phrygian, much like Db/C or Dbmaj7b5/C. B-/C is a very ambiguous sound that can be Lydian, but also diminished.

Of course, it's possible to put any chord sound over any other chord sound. When I played in the great bassist Cecil McBee's band, his music featured composite chords like Gmaj7/Eb-7/D. It wasn't always clear to me what I should do over those, but the search was very challenging and provocative. Messiaen has piano pieces that put shifting major 6ths over one another. More simply, an A triad played over an Eb triad, (the Polytone Amp chord) results is an Eb7b9#11 chord, but we still hear those warring triads. So voicing chords with regard to the upper structure versus the lower structure results in a certain energetic harmonic feeling.

However, when using slash chords you should be sure that this is the sound you want, not the simpler chord symbol name. Intuitive composers who aren't aware that these chords have functional relatives will use these voicings because they can find them and, for the same reason that they are clear and easy to find, they are limiting to pianists who have a more complex understanding of the wide palette of available piano voicings for chords. If you don't know much about diminished voicings, B/C is quite a novelty, but if you've worked with a lot of diminished sounds at the piano, it's one of a family of chords and voicings. This also goes for writing bass lines and drum parts if you are not a bassist or a drummer. Keep in mind that you are writing for experts on their instruments and you want to give them the latitude to interpret your music in ways that allow them to bring their knowledge and expertise to the performance. It's wise not to handcuff your bandmates by being overly specific unless you are certain that that is exactly the effect that you want.

Often, students with a background in classical harmony use many inversions: inversions of triads, inversions of sevenths, inversions of chords without tensions, inversions of chords with tensions. While you can't say that this is wrong (there are wonderful examples of this in great jazz compositions and arrangements), very often using inversions is a way of obscuring the harmonic function of a chord. If I have a complex dominant with a lot of tensions in it—those tensions are heard and understood in relation to the root of the chord. So putting all of that over the fifth of the chord or some other bass note confuses my sense of the functions of the notes of the chord.

For example, a D7(no 5) b9, b13/Ab could be expressed much more simply as an Ab9#11. Put the same chord over an F# and it becomes an F#maj7#5#11. However, sometimes a complex upper structure over a bass note creates something new that can't be named more simply. Sometimes, even if there is a simpler name, the slash chord label gives the player a more modal sense of how the song might be approached.

Here's a tune of mine that I recorded many years ago on a CD called "Handmade," (Palmetto Records, 1998). I chose to label D7#9/F# instead of F#maj7 #5, #11, even though the notes are the same (assuming that the D7#9 comes from the altered scale.) I guess this is in part because the melody, while somewhat modal goes back and forth from a D7 altered sound to a D7b9 diminished sound. Labeling the chord D7#9/F# allows me to be a little ambiguous about what's happening on that part of the scale. (When the Bb occurs in the melody, an altered scale is implied; when the B natural occurs, a D13b9 or half step/whole step diminished scale is suggested.) In bar 14, the Dma7/A (another slash or inverted chord with a #11 in the melody) is more easily understood with this name (than as an Amaj13natural11.)

Chapter 13

Slash Chords

(CD Track 98)

In Passing

Here are the changes to one of my favorite Kenny Kirkland tunes, "Chance," from his CD, "Kenny Kirkland." In it, he blends slash chord harmony beautifully with more traditional chordal structures. Interested students should research the melody of this tune for a sense of how he connects these modern chords with a hauntingly beautiful melodic line.

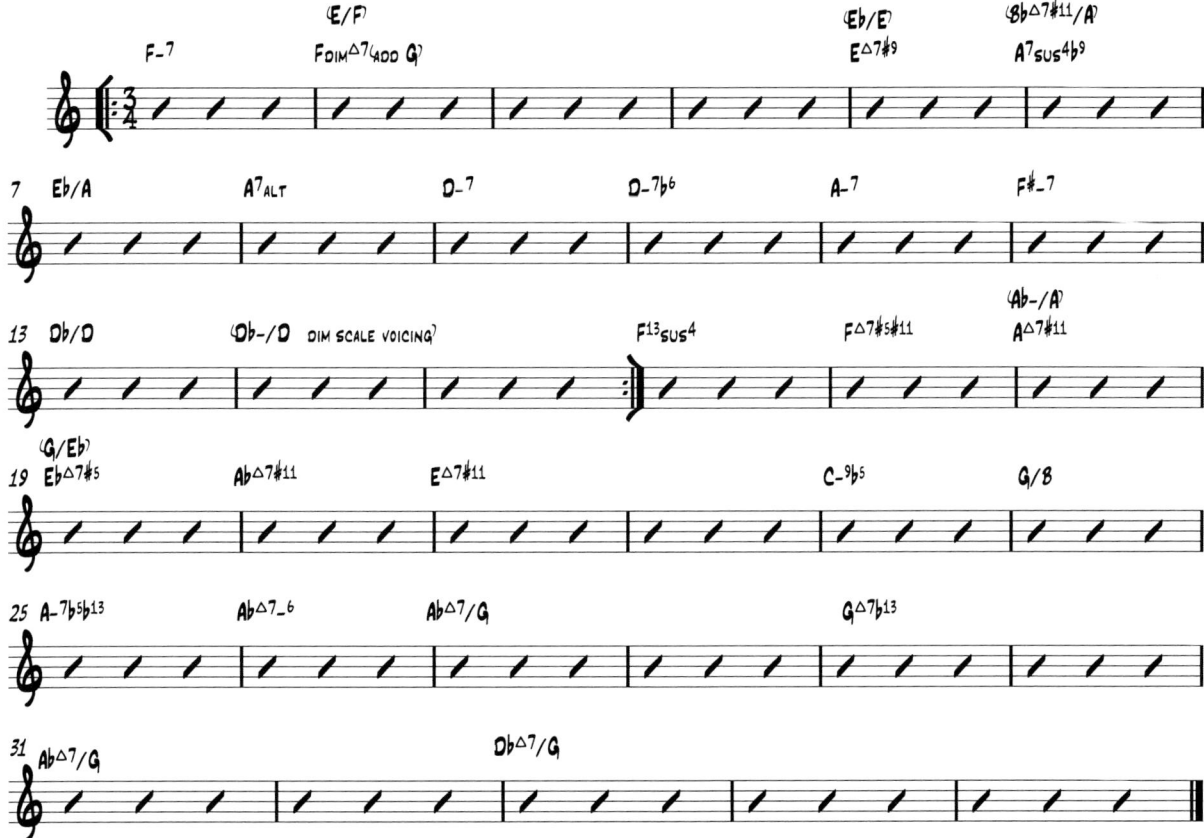

In addition to major triad upper structures, additional tensions are sometimes used (bars 2, 6) additional chord tones below the upper structure (bar 5 Eb/E + the third of the E in the lower half of the chord makes the E major7 #9, #11 sound) and upper structures that are seventh chords or minor triads (bars 6, 14, 18). Particularly interesting upper structures are the Db-/D and Ab-/A (1, 7, #11, 9), an indeterminate chord without a third in it (suggesting lydian or diminished major 7.) In bar 13, the Db-/D suggests diminished (when the melody is added) and in bar 18 the Ab-/A suggests Lydian major. Also significant is the Gmaj7b13, which is a major#5 with the natural 5 in the chord. The melody of this tune beautifully traces a simple melodic line over these complex chord changes.

Try and write some progressions that use slash chords. Feel free to explore your own upper structure sounds over different bass notes. As we saw in "Chance," starting with some simple upper structure sounds can lead to more varied types of slash chord harmony. As you refine your palette you can find a vocabulary of chords that moves in and out of slash chord and root-based harmonic territory.

CHAPTER 14 – HARMONIZING A BASS LINE

This next technique is one that is used both in tonal situations and chromatic harmonic situations. As you probably noticed in our examination of the first two techniques, what happens in the bass is of paramount importance to defining harmony. Given a melody, I can construct a bass line that harmonizes well with it. Once I've done that, I have a series of melody notes and bass notes (the top and bottom of our chords) that are missing internal voices that define chord qualities. At that point, you can use the first technique we discussed ("same root, different chord quality") and fill in the internal voices of the chords.

Here is a fairly famous example. These two measures of the standard "Yesterdays" are often harmonized with a bass line in contrary motion to the melody. The melody ascends. The bass line descends. Here's the way the tune often appears in fake books.

I can write a bass line that compliments the melody extending this idea of contrary motion.

I'm using mostly half-steps and that increases the sense of harmonic function because, as we saw in the passing chord chapter, half-steps are a very logical way to connect chords. But I can use any intervals that I want. The important thing is to find a bass line that feels like a strong and effective counter line to the melody.

Once I have a bass line, I can fill in chord qualities. If I choose very consonant qualities, then this passage will sound functional and the harmony feels logical and "inside."

(CD Track 99)

(Note that I chose to keep the half step feeling by using a half step up ii-V7 in the third bar to lead to the B-7 E7 in the fourth bar).

If I choose different, less functional feeling chord qualities, the same passage takes on a different, more "outside" character.

CHAPTER 14

HARMONIZING A BASS LINE

(CD TRACK 100)

Slash chords and more tense harmony make the passage feel even more "outside", modern and dissonant.

(CD TRACK 101)

Of course, I could start my bass line somewhere less connected to the original tune's harmony. Here's another bass line that I've harmonized that again moves in contrary motion but begins on an Ab.

(CD TRACK 102)

Try this yourself. Here's the melody without chords so you can add your own.

Here are three short passages from a reharmonization of mind of the tune "Round Midnight," that often re-harmonized standard. I've used the same sort of contrary motion concept to harmonize these. (The rhythm is stretched out a bit from the original. In this particular version of the tune I am playing rubato, so how the rhythm is written is not an issue.)

The first is the opening phrase of the tune.

CHAPTER 14

HARMONIZING A BASS LINE

(CD Track 103)

The first two chords are not really namable. The counter line in the lowest voice is really a tenor line, without a clear bass function until we get destination of this line, the A7sus4.

Here's another excerpt, from the 3rd bar of the tune.

(CD Track 104)

This time, the lines both start on the Eb and then move in contrary motion in half steps until we reach the C13b9 chord, the V7 of F.

One last excerpt, this from the 5th bar of the tune.

(CD track 105)

Again, the bass notes move in contrary motion, but in different intervals. There's no real harmonic reason for the particular note choice of bass notes—I just felt these sounds fit the melody well.

Notice that while I chose somewhat non-functional chord sounds for the above excerpts, like major7#5, 7sus4 and sus4(3) chords, I also used a major 7th and a lot of minor7ths. If I use tense sounds only, they quickly get worn out and lose their surprising quality.

Try re-harmonizing the above passages using the contrary motion idea. Challenge yourself to create several different harmonizations using the same bass line and experiment with both half-steps and whole-steps (or other intervals) in the line. Remember, if your bass line doesn't feel strong by itself, then the re-harmonization will probably not be successful.

Chapter 15 – Chords built in 4ths

Functional harmony springs from triads and triads are pairs of stacked thirds. If I leave the third out of a chord, there is a good deal more harmonic ambiguity. A chord that is not major or minor doesn't have a clear harmonic function.

This is one of the reasons that dominant7th sus4 chords are used so often in modern music. They are ambiguous. If I resolve the 4th to a third, then the sus4 chord acts like a subdominant but if the suspension is left unresolved, it has a hanging, indefinite feeling that can seem either dry and mysterious or warm and rich-sounding, depending on how it's voiced.

In the same way that we made third-based diatonic triads and seventh chords from the major scale, we can make diatonic 4th chords. Using the dorian minor scale, below are diatonic chords in fourths (or "quartal" harmony).

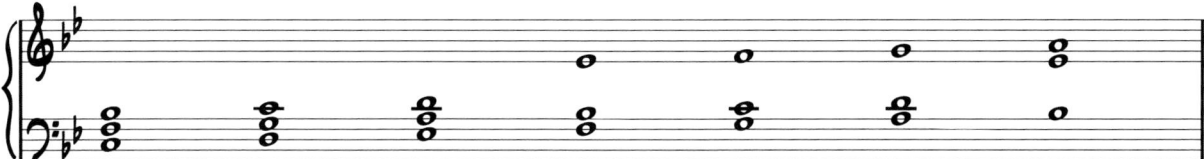

Stacking another fourth, I can make 4 voice chords.

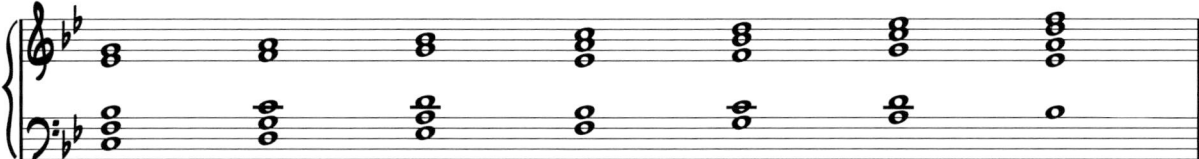

Or 5 voice chords

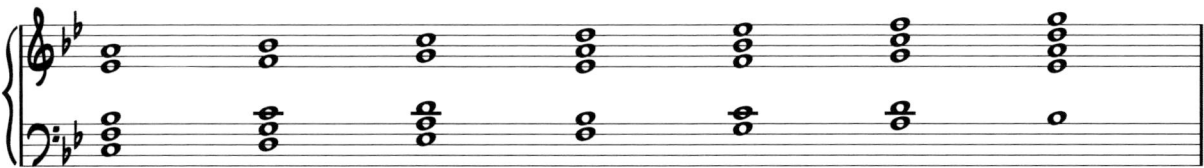

In addition to these voicings, another very well known fourth voicing, the "So What" voicing, made famous by the Miles Davis tune, is constructed by placing a 3rd on top of a 4 note fourth voicing.

CHAPTER 15 — CHORDS BUILT IN 4THS

You no doubt have noticed that these fourth voicings (even the non-"So What" voicings) are not constructed entirely of fourths. Since they are diatonic voicings, the asymmetry of the scale creates different combinations of fourths and tritones as we build on different scale degrees. When constructing chords from thirds, these different combinations resulted in different chord qualities. Since fourth voicings don't have different chord qualities per se, these differences are less easy to label.

In general, although there is no hard and fast rule here, a tritone occurring anywhere in the chord other than between the two bottom voices of the chord, tends to weaken the voicing. Also, any chord that has an internal b9 interval also tends to be a weaker voicing. (Exceptions to this result from the fact that we are moving into contexts with freer use of harmonic dissonance and functional ambiguity.) So if we eliminate all of these "weak" voicings, we are left with:

For three note voicings

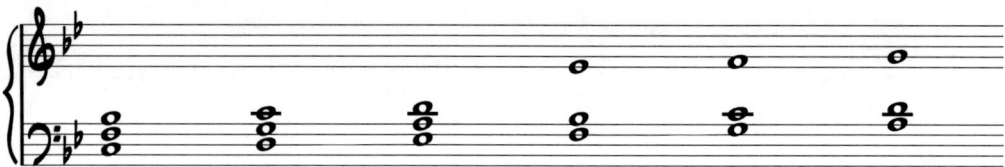

For four note voicings

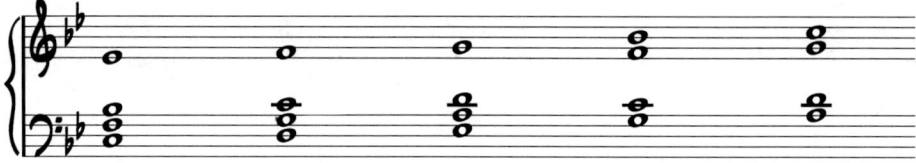

For five note voicings

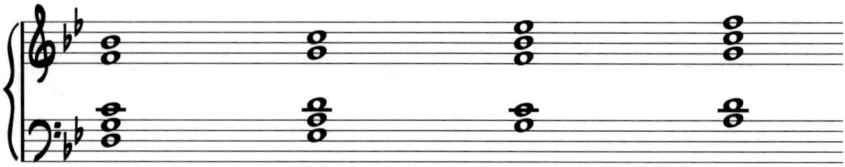

For "So What" voicings

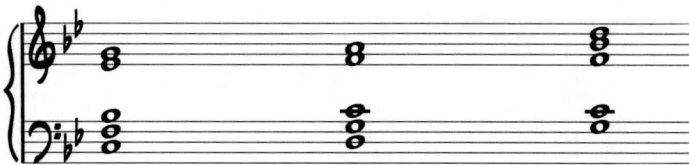

CHORDS BUILT IN 4THS — CHAPTER 15

These fourth voicings have another interesting quality and that is that they are "fold-up-able." (I'm indebted for this explanation to the fine trumpeter, arranger and educator Michael Mossman.) That is, if I want to make a fourth voicing tighter feeling (in the same way I can keep third-based voicings in close position or open position) or if I want to harmonize melodies in lower registers, I can move a voice (or voices) down an octave to make tighter feeling variations of these voicings. As fourth voicings move closer together, they become combinations of fourths and whole steps and eventually clusters.

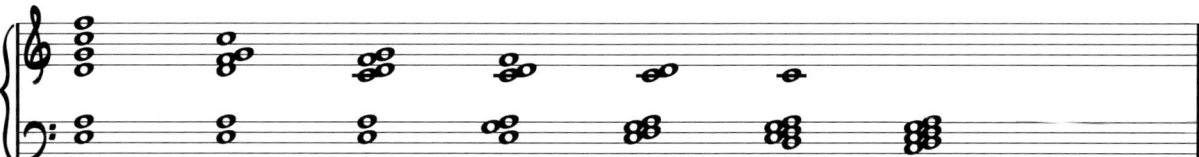

The 6-note stacked fourth voicing above folds up in progressive steps. Each time we move to the right, we lower the top voice an octave until we reach the final voicing, a cluster. The final cluster voicing isn't necessarily useable—you get to determine just how many seconds you want in the voicing, and how far you want to go with this concept.

My point here is that combinations of stacked fourth voicings and fourth voicings with octave displacements notes will work well together in arrangements.

The two voicings above will register on the ear as "fourth voicings" even though one voicing consists of two fourths and the other consists of a whole step and a fourth. Arrangers use these related voicing structures in solis and fast moving lines because the sound is smooth and compatible when you hear this voicing structure moving in rhythmic values of short duration.

Since the fourth voicings of the dorian scale don't break down into differentiated chord qualities, I tend to think about these voicings modally. Play through the C Dorian voicings with a C in the bass and these chords sound like C-7. With an Eb in the bass they give you Ebmaj7 sounds and with an F in the bass, they sound like F7sus4 chords. These are the most common chords associated with these voicings because of the lack of "avoid" notes in these scales. (I could, for example, put an A in the bass and use the above voicings for A-7b5 chords (since the A Locrian scale has the same notes as C dorian) but the Bb and F in these voicings tend to clash. F, Eb and C as bass notes create less of these kind of clashes in the harmony.)

Chapter 15 — Chords built in 4ths

I can also construct fourth voicings for other chords than the above using combinations of 3rds fourths, and tritones. In general, using fourths in voicings of mixed intervals brings a quartal sound and feeling to chords that are functionally clear.

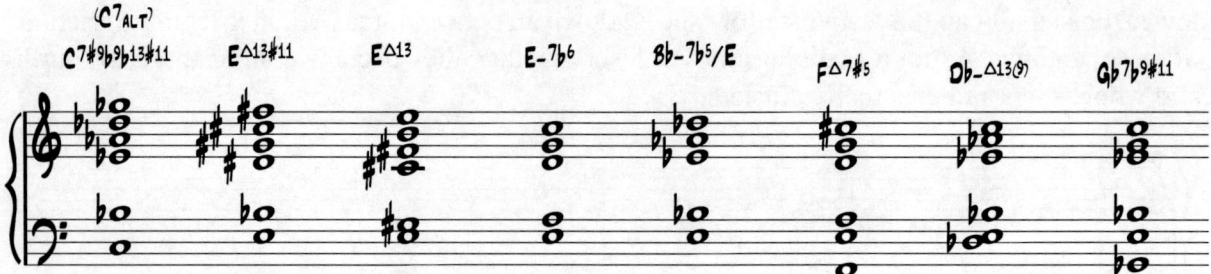

Another way to use fourth voicings is as upper structures of chords. These sounds which can be so mysterious and incomplete sounding make interesting voicing choices, giving a certain dryness to chord progressions.

Let's look at an example of this. Here are some of the voicings that Herbie Hancock uses on Miles Davis classic recording of Wayne Shorter's tune, "Nefertiti." These voicings are transcribed here without rhythms, focusing only the harmonic choices. Let's look at the first four bars of this tune, as Herbie plays it in different choruses:

the same four bars from a later chorus

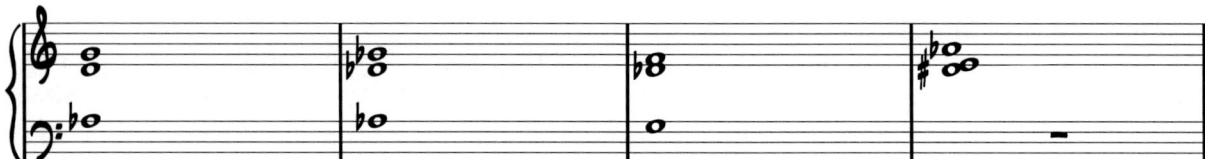

(Actually, to be consistent, I should call the second chord of the progression an Ab7sus4 chord, but I am following an interview with Herbie Hancock (from Ethan Iverson's blog, "Do the Math") that quotes Herbie as labeling the chord that way.)

Notice how simple the structures are for these first few chords, in the above choruses. Fourths predominate, and they are connected by beautiful voice-leading. The top note of the chord is also very important, creating a counter line to the melody of the song. However, most important for our discussion here, is the way he uses fourth upper structures (in this case, without filling in the lower parts of the chord. You can see this particularly clearly on the G-7b5 chord change, in the

CHORDS BUILT IN 4THS — CHAPTER 15

first chorus example above, the fourth of C to F, the 4th and 7th of the chord, has a Db inside it. The second G-7b5 is stacked fourths, the flatted fifth left out of the voicing. In the last example, while not really a fourth voicing offers an example of great voice-leading from the Ab11 chord.

Here's another four bar piece of the tune:

and again, from a later chorus

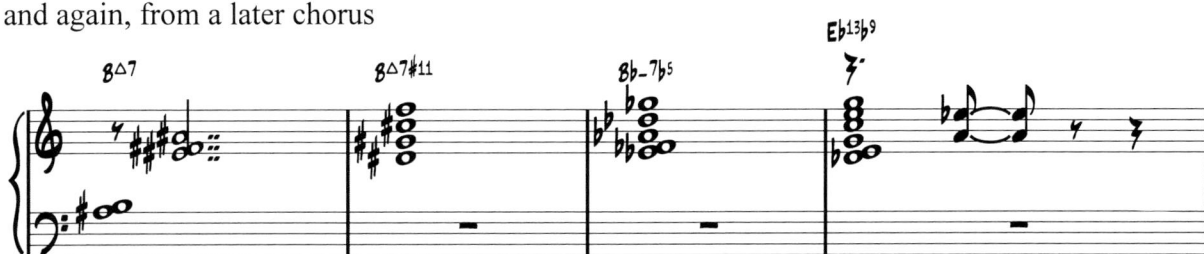

Again, you can see many fourth combinations here. The first Bmaj7 is two fourths, one in each hand, one with a whole step inside it and one with a half step inside it. The second bar Bmaj7s are variations on the "So What" voicing. Again, the Bb-7b5 is constructed from mostly fourths as well.

Here's another four bar section

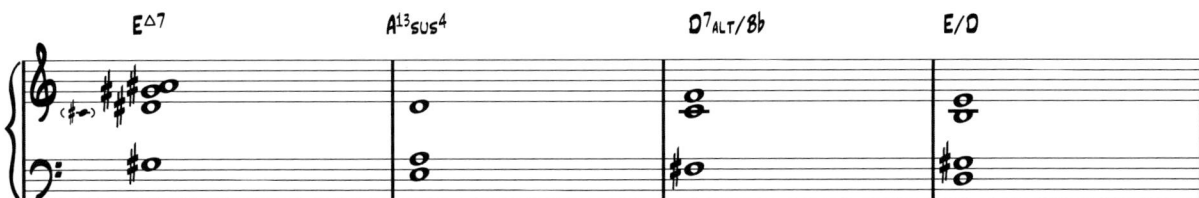

a later variation of the same four bars.

E major7 again gets the fourth treatment: stacked fourths plus two thirds in the second example, fourths and whole steps in the first example. A7sus4 is stripped to its essential fourth structure, followed with good voice-leading to the D7altered chord/Bb. Adding the F# in the second four bars makes the E triad a stacked fourth structure with a whole step inside it.

Herbie Hancock, truly a master of voicings, uses these ambiguous sounds to paint colors on this tune, but his use of fourth structures is ingenious and beautifully realized through the kind of voice-leading he employs to connect these chords.

One last word on this topic comes from a friend of mine who was working with Herbie. On the way to a gig Herbie suggested to the band members: "Tonight, let's not play any thirds of chords." That kind of exploration—harmonic "tinkering"—is typical of Herbie's comping. He continually re-examines the harmony of songs, finding unique structures and re-interpreting harmonies within even very familiar chord progressions. And the idea of eliminating thirds (which is central to quartal thinking) is often a part of his harmonic explorations.

Chapter 16 – "Giant Steps"

"Giant Steps" changes, sometimes called 'Coltrane changes' are the creation (or perhaps "discovery" is a better word) of John Coltrane, first heard on his 1959 recording, "Giant Steps." Technically, it doesn't really belong in our list of non-functional re-harmonization techniques because it is a very functional set of chord changes. Still, we are going to look at the technique briefly here, because it is another "modern" tool used in jazz harmony and, even though it is a functional chord progression, it stretches the boundary of the ii-V-I relationship through superimposing other chords over these changes.

In the late 1950s, Coltrane experimented with a lot of different sets of chord changes before moving to more open, modal forms. Tunes like "Straight Street", "Moment's Notice" and "Lazybird" pushed the envelope of bebop harmony and the use of rapidly changing chords and chord scales. These tunes primarily focused on ii-Vs that moved up and down various intervals. One could argue that these tunes broke from bebop harmony in their extreme use of modulation. However, these tunes are conceptually connected to bebop in that they use added ii-Vs, often up and down half-steps, and other superimpositions of chords, in effect extending harmonic ideas developed in the bebop period. "Giant Steps" comes toward the end of this period of Coltrane's development and represents an extreme in this approach to chord progressions.

The changes we think of as "Giant Steps" changes come from the first two bars of the tune of the same name. The "Giant Steps" pattern is one of two-beat chord changes that start on a Imaj7 then go up a minor third to a dominant7 that resolves up a fourth to another maj7, which goes up a minor third to another dominant7, which resolves up a fourth to a maj7 (Bmaj7/ D7/ Gmaj7/ Bb7/ Ebmaj7). These changes are part of a progression which we find in the Coltrane tune "Countdown" among many others, and is a re-harmonization of a ii-V-I Maj7 cadence. The complete pattern starts on a ii-7, goes up a half step to a dominant chord and then the same pattern as "Giant Steps" begins, up a fourth to a maj7, up a minor third to a dominant, up a fourth to a maj7, up a minor third to a dominant (the V7 of the cadence) up a fourth to the I maj7 (E-7/ F7/ Bbmaj7/ Db7 /Gbmaj7/ A7/ Dmaj7. The crucial thing to notice here is that this is a re-harmonization of the progression: E-7/A7/Dmaj7.) These changes are sometimes called "three key changes" because they incorporate three key centers (Bbma7, Gbmaj7 and Dmaj7) a third apart. (Or in the tune "Giant Steps" B major, Eb major and G major.) In each case, the three tonal centers are preceded by dominant7s. Coltrane wrote many re-harmonizations of standards utilizing this three key concept. Sometimes he incorporated this technique in re-harmonizations of standards ("But Not For Me," "Body and Soul"). Sometimes he used a standard chord progression as a jumping off point to create a new song, loosely derived from the cadences of the original tune ("Countdown" based on "Tune Up," "Satellite" based on "How High the Moon," "26-2" based on "Confirmation," "Fifth House" based on "What Is This Thing Called Love"). Sometimes he created new tunes that weren't based on standard tunes, such as "Giant Steps."

Since these Coltrane changes are a pattern and since, as Trane employed them, they only follow the melody loosely, it's relatively easy to apply them to other standards that have sections of ii-7 V7 Imaj7, such as the bridge of "Cherokee."

Chapter 16

"Giant Steps"

(CD Track 106)

"GIANT STEPS"   CHAPTER 16

The first 12 bars of the bridge use the same strategy as "Countdown". The last four bars work backward from F7 in the last bar of the bridge to the C7 in the 14th bar. The Gmaj7 to G-7 (bar 12 and 13) make a transition between these two sections. The last four bars could have been handled many ways. I also tried to vary the melody while still alluding to the melodic material from the original bridge.

These 3 key changes reflect Coltrane's interest in superimposition. Essentially, he creates a harmonic mosaic, where keys that are fairly far apart are placed next to each other. In Coltrane's recordings of these kinds of tunes, he sticks very close to the Mixolydian/Ionian scale options. His goal is to put B major next to G major next to Eb major, and so he doesn't use altered dominant sounds much. He tries to give us those 3 keys as clearly as possible, playing right through the middle of each chord change, using patterns that define the harmony clearly and somewhat simply. For this reason, Coltrane changes generally get natural tensions and are most effective when the melody is altered to fit with these chord sounds.

Another sometimes overlooked point about these "Giant Steps" tunes is how good, albeit simple, Coltrane's melodies over these kind of changes are. Whether he is creating a solo-like line on "26-2" or a melody in half-notes on "Giant Steps" or "Countdown," his melodies are memorable. When he uses this device in re-harmonizations of standards he ends up changing the melody significantly, creating strong new melodies on the 3-key parts of the tune. No attempt is made to keep the original melody in these situations, which makes this re-harmonization technique different from the others we've studied.

Another important point about Coltrane changes on standards is that the harmonic rhythm is usually even, with the same number of beats on each chord in the progression (except for the final chord). On some of his re-harmonizations, the three key changes come while the melody is holding a long note ("Body and Soul") while on others Coltrane adapts a melody in motion to this harmonic device ("But Not for Me"). On "26-2" he weaves in and out of these changes, connecting them in surprising and subtle ways.

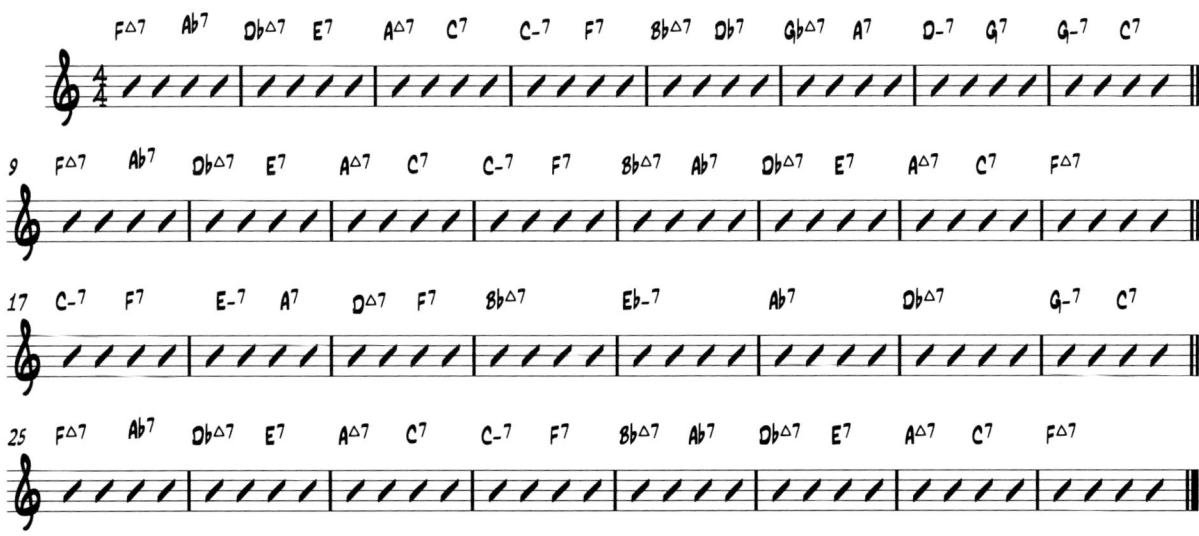

Chapter 16

In this tune, Coltrane does something different from either the "Countdown" progression or the "Giant Steps" progression. Bars 1 through 3 above use the "Countdown" pattern going from Ab7 all the way to cadence finally on F, but we start on the I chord (F maj7) instead of the ii-7 chord (G-7). In Bar 4 where we'd expect the resolution to the F major 7th to occur, we get C-7 F7 instead, a ii-V to the IV chord, in keeping with what happens on the song "Confirmation". Then the pattern begins again on the IV chord. In bar 7, where we'd expect a resolution to D major7 (if we were following the "Giant Steps" pattern) we instead get a D-7 G7 that leads to G-7 C7, taking us back to the top of the form and the I major7 chord. (Again, this comes from "Confirmation".) In bar 13 we return to the IV chord but this time, Ab7 follows this chord which is a kind of bluesy bVII7 feeling change, which again starts the "Giant Steps" pattern, this time cadencing on Fmaj7 in the bar before the bridge. The bridge starts with a ii-V to D but quickly segues to Bb major, keeping up the 3 key idea by connecting two keys a major third apart. The rest of the bridge is the same as the normal changes to "Confirmation." It's ingenious the way Coltrane both makes a fascinating blowing form based on three key changes and at the same time drawing elements from "Confirmation" to create a kind of re-imagining of that tune.

I'll end this chapter with a nice example of the effective use of "Giant Steps" changes as a compositional device written by one of my harmony students, Marius Duboule. The tune is called Tokuchō and is based on the Monk tune "Nutty".

"GIANT STEPS" — CHAPTER 16

Try creating some of your own reharmonizations or more extreme re-creations of standard tunes using "Giant Steps" or "Countdown" changes. See if you can find strong progressions that make interesting variations on these standards and also try to find interesting melodies of half-notes or 8th note lines as Coltrane does so effectively on these songs.

CHAPTER 17 – COLOR CHORDS

Color chord re-harmonization is a somewhat vague label for re-harmonizations not based on harmonic function. When students in my Harmony I class bring in re-harmonizations that contain passages in which none of the techniques we're studying seem to be present: no tritone substitutes, no passing chords, no diatonic substitutes or modal interchange chords, I'll say, this is a "color chord" re-harmonization. This means, essentially, that the student chose those chords at random because he or she liked something in the harmonic colors, but there isn't a clear logical connection between the chords. Of course, there's nothing wrong with choosing a chord change because you like the sound of it—at the end of the day, that's what we all do all the time, whether there is some appealing logic to a progression or not. However, I want the chords to feel like there is some reason why I chose one over the other. In cases where chords are functioning as we saw them function in the first part of this book, the logical connection between chords is clear. But in cases where there isn't such a clear harmonic logic, I still want the chord changes to have a feeling of inevitability.

There are some reasons that chords sound good one after the other, even when there's no clear reason for choosing one in particular. One way chords follow each other is based on "notes versus quality." This idea is represented by the diagram below. On one side of the line we have "notes" and on the other side "chord quality." If two chords have the same chord qualities, they usually connect smoothly, even though they may have few notes in common. For example, if I have a chord progression where say, a G-7 is followed by an Ab-7, the chord qualities are the same and the Ab-7 sounds logically connected to the G-7, but the notes that are available on these chords are very different.

I can also connect chords using the opposite approach. A B-7 followed by a Cmajor 7 (#11) is an example of two chords with very different chord qualities that have chord scales that share most of the same notes.

So to summarize, non-functional chords have a logical connection to each other if either the notes of the chord scales or the chord qualities themselves are the same or similar.

QUALITY	NOTES
SAME ⇨	DIFFERENT
DIFFERENT ⇦	SAME or SIMILAR

There are many examples of tunes that have chord changes connected by either similar chord qualities (and different notes in their chord scales) or different chord qualities (and similar notes in their chord scales). Joe Henderson's "Inner Urge" is a good example of both of these ways of connecting chords.

COLOR CHORDS   CHAPTER 17

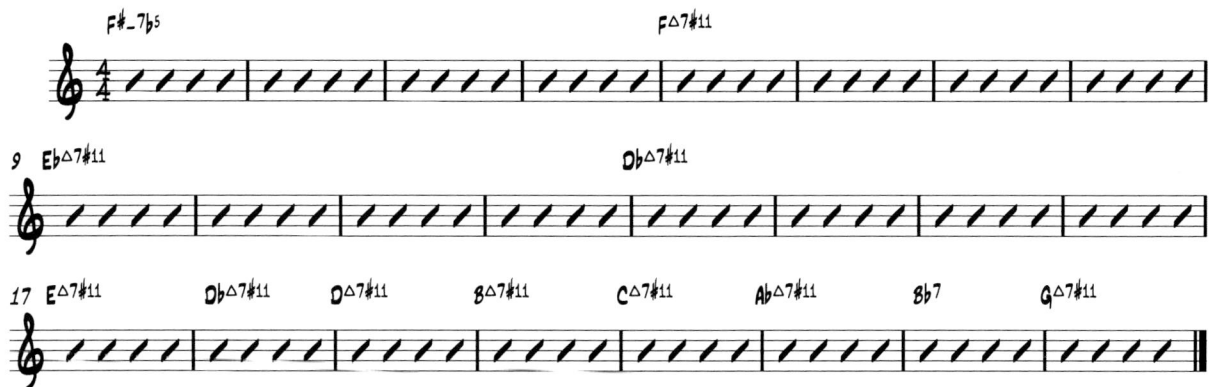

This tune is constructed almost entirely of major7th chords, moving mostly down in whole steps, up in half steps or down in thirds (chords that are connected by their same chord qualities). However, the last chord of the tune, the G major 7 (#11) leads back to the F#-7b5 and this is an example of two chords with different qualities connected by their similar chord scales. (Another example of this is the first and second chords of the tune, the F#-7b5 that is followed by F major 7.)

Examples of tunes that have a lot of chords of the same quality include Bill Evans' all major7th tune "TTTT" and his minor 7th filled "Time Remembered." The B section of "Black Narcissus," another Joe Henderson tune, provides another example, also using major 7ths. Kenny Kirkland's "Chance" (discussed above in the slash chord chapter) has a section of several major7ths in a row, and a section of minor sevenths. This technique is so common in modern jazz compositions that you can almost open a fake book at random and find it. These progressions (or parts of chord progressions) make sense because the chord qualities are the same and work through the connection of like thing to like thing.

There are also many tunes that contain chords that have a lot of common tones, or common tones between their chord scales, or between important notes in their chord scales. The first two chords of Bill Evans' "Time Remembered" are B-7 to Cmaj#11, the first four chords of "Nardis": E-7/ Fmaj7/ B7#9/Cmaj#11, contain two such connections between the first and second and between the third and fourth chords. Looking back at the "Nefertiti" chord changes, we can see these kind of 'like notes versus different chord qualities/different notes versus like chord qualities' approach operating in the way chords are connected one to the other. The first chord, Abmaj7#11 leads to an Ab7sus4(3), with many important common tones but two very different chord qualities. The next change shares the important Db, everything except the root, really. The relationship between the C7alt and the Bmaj7 is a common tone connection, as is the B major7 to the Bb-7b5, the Eb7alt to the Emaj7, the E/D to the B-9, the Eb13#11(no 3) to the Bb-maj7. Common tone relationships, particularly between the upper structures, connect most of the harmony in this tune.

Let's look at a tune of mine. This is a song called "Tom Harrell" that I recorded on a CD called "Handmade." Here's the first 9 bars of the tune:

151

CHAPTER 17

COLOR CHORDS

(CD TRACK 107)

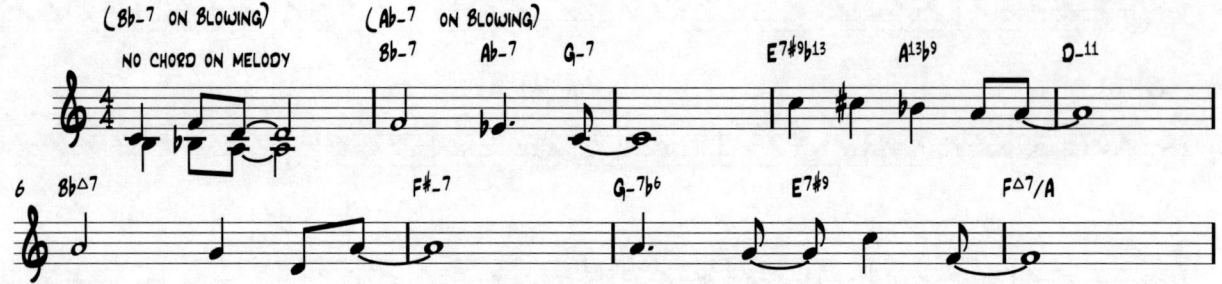

In this tune, like many modern jazz compositions, a mix of functional and non-functional harmony is employed. Actually, this tune is a lot more functional than many of the tunes I write but I was trying to get at something that I've really liked in certain of Tom Harrell's compositions, a certain kind of movement chord to chord, moving in and out of functional and non-functional harmony. I didn't write this tune thinking about harmonic rules. However, I can analyze it to understand what effect certain harmonic choices have. Sometimes I'll challenge myself to write consciously using a particular harmonic idea that came from something that I wrote intuitively.

The first three chords are all the same chord quality, minor7ths. Then the tune modulates into D minor. The Bbmaj7 is a bVImaj7, a common place to go to in D minor. The next chord change, the F#-7 is interesting to me, because there's no functional reason to go there. The connection is the A natural, and I like the sudden juxtaposition of this harmony after the Bbmaj7, both chords harmonizing that same note. The first section ends in the related key of Fmaj/A.

Try to analyze some of your favorite modern tunes, such as songs by Wayne Shorter, Herbie Hancock, Bill Evans, Tom Harrell and others. Analyze the connections between chords that aren't based on ii-V, V7 to I or other functional harmonic relationships. Look for similarities in chord quality and common tone relationships.

Also, try and analyze your own music. Much of what we write is done intuitively and that's fine. However, after you've written something intuitively, you can analyze it and write other tunes exploring similar harmonic ground. Think of Coltrane writing "Giant Steps," "Fifth House," "Satellite" and the many other tunes exploring the "Giant Steps" progression. The marriage of intuition with rational development and exploration of ideas and harmonic structures that interest you can be extremely productive.

Here's one more tune of mine. This is from the same recording I mentioned above, "Handmade," and is called "Fairy Tale."

Chapter 17

Color Chords

(CD Track 108)

This tune explores a rhythmic cell through a chord progression. It's a good example of color chord relationships because most of the connections between chords are based on common tone relationships (bar 9 and 10, 10 and 11, 11 and 12, 13~18, 19 and 20, 21 and 22, 26 and 27, 30 and 31) and similar chord qualities (24 and 25, 28~32).

Try using the above concepts for your own color chord progressions. Try writing a chord progression that interests you using the idea of chords connected by similar notes and then chords connected by similar chord qualities. See if this generates a progression that is different from other compositions that you've written in the past. Then try writing a melody over this unusual progression. These are ideas that you can return to in future compositions. (For more on this and other compositional strategies, see "Appendix A: Tips for Composers.")

CHAPTER 18 – PARALLEL CHORDS THAT USE EXACT TRANSPOSITION (PLANING)

Another way that chords can be connected is through parallel movement. Parallel chords are chords in which each voice moves in the same direction. In the chapter on fourth voicings, we saw a lot of voicings moving (in parallel motion) up a scale. This kind of movement, in which each voice moves to the adjacent scale degree results in different chord qualities and voicing structures because of the asymmetric nature of the chord scale.

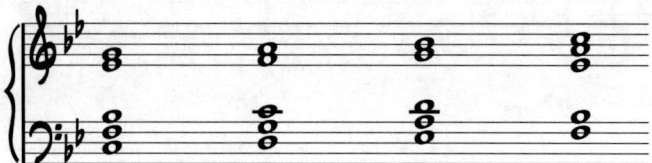

The voicings above are the "So What" voicing moving up a dorian scale. The first two voicings are exactly the same intervals in relation to the root of each chord—the second voice is a fourth above the root, the third voice is a fourth above the second, the fourth voice is a fourth above the third and the top voice is a major third above that. The third chord has a different structure, because some voices are a half step above the last chord and some voices are a whole step, so this chord is root, tritone, fourth, fourth, minor third.

When I move a voicing up a scale, allowing the scale to affect the voicing structure of each chord, this kind of movement is called a tonal transposition.

An "exact" or "perfect" transposition is different. Whatever interval the melody moves, the root and all the internal voices move the exact same interval. Here is an example of an exact transposition using the same "So What" voicing. This comes from a tune by McCoy Tyner (from the drum trades on the tune "Inception" from the album of the same name.) All of the voices move up in whole steps and each voicing is root, fourth, fourth, fourth, major third.

In exact transpositions, the voicing structure is unperturbed: every voicing is exactly the same as the last, but transposed a particular interval away from the previous voicing. This kind of parallel movement is also sometimes called "planing."

Exact transposition is a powerful harmonic tool. It takes you out of the key, so it brings a kind of exotic chromaticism to tonal situations. If the melody line that I am harmonizing is strong, then we hear the melody and the implication of the normal diatonic harmony is there, but the voicing structure moving parallel to the melody brings in notes not usually associated with that key. It is a chromatic intervallic approach, so it's outside of the harmony, but again when used sensitively, it feels both in a key and out of the key at the same time. In the above example on "Inception" the tune is a C minor blues. The first two voicings are in C minor, the third takes us out of the key (E natural and B natural) and the last three chords take us further out of the key but finally point us back toward C-11 (the next voicing in the pattern.)

Examples of transposition, both exact and tonal, are ubiquitous in modern jazz arrangements. Examples of tonal transposition include: Gil Evans' famous counterline in the brass on Summertime:

Here's a passage of diatonic triads from Bill Evans' solo version of "All the Things You Are". (Transcribed by Keith Yaun.)

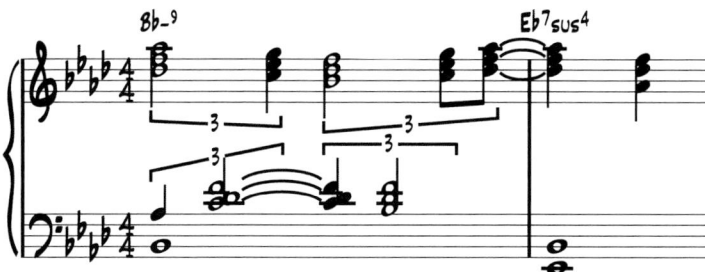

The triads over Bb minor7 are tonal transpositions, each voice of the triad moving up or down the chord scale, so the chord qualities move between major and minor. Bill Evans often uses triad upper structures moving up a chord scale.

Exact transposition can be very liberating in an arrangement and on a personal level, it's something that I've been working on more and more in recent years. As a pianist, one of the difficulties this technique presents, is that one has to keep the voicing structure very strongly in mind without reference to chord changes. Mostly, our sense of voicings is connected to what the available notes are on chords and is conceived relative to a bass note. For example, 1,4,7,9,3,5 on a minor chord is relatively easy to play in any key. It's more difficult to think: melody note, then major third below, half step below that, major third, fourth, fourth. However, if I am moving some combination of different intervals stacked vertically to harmonize with a melody or melodic line, I'm thinking of the intervals I am playing in this way. Pianists tend to think of chords as being built up from the root and this kind of harmonization is a top down approach.

Chapter 18 — Parallel chords that use exact transposition (planing)

Any close position voicing (all the notes of the chord are within an octave), drop 2 voicing, as well as fourth voicings that aren't extremely wide, have potential to work in this sort of exact transposition situation. Open voicings (voicings wider than an octave) can be used as well, but chords that retain a strong root function will sound like re-harmonizations with every change sounding like a new chord, whereas the sound of smaller chords moving by interval tends to be more ambiguous as to what the roots of the chords are. Range also plays a role here, with higher voicings (of all widths) sounding more ambiguous, less like moving chord changes with a changing root function, but there's no hard and fast rules here and you can let your ears guide you.

Within a tonal context, short passages of exact transposition really open up the harmony, particularly if the voicing is harmonically rich, or intervallically interesting. Personally, I am particularly attracted to interval sounds that have a lot of ambiguity, like fourths and fifths + half steps or whole steps, minor 6ths and half steps, or diminished scale stacked in unusual intervals.

Here are some examples. First, "Caravan", using a major6b9 voicing structure (diminished scale).

(CD Track 109)

Here's the first four bars of "Polka Dots and Moonbeams" using a whole step + a major triad in 2nd inversion voicing structure.

(CD Track 110)

Here's a short excerpt from "Round Midnight" using exact transposition (half step + a major third) over a pedal.

PARALLEL CHORDS THAT USE EXACT TRANSPOSITION (PLANING)   CHAPTER 18

It's important to look for interesting interval combinations to transpose. I keep a record of interval stacks that I'm interested in. I could call them chords, but I am trying to differentiate between chords that can be defined as having a certain quality and this harmonic material which is more ambiguous than that. Actually, that's really what this is about: being able to define vertical combinations of interval sounds as something other than "chords." Maybe it will be clearer if I show you some of the combinations I've been working on. Here's a very consonant sounding structure.

The voicing above is major7 over its third or a minor triad with a b6th added. It's voiced as two fifths with a half-step in between. The appeal of this sound to me in the above context isn't really so much about the chord quality, it's the stacked fifths with the half step crunch in between. To transpose it exactly, I don't really want to get distracted by the 'minor b6th-ness' of the voicing— it's not going to function like that chord anyway, it's just going to move with all the voices in locked step underneath whatever melodic shape the top note of these transposed voicings are making—it's the fifths and half-step I want to think about.

(CD Track 111)

A more tense sound comes from a fifth with a tritone connected by a half step. Again, I could name this chord: Gbmaj7#11/Bb, but first of all, that name is pretty complex and requires some thought to construct the chord from it, and second of all, it's not functioning in any way like that chord. It's just a sound, which I am going to transpose underneath a melodic shape.

(CD Track 112)

CHAPTER 18
PARALLEL CHORDS THAT USE EXACT TRANSPOSITION (PLANING)

Here are some other sounds I've been playing with. The first is an inversion of a D dim major7 (or a fourth and a minor third, connected by a half-step.)

A fifth, a half step and a minor third

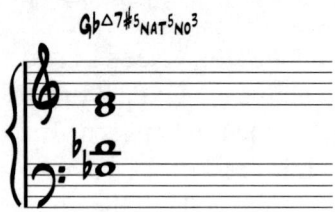

half step, whole step and a fourth

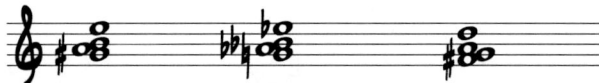

A half step and a minor 6th

You should try this yourself. Make up your own interval combinations, anything that appeals to you and then try and adapt them to tunes, or use them as a compositional tool. I'd like to say that the possibilities are limitless, and of course they are, but I want to stress that having wide-open possibilities means that you have to find sounds and develop them in a way that creates an inner logic of your own devising. Just because we are in a world of freedom harmonically, that doesn't mean that you can do just anything. Of course, you CAN do just anything, but if you pick harmonic structures out of a hat, it often sounds random and "non-purposeful."

This may seem like a strange aside, but I'm going to make it anyway. I went to a movie that a lot of people liked, a film about being confused in a foreign culture. (No, not that movie, a different one.) Anyway, I really didn't enjoy it much and I found myself explaining to a lot of people who did like it why I didn't. Actually, I didn't really know why I didn't like it. Contrary to how I may seem in this book, I really don't have all the answers. So, eventually I figured out that I thought it was too easy to be confused and not get it, which was the theme of this movie, at least for me. Being confused and not getting it is the natural state of being, at least for a lot of us. So (stay with me here) it's kind of the same thing with harmony. Given a wide-open non-functional harmonic frame, you can play a lot of random stuff and it's going to sound like random stuff. What you need to do, I think, is find patterns that create harmonic logic.

Of course, harmonic logic is in the ear of the behearer (to quote Dewey Redman again) and what might sound beautiful and inevitable to me, may sound random and disconnected to you. (Hence, the riot that ensued when people first heard Stravinsky's "Rite of Spring.")

Anyway, end of polemic and movie reviews. Onward.

Let's return to the Hank Jones transcription we looked at earlier. The harmonic movement that we analyzed earlier was functional. However, Hank Jones uses a lot of parallel harmonic movement in this piece. Here's an example from bar 9, the pickups to the second A section:

These are parallel fourths (five note voicings) that follow the melody exactly transposing this voicing.

Here's a short example from bar 17, a short section that has two parallel voicings functioning as passing chords.

Here in the pickups to the last A section he uses parallel diminished voicings much in the manner of the "Caravan" above.

Chapter 18 PARALLEL CHORDS THAT USE EXACT TRANSPOSITION (PLANING)

This technique continues into the Last A section, using a few different parallel diminished voicings, and then mixing these diminished sounds.

These instances of exact transposition give an open feeling to the arrangement, a feeling of unpredictability. They allow Hank to leave the normal chord progression for several bars at a time, harmonizing the melody in a particularly rich and colorful way, but without sacrificing the sense of logical connection between chords. We don't even feel that we've entirely left the key, since the parallel sounds are following a melody that is very much in the key of F. We hear the "out" harmony, but it resolves, a colorful moment that we hear as a logical extension of what he played earlier. (It's worth noting that Hank Jones uses exact transposition most extensively in the last A section of the piece, after he has played two earlier A sections that use more functional harmonic language.)

Now would be a good time to go back to one of the functional arrangements that you did in the first half of the book to see if you can use exact transposition in a few places in the same way that we saw above, increasing the harmonic color and creating a momentary chromatic section of your arrangement, without losing the overall sense of working within a compatible harmonic vocabulary for the piece. Try this repeatedly in your arrangements and re-harmonizations of standards or original compositions. (Again, for more ideas of compositional strategies, refer to "Appendix A: Tips for Composers.")

Chapter 19 – Pedals

A pedal (sometimes called pedal point or bass pedal) is when changing harmony occurs as an upper structure over a held note in the bass. (Bass players have some freedom in interpreting the bass part to make ostinatos (repeating bass figures) or other types of bass lines out of these one-note situations, but it's important for them to keep returning to the pedal note since this is the defining sound of the harmony during a pedal section of a tune.) Pedals or pedal points can occur in other voices (sometimes referred to as inverted pedal point) but these have much less impact on the harmony of the tune.

The most common type of pedal is a pedal on the fifth of the key. This can happen at many points in a tune, but is most common as a kind of suspension in the bass during a ii-V or turnaround. When a V pedal occurs in one of these places, it acts functionally like a dominant.

Often V pedals occur in introductions to a tune. A famous example is on Miles Davis' "Someday My Prince Will Come" in which Paul Chambers repeatedly plays quarter note Fs continuing into the tune in Bb major. V pedals often occur in original compositions such as Bill Evans' "Turn Out the Stars".

Another famous Miles Davis arrangement that features a V pedal on the A sections is "All of You".

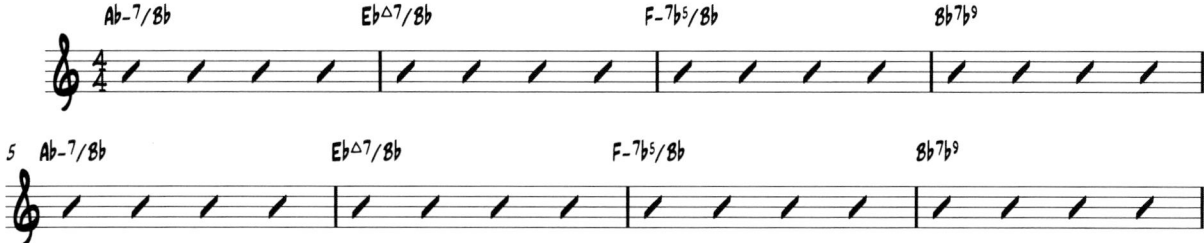

Pedals also occur in standard tunes, perhaps most famously in the A sections of Green Dolphin Street.

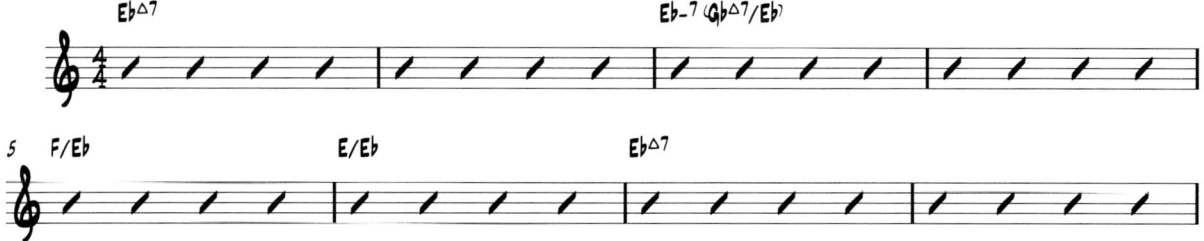

This pedal is a little more unusual because it is a I pedal. It gives this song its suspended somewhat moody feeling.

CHAPTER 19

All of the above examples are tonal. However, the feeling of a pedal is one of suspension—of a lack of harmonic motion, at least, of root motion. This feeling is enhanced by the superimposition of harmonic movement over the bass note—the bass sound contrasts with the harmony moving above it.

Pedals are widely used in modern jazz compositions and arrangements. Another famous pedal is John Coltrane's arrangement of "Body and Soul", in which an Ab in the bass transforms the first chord change of that tune into a suspended Ab7 kind of sound. He employs a similar device in his tune "Fifth House," a song based on the standard, "What Is This Thing Called Love." In this tune, an ostinato of C, G and octave C is played in the bass while the sax plays the melody (written over a "Giant Steps" progression) without piano comping. This is a somewhat more involved use of a pedal where a long and complex progression occurs over a static bass, but functionally it is a similar idea: a C (ish) pedal happens under a Giant Steps progression leading to F- and continues under the Giant steps progression leading to C. This is basically two pedals (V under ii-V- i in F- and I under ii-V-I in C—remember that "Giant Steps" is a 3 key variation on a ii-V-I cadence.)

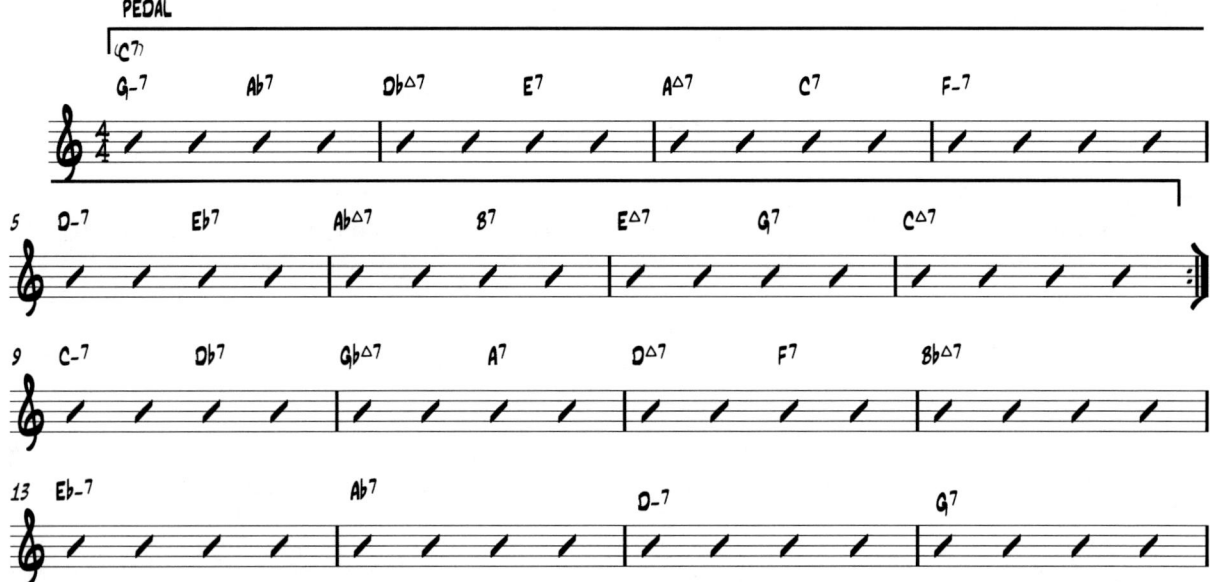

Coltrane solos on the superimposed chord changes, but tends to adhere more rigidly to the progressions in bars 5 through 8 and 9 through 12 than in bars 1 through 4. At any rate, the absence of piano comping gives him the option of playing over the A sections with a greater degree of harmonic freedom, sometimes referencing the original G-7b5 C7, F-.

Herbie Hancock's "Dolphin Dance" is another modern jazz tune that employs pedal sections.

Pedals **CHAPTER 19**

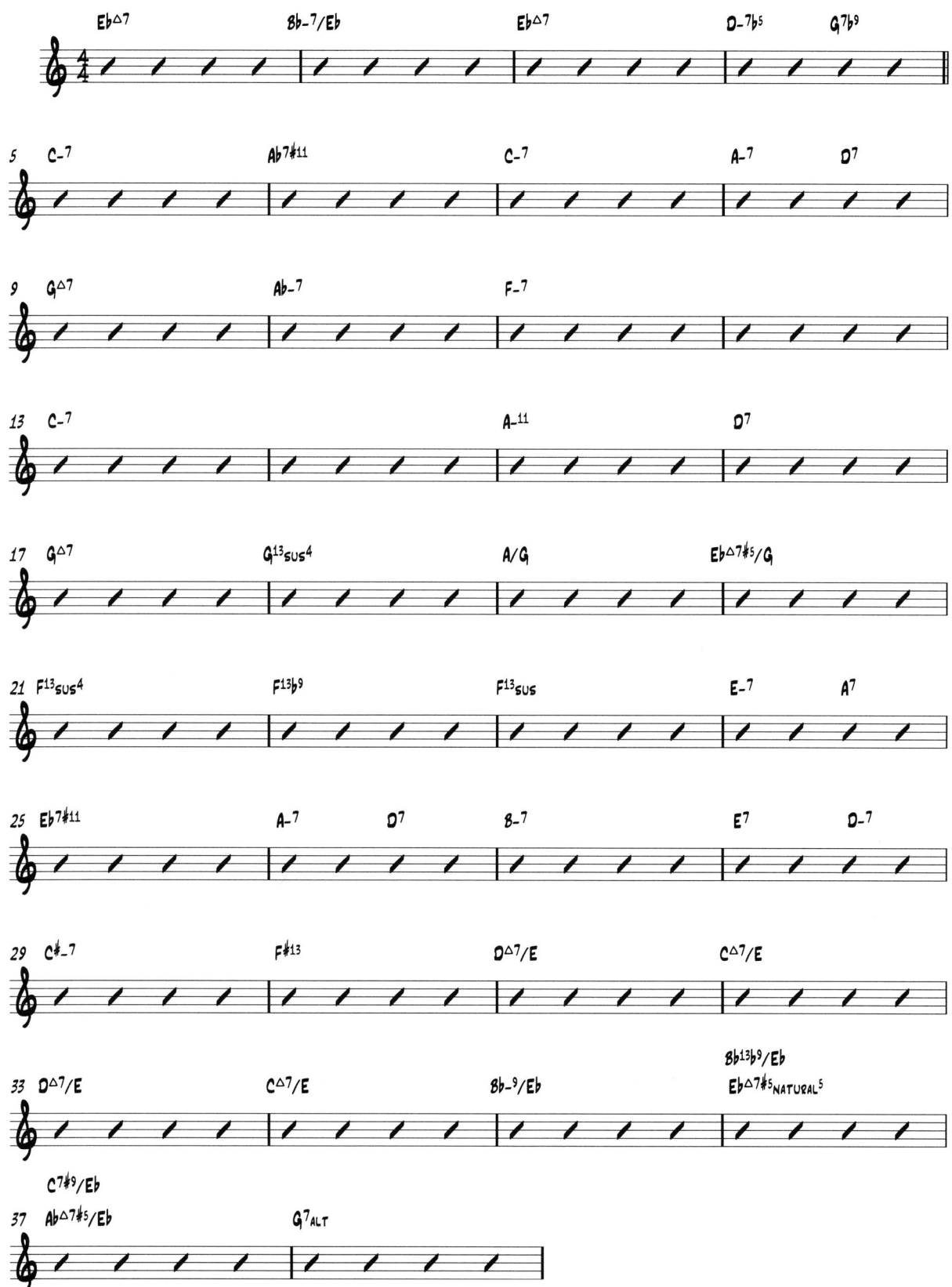

Bars 1 through 3, 17 through 20, 21 through 23, 31 to 34 and 35 to 37 are all pedals. (There is some variation in how Herbie Hancock interprets the last four bars of the tune, which only goes to show that pedal sections of songs allow for greater harmonic freedom. Bar 36 has a diminished quality and bar 37 feels like a ii chord in the key of Eb, with the above chords as upper structures of an F-major7 over Eb, more or less. Herbie has performed and recorded this song many times and changes the harmony in different performances. The above chord changes are an approximate guide, not the last word on the "correct" changes for the tune.)

Because pedal sections of tunes impose harmony over one note, they tend to be very liberating for the soloist. Over a pedal, it's easy to vary the harmony from the given chord change to other superimposed chord changes, especially (although not exclusively) for pianists who can easily superimpose harmony with left hand voicings. If the pedal continues for a while, the harmony often gets freer and freer, with the soloists "side-slipping" (this term means exactly what it sounds like: moving up and down from the original chord change in half-steps) into chromatic free improvisation and then returning to the original upper structure harmony.

Some pedal tunes have no other sections, they are entirely over a single bass note. This type of tune is different from a modal tune in that a modal tune is over one harmony or one chord scale. A pedal tune is over one bass note, but may have many different harmonies superimposed over it. Or, sometimes the harmony is unspecified, but the melody is chromatic or implies something other than one scale. (These distinctions are not always so clearly delineated in actual performance, where improvisers play what they hear and superimpose as they wish. However, the melodies of modal tunes like "Impressions" and "Milestones" are clearly written over one chord scale, and pedal tunes are not.)

"Pendulum," a tune by Richie Beirach, recorded both as a trio piece and with the Dave Liebman Quintet with Randy Brecker, is the latter type of pedal tune. In fact, when I first moved to New York, I used to hear the band *Quest* a lot (Dave Liebman, Richie Beirach, Ron McClure and Billy Hart) and this band played many tunes built around pedal points. I remember hearing Ron McClure, complaining half-kiddingly (I think he was half-kidding) that everyone else in the band was playing all kinds of interesting superimposed harmony while he's stuck playing "G" all night long.

Of course, using a pedal is always an option as a re-harmonization tool. This is from a re-harmonization of mine of "Darn that Dream." The first two bars of the first and last A sections use two different pedals: F and G.

And here's one last pedal arrangement, this time of the standard, "The Party's Over." This is a pretty standard V pedal but the pedal increases the ambiguity and eeriness the treatment of the melody (no comping, only two horn lines) putting the emphasis on the counterpoint between the two horns.

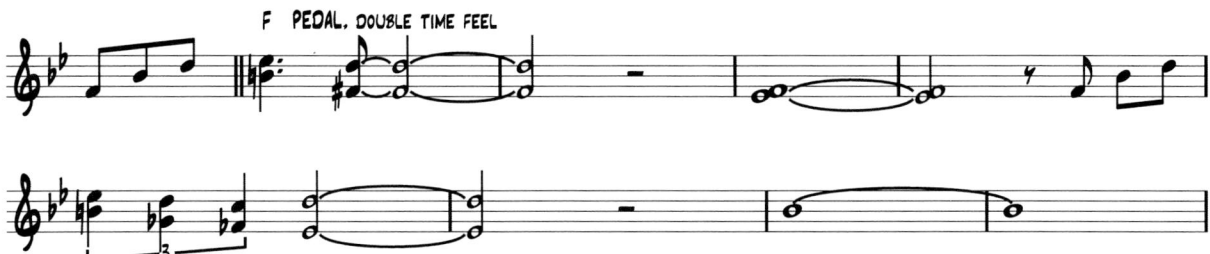

CHAPTER 20 – CHORD SUBTRACTION

Most of the harmonic techniques that we've looked at have one thing in common: they add chords to the chord progression of a song. However, re-harmonization can work the opposite way: we can get rid of chords instead of adding.

This is something that we looked at a bit when we were looking for the "right" chords on standard tunes. By looking at many versions of a standard, we develop a sense of what is the elemental harmony, the most basic, pared-down version of the tune—its deep structure. One way to omit chords is by leaving out all but the most essential, elemental parts of the progression. For example, in "Body and Soul," the deep structure is that the tune begins on a ii-7 chord and eventually resolves to I. There is some harmonic movement that gets us back to the ii-7 chord and then something leads to the vi-7. The first and second endings both move from this vi- back to the I, the second ending adds a V7/bII which is a sudden modulation up a half step. The bridge is mostly turn-arounds in this new key of bII (with a brief appearance by the iv-). The I maj7 of this key becomes a minor7 chord and this is the pivot chord (ii-7) to the next key (VII in relation to the original key of the tune) and again, it's turnarounds in this key, connecting by dominants moving down in half-steps at the end of the bridge to lead to a V7/ii in the original key. Something like this:

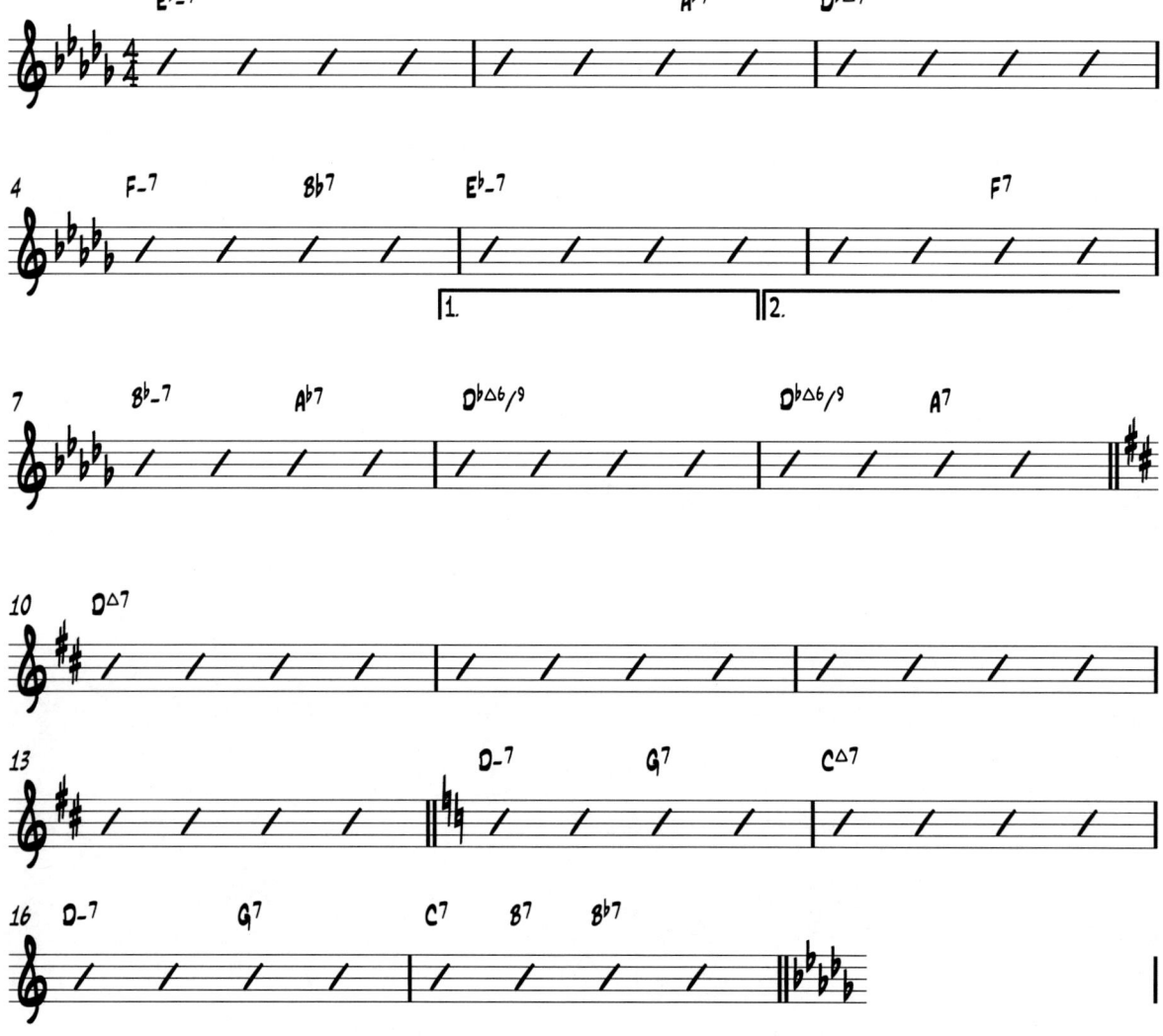

The changes to the deep structure of a tune can't really be written down definitively—there isn't one set of changes that ARE the deep structure. It's more of a platonic ideal. For every player the deep structure may be a bit different or each time I play the tune, I may consider different chords to be part of the fundamental harmony or not. I might decide that a ii-V, for example, is absolutely essential to the tune, or I can use a V functioning chord instead, or just the ii-7 functioning chord or something indeterminate that resolves to the target chord. In bar 16, can that ii-V be left out altogether? How about the B7 that comes in the next bar? Is the Bb7 that usually comes in the second half of the first measure of the tune essential, or something that might be omitted as I've done above? Of course, this depends, to some extent on what we mean by essential and the context that you are playing in. If I am playing the melody with a vocalist, or if I am playing through the tune in an improvised way without prior discussion of the chord changes, I probably will want to play the tune much as the other players are expecting to avoid unpleasant surprises. If I am playing the song solo or voicing the melody in a different, more impressionistic way, I can do something different. Being able to imagine the tune stripped down to its bare essentials allows me to build it up again in different ways using different harmony. If the Bb7 is an essential unchangeable part of this tune, then the famous Coltrane arrangement can't exist, because it omits this chord change.

So playing a modal feeling introduction, ostinato or other kind of figure that continues into the tune, as Trane does, is one approach that is possible by subtracting chords. Tunes that use turnaround harmony extensively often make effective modal tunes. "Softly as in a Morning Sunrise" is one such tune. Many years ago, I played in a house band for Sonny Stitt. When he played this tune it was very obvious that he was thinking of minor turnaround harmony, spelling out the chords very completely in his solo. Mere inexperienced youth that I was, I had only thought of this tune as a minor modal tune along the lines of Coltrane's version of it and so I was surprised to hear turnaround harmony in his solo lines. Of course, the minor turnaround harmony came first and is closer to the original harmony of the song, but for jazz students, with Trane's version already more than 45 years old, it's quite likely to be the dominant version in young players' experience.

Modalizing a tune tends to give you more freedom with the amount of chromatic or dissonant harmonic material you can add to it. You can use many of the techniques we've been discussing more easily in a modal context. Slash chord re-harmonization, exact and tonal transposition, chromatic side-slipping, and treating the I chord harmony as a kind of pedal for superimposition of upper structure chords and chromatic material are all more easily used in one chord situations.

Another way to make a tune modal is to analyze the note set of the melody. For example, in "Here's that Rainy Day" the melody of the first four bars is the first four notes of a Bb pentatonic (with one note outside of the pentatonic, the often mis-played B natural in the third bar.)

The harmonic underlying structure of the tune is that it begins on a I major and then modulates to the bVI major key, but I don't necessarily have to respect that. I am going to change the tune a bit more radically if I break with the functionality of the song's deep structure, but that's what we are checking out here. So, I can harmonize the first four bars with any sound that compliments the first four notes of the Bb pentatonic scale, such as a D7altered, an Eb major 9, a Gbmaj7#5, an F-7, and Abmaj7#11 or a Bbmaj7, among others. Some of these harmonizations will sound tense and all of these modal approaches will alter the feeling of the song (especially because they ignore the modulation that is an important structural feature of the harmony of this tune) but if I like this effect, I can continue. The next note set of the melody is A, B, C, D, F#, and these notes are harmonizable with Cmaj7#11, D13, E-7b6, B13b9 or any dom13b9 chord up in minor thirds (through the diminished scale) and on and on. This more radical deconstruction of the harmony based on the notes of the melody takes the tune apart, but still preserves a certain logical thread through the harmonic demolition.

Tunes with relatively few notes in the melody are the most available for this kind of re-harmonization.

Chord subtraction doesn't have to be done in quite so radical a manner to be effective in freeing up the harmony of a song. In my book, "The Jazz Musician's Guide to Creative Practicing," I wrote about how as the tune progresses, chorus to chorus, for some musicians the underlying harmony becomes more and more simplified and the player plays more freely over it. As I said above in the pedal section, playing over simplified harmony allows more freedom for the soloist to play more chromatically or to superimpose different harmonies. It's a lot easier to do these things over one chord change per bar, or every two or four bars, than when you are playing over a new harmony every two beats.

Modern jazz harmony has tended to go in two different directions. One direction is toward more complex and busier progressions ("Giant Steps" and "Countdown" being two prominent examples of this) and the other is toward more space and openness: pedals and modal playing (think of Coltrane recordings like "Transition" and "India") over which more harmonic superimposition and chromaticism can take place. In my last book, I mentioned a wonderful article by Richie Beirach for Keyboard magazine called "Somewhere Over the Changes" in which he described how as he soloed chorus after chorus on a blues, the chord progression he was playing became simpler and simpler (I for four bars, IV for two bars, I for two bars, V7, IV7, I for two bars) as the kind of lines he played over those changes became more chromatic and complex.

So we have another inverse relationship. Simplifying the harmony allows the line to become more ambiguous, chromatic and pan tonal. Making the harmony more complex creates a busier and somewhat richer harmonic form, but often leads to simpler chord spelling in lines.

For this reason, many modern tunes are simplified, more highly chromatic versions of busier harmonic forms. Rhythm changes provides a good example here. The deep structure of rhythm changes is something like this:

CHORD SUBTRACTION — CHAPTER 20

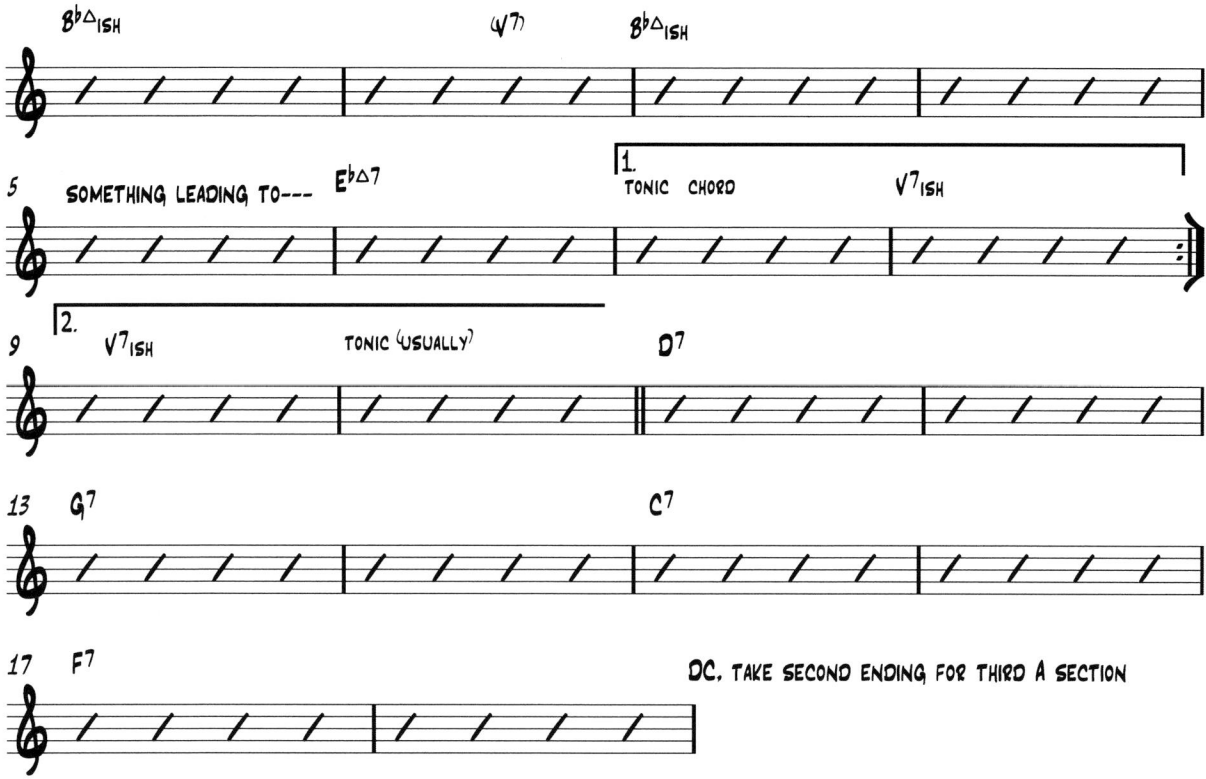

Tunes such as Wynton Marsalis' "Hesitation" offer a modern take on this form. Instead of turnarounds, we get the basic harmony in chromatic fragments (in the case of "Hesitation, with modulations). Often, when I compose something based on more traditional harmony or using a form like rhythm changes or blues, I try to think of the basic harmony as a sketch, or like a pedal that I can adapt or vary as I wish. Or sometimes I think of the chord change occurring on the downbeat of the measure, but the rest of the measure between the point of one chord change and another as "free" or open.

Here's an example of a tune of mine that explores this idea. It's a blues called "Blutocracy", from my recording "Communication Theory." (Palmetto Records, 2000). I wrote this tune thinking of the roots of a blues but with a very open chromatic sense of what could be played on them. The harmonic structure is simple and pedal-like because the line is chromatic and complex.

CHAPTER 20

CHORD SUBTRACTION

(CD TRACK 113)

One other concept should be mentioned here and I won't spend a lot of time on it because I covered it much more thoroughly in my earlier book, "The Jazz Musician's Guide to Creative Practice." Variations in harmonic rhythm can have a huge impact on the harmony of tunes. A lead sheet may tell me that the Bb7 comes on beat one of the third measure of the tune, but I don't have to play it there—I can delay it, or play it early or leave it out entirely. This concept is more connected to line playing and therefore not really within the scope of this book, but it can also be utilized in writing and arranging to great effect.

CHAPTER 21 – UNAVAILABLE TENSIONS

There's a great moment in the bridge of "Ruby, My Dear" where Monk hesitates for a moment before playing C minor on the downbeat. When he plays the voicing it has this extra fuzziness in it, he's playing a C minor7 with a major 7th next to the b7. When I figured out what that was, I was really knocked out by it. We often are so used to things being as we expect them to be that our ears aren't open to other possibilities.

And of course, why not play a minor and major7 next to each other in a cluster? Well, actually, there are fairly good reasons not to, one of them being that it's a little unclear what chord scale to play with such a voicing. And sure enough, for this and other reasons, including habit and a sense of what the normal amount of tension and dissonance in minor 7th voicings usually should be, 99.99 percent of the time pianists play either a C minor7 or a C minor major7 and almost never play a chord with both sevenths in it. Which is why when Monk plays the double 7th minor chord, it is so striking and effective.

When we discussed available tensions way back when, I made the point that these tensions get used something like 90 percent of the time. Sometimes I have beginning students who, when they voice chords, try to create "original" chord sounds by using "unavailable" tensions when they haven't mastered finding the available ones yet. With these students, I usually ask if they are interested in internalizing the jazz theoretical framework and harmonic language that's in use most of the time by players like: Duke Ellington, Oscar Peterson, Bill Evans, Hank Jones, Herbie Hancock and so on. I am open to the idea that some players and some students may be focused on going in their own direction and don't want to learn the traditional jazz harmonic vocabulary. There are geniuses of course, as well as searching people who are intent on creating their own harmonic language. But, usually, students who are working "outside of the box" stumble on more extreme harmonic ideas and dissonant vocabulary for a lack of understanding, either not knowing about the "inside" sounds of harmony, or making mistakes while trying to express this harmonic language. Very often, students who make the most extreme harmonic choices aren't really "hearing" these choices. Still, I always encourage students whose re-harmonization taste is taking them in odd directions to keep going and develop their own personal harmonic likes while continuing to study and learn more about the harmonic details of some of the great players in the jazz tradition.

Okay, but saying something is true 90 or even 99 percent of the time, begs the question; when isn't it true? The answer is something like: whenever you want to stretch the harmonic boundaries of your playing and writing, but also one might equally well say: you can use these less often-used chord changes, these "unavailable tensions" when you hear them. And that's pretty much the key. Monk uses this unusual sound on a minor chord and it comes as a revelation when you hear it because of the strength of his intention. There was a point where some listeners thought that Monk had no technique and was using arbitrary sounding dissonances. Nothing could be further from the truth, at least, in my opinion, and nowadays that's become the standard take on his playing. Monk chose these unique sounds and harmonies just as Jackson Pollack brought extreme intentionality to his drip paintings, or Stravinsky to the "savage" modern sounds of the "Rite of Spring."

CHAPTER 21

So as you ponder the possibilities of adding "unavailable tensions" or tensions that break the "rules" here's a few chord qualities to start you off.

1. Major 7 natural 11 chord. I remember noticing this harmony as the last chord of a Thad Jones arrangement. He uses the whole seven note major scale and it gives the chord a kind of homespun major feeling that you don't get from either a #11 or a chord without an 11 in it. Obviously, this is a chord that is derived from the major scale, featuring a note that we are usually taught to avoid.

2. Major 7 sharp 9 or B/C (with the 3rd of the C chord below the B triad.) Sometimes used as a kind of ending chord, such as on "Moment's Notice" but now heard more and more in contemporary jazz writing. This chord can be derived from a G harmonic major scale (a G harmonic minor scale with major third instead of a minor third).

3. Major13b9 chord voiced like an A triad plus a 9 over C. (This chord can be derived from an augmented scale. It can also be derived from a diminished scale that is constructed from two different diminished scale fragments: C, C#, D#, E, F#, G#, A, B—this is a very cool and unusual scale that starts half, whole, half, whole, and then continues whole, half, whole, half.)

4. Major7 #5 natural 5 chord or Abmaj7#5/C. (This chord can also be derived from the augmented scale, as well as from the C6/Bdim7 pair—the C major bebop scale.)

UNAVAILABLE TENSIONS   CHAPTER 21

5. Maj7 #5 #9. (Also derived from the augmented scale)

6. C minor major7 with a b7. See above, Monk.

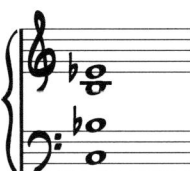

7. C minor major9 b6 or Ab-/C derived from the C harmonic minor scale.

8. C minor7 b9 from Locrian or Phrygian.

9. Cminor7b5b9 from locrian.

10. Cminor7 b5 natural 13 (or D/C-7b5). Locrian natural 6 scale is a somewhat less common scale that fits this chord.

CHAPTER 21 UNAVAILABLE TENSIONS

11. Near diminished voicings. Voicings based on a diminished scale with one note added that isn't in the scale.

Actually, we can break these chords with unavailable tensions down into two different categories. Some chords above are based on common chord scales containing what are usually thought of as "avoid" notes, that is, notes that are usually not stressed melodically or harmonized vertically, such as the 11th on a major 7 chord, the b9 on a minor7b5, the b13 on a min maj7 (from harmonic minor). To find these unusual voicings I am thinking of the whole scale without regard to the usually unavailable parts of the scale. Thinking of chords as scales is a way to increase the variety of your voicings even in functional harmonic situations. You can imagine the notes of the scale and then assemble the scale vertically, trying to find interesting intervals to place one on top of the other. For example, here are a few vertical constructions for a harmonic minor scale.

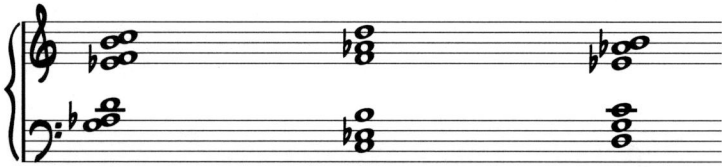

Some chords above aren't derived from common scales. Of course, I can always create a scale that will fit a given chord, however complex. Some of the scales listed above, like harmonic minor modes, the harmonic major scale, the augmented scale and others, through continued usage may become integrated into our mainstream harmonic vocabulary. In any case, whenever you encounter an unusual chord with a tension combination or chord tone combination that you haven't seen before, you can always work from the normal scale adding the altered tensions and chord tones. So a scale for a C-7 with a major 7 can be a dorian scale plus the major 7. A Cmajor 7 with a b9 can be a C major Ionian scale with the 2nd degree flatted. There may be other options (some of which are listed above) but you can always create a scale that fits any chord.

Here are a few examples of these chords in action. First, "Embraceable You."

(CD Track 114)

This technique often leads to a somewhat dark interpretation of the piece.

I also did a solo version of this song on my recording, "Leaving Home" that featured a lot of chord changes with unavailable tensions. As a pianist, these kind of arrangements can be challenging to play, because you want to try to give more weight to certain notes in the voicing to bring out the melody and to create a kind of fuzziness around the "wrong notes" that are present in the voicing.

Here's "You Don't Know What Love Is".

(CD Track 115)

Again, this is a pretty dark in mood. Very often if I am using this type of harmony I will place it against passages of more traditional harmonic material, such as triads or incomplete chords (the last type of non-functional re-harmonization we have to talk about in the next chapter). One of the nice things about this harmonic palette, though, is that these voicings have a through-composed feeling. I am not playing any common jazz voicings that can make a melody chorus feel hackneyed or clichéd. Again, it's all in how you put these things together. Players such as Martial Solal, Jason Moran and Richie Beirach exploit this kind of harmony very effectively. Kurt Rosenwinkel, Dave Douglas, Lage Lund and other contemporary writers are very good at using voicings with unusual tensions in a varied way, creating new sounds, not of all of which are as dark as the above harmonizations. For those of you interested in these harmonic ideas, you should continue to explore these tunes. In my harmony class, students transcribe original compositions that employ these techniques, seeing how each composer explores the palette of "unavailable" tensions in his or her unique way.

CHAPTER 22 – INCOMPLETE CHORDS

another way to mystery leaving.
    S p a c e s……silen.
        T   Un
      Fin   ish   (ed)

Okay, so, e e cummings, I'm not. But our last topic in the rules of non-functionality is chords that are incomplete so I thought a bit of "poetry" would make a nice lead-in. Like all of these other techniques, this one has a completely functional tonal application. That's because when I hear an incomplete chord, the tonal context will allow me to fill in the missing notes.

An incomplete chord is any chord that is missing fundamental chord tones. For dominant, major 7th, minor7th and minor major7th chords, the fundamental chord tones are 1, 3 and 7. For all other chord types, add the fifth to these tones. I can leave out any of these notes to make an incomplete chord.

Leaving out the root is the first option. While this sounds impossible (after all, if you are playing a chord, something has to be the bottom voice) it happens often. That's because a root is not just the bottom note of the chord, but a note that happens in a certain bass note register. Roots tend to occur down below middle C, usually a fifth to about an octave below that, down to the low E of the bass. Notes played at the bottom of chords in this range have a bass function. Often, voicings in the middle of the piano have a kind of rootless sound, especially if the voicing is one that is often used as a "non-root" structure. For example, left hand voicings of the type that pianists use when there is a bassist playing the root become harmonically ambiguous in a solo context. (For more information about non-root left hand voicings, see Appendix B, Piano Basics.) A good example of this comes from a solo version of the song "When I Fall In Love" by Bill Evans (from "the Solo Sessions"). In this particular version, Bill plays chords that give a faint suggestion of the underlying harmony. I've had students transcribe this tune and when they label the chord changes, dutifully using the bottom note of each voicing as the root, they come up with an extremely complicated and confusing re-harmonization of this tune. However, if we look at these voicings for what they are, typical rootless voicings for fairly common chords, the progression starts to look a lot more normal. This isn't just theoretical tinkering—to people (especially pianists, rather obviously) who are familiar with these non-root voicings, the implied roots are heard. So this is an example of where our brains fill in the rest of this incomplete chord sound. Nonetheless, the effect is very haunting and tantalizing—placing the melody in a very spacious and subtle frame. (One quick aside here: I've occasionally heard piano teachers admonish students not to use these rootless chords when they play solo. This is one of those oft-repeated rules that contains a valid point about bass function in solo contexts, but can be turned into dogma. There are many fine examples of great pianists breaking this particular rule.)

Far more common than incomplete chords that leave out the root, are voicings that leave out the third or the seventh of the chord. If I leave out the seventh, the harmony may become triadic, but usually, triads aren't considered incomplete 7th chords, they're complete triads. More often in this context, an incomplete chord that leaves out the 7th is one that has other upper structure notes that you don't usually find on triads. A common chord that is an alternative to a seventh chord is the 6/9 chord. I don't see this kind of labeling as much as I used to and this term may be fading into oblivion, but what is usually meant is what I would call a major 6th chord, with the available 9th added. A nice (and fairly common) fourth voicing for this chord is

So, while this technically qualifies as an incomplete major7th, it really is a very complete chord (a major 6th).

What I am referring to as incomplete voicings are more ambiguous. There's something undefined and indeterminate about them.

Here are some incomplete voicings that leave out the 7th of a (theoretically) major7th chord.

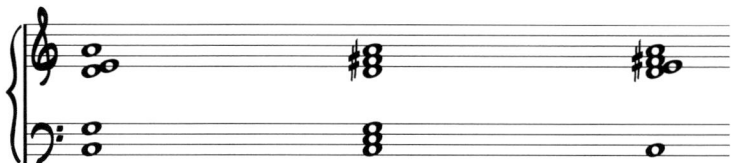

Of course, without the seventh, the above voicings might suggest C13#11, a dominant chord. So in this case, the voicings are ambiguous as to what that missing seventh might be. However, if altered tensions are present, then I will assume that the missing seventh is a dominant seventh because altered tensions are primarily associated with dominant chords.

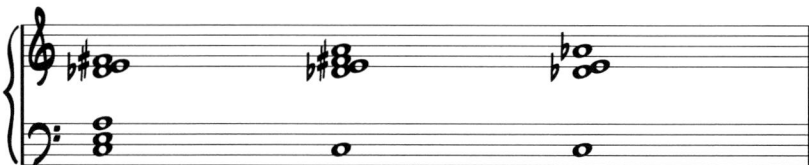

Voicings that leave out the third are even more ambiguous. Harmonically speaking, whether a chord is major or minor is one of the most basic things I can know about a chord. Without this defining characteristic, these chords have a slightly hollow feeling.

We've already encountered one such chord and that's the dom7sus4. The strong appeal of this chord is its neutral, ambiguous feeling. We can extend this idea of suspension in two directions. One is that we can add suspended 4ths to other chord qualities such as major sevenths and minor7b5 chords.

Chapter 22 — Incomplete chords

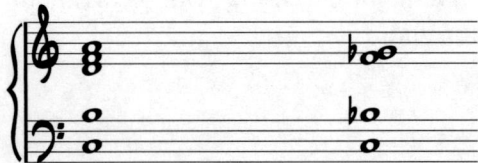

The fourth is a natural choice for suspension in major chords because it leads to the third by half step. But I can also suspend the 2nd if I want. This chord (without a 7th) is sometimes referred to as a C2. It's heard fairly often in pop music (and more recently, jazz) contexts.

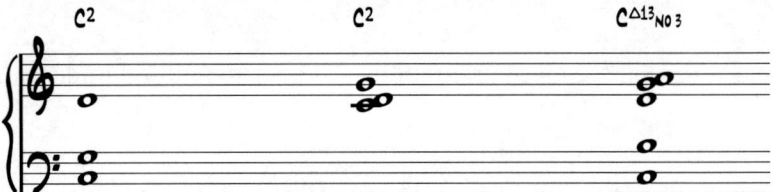

I can also make dominant, major 7ths minor7b5 chords with suspended2s.

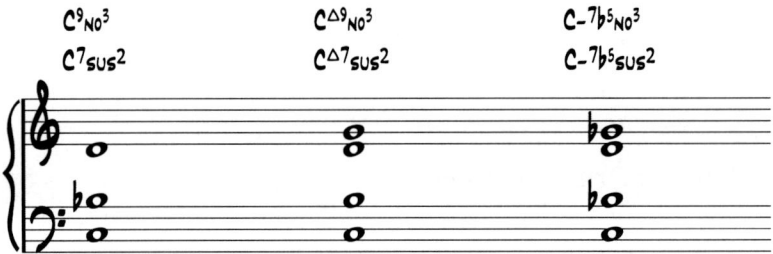

(How we choose to label incomplete chord sounds is a matter of personal preference. I guess I'd prefer to see G/C for the Cmaj7sus2 chord because I can find those notes a lot faster. This, by the way, is a beautiful voicing for a major sound (or a minor major sound for that matter). Similarly, Bb+/C would be a lot easier to locate on the piano for most of us than C-9b5no3 or C-7b5sus2. I was really thinking of these sus2 chords more as a class of chords here, than as a preferred labeling system.)

I can leave more notes out. Fifths and roots, the stuff of rock power chords, are powerful and indeterminate. These are sometimes labeled C5

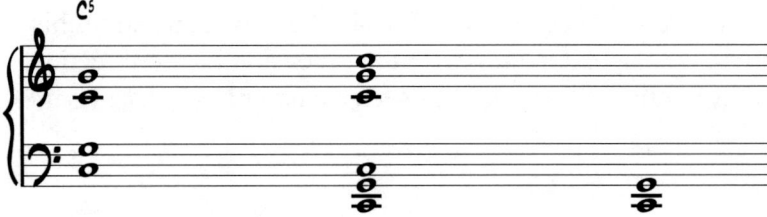

INCOMPLETE CHORDS CHAPTER 22

I can add to this any combinations of major 7ths and tensions associated with these sounds. These chords are named according to whatever chord tones and tensions are associated with them always with the suffix "(no 3)" added. (With the "no 3" either in parentheses or without parentheses depending on the legibility of the font used to write the chord symbol.)

If I use dominant 7 and the tensions associated with these chords without a third, I get a lot of sounds, some of which may sound like complete chords of a different quality. I remember reading through some of Tom Harrell's music and I got to a chord that was labeled a C7 altered, but had a written-out voicing below it with the notes of a C-7b5 b13 if I am remembering correctly. When I asked Tom about it, he said, "I shouldn't say this, but a lot of times, piano players play the same voicings…" Piano players can expand their sense of what sorts of voicings are possible and not rely on tried and true voicings that we've heard a lot already. This is such an interesting idea to me and it backs up a problem that I often see with piano students. They learn some very complete and very full left hand non-root voicings for all the basic chord types and then when they see a G-7, they play the 3,5,7,9 voicing and when they see a C7altered they play the 3, b13, 7, #9 voicing. While these voicings have their place (and have been used effectively by practically every great jazz pianist) students tend to think that they ought to be used all the time, that there should be a complete harmonic sketch of every chord quality in the left hand (minus the root, the bassist has that) while the right hand plays lines over these chords. Hearing this surplus of harmonic info, the right hand can sound superfluous. I want to hear space, and incomplete chord sounds, or melodic (and of course, rhythmic) counterpoint in the left hand, not every single chord sound spelled out completely.

This reminds me of a story. I went to hear the great pianist Kenny Werner playing with the Vanguard Orchestra on a Monday night at the Village Vanguard. I used to sub regularly for Kenny with this band and so I was interested in checking out how he approached the music. On a particular tune, Kenny was comping for a trumpet player who was a very traditional be-bop sort of player. Kenny was playing a lot of extremely unusual chords and voicings, radical harmonic choices that had little to do with the normal progression of the piece. After the set, I asked Kenny about what he was up to and he said, 'It was great! The trumpet player was playing all of the harmony of the tune so I was free to play whatever chords I wanted!'

This approach was probably a bit disturbing to the traditional trumpet player, but there's a lot to learn from it. More piano students might take a page from Kenny's book and not repeat the harmonic information of every chord in both hands when they comp for others or themselves.

So having said all that, here are some incomplete sounds over C7 no 3 using different tension combinations.

Again, as I mentioned above, the fact that these chords can be interpreted in more than one way (as minor7b5 chords if the missing third is minor), shouldn't keep you from using these ambiguous sounds as a way of changing the harmonic color of dominant chords. Being artfully ambiguous as a comper, arranger or composer tends to gives soloists more options, something they usually appreciate. (A great guitarist once told me to comp harmonic movement without comping the harmony of the piece—something for compers to meditate on.) Harmonic clarity and ambiguity are options that you want to add to your harmonic tool box. It's rare that I find young jazz musicians who are overly ambiguous in their voicings and arrangements, unless it's from an unintended inability to play strong clear voicings when the harmony becomes complex. Usually, students interpret chord changes overly literally. Modern jazz compositions, such as Wayne Shorter's "Atlantis," contain chords that are ambiguous and incomplete. Very often the choice of voicing is determined by voice-leading or other melodic considerations.

Here's an example of a tune of mine built primarily around the concept of incomplete voicings. It's called "Scriabining". It uses triadic harmony and ambiguous incomplete sounds to create a harmonic texture that is both modern and open-ended feeling.

Perhaps you can take it from here and come up with your own combinations of complete and incomplete sounds.

You have to approach all this with a lot of humility, it seems to me. Sometimes, I'll write something quite complex, a harmony that I haven't seen before specifically, or a chord that can't be named easily, and after playing on the tune for a while, I realize that something simpler would have worked just as well. I am often reminded of the time I had a rather stubborn student bring in a tune with the chord changes: C-6 to F7 to Bbmaj7. I asked him if he REALLY needed that chord to be a C-6, or might it actually be better and simpler as a C-7 since the C-6 in this context, to my ears anyway, was a weaker choice than C-7, harder to voice and minimizing the effect of the dominant that came in the next bar. "Oh no," he assured me, "I'm the composer and that's what I want. It has to be that." Well, true he was the composer, but that doesn't prevent him from being wrong. In general, especially in the world of non-functionality, as I said earlier, you have to want that particular chord and not another. Intention matters.

So occasionally, I'll change a chord on a tune of mine that I've played for a while, something that I originally understood as an incomplete chord sound that I now hear as something simpler; a sound that used to be special and could be nothing else but over time has morphed into a more commonly used chord sound. That's not always (or perhaps ever) a bad thing, because I now can understand what was once a special case chord within a larger harmonic context that gives me greater freedom as an improviser over that particular harmony.

CHAPTER 23 – CONCLUSIONS

With that, we've finished are exploration of non-functional re-harmonization techniques. To review, we've discussed the following harmonic options for non-functional situations.

1. Same root, different chord quality
2. Slash Chords
3. Harmonizing a bass line
4. Chords based on fourths
5. Giant steps
6. Color chords
7. Parallel chords
8. Pedals
9. Chord subtraction
10. Unavailable tensions
11. Incomplete chords

At this point, I generally ask students to create their own re-harmonization of a standard, referring to the list of techniques above. Of course, in actual practice, these techniques can be used whenever you wish, dovetailed into functional re-harmonizations for variety's sake and personal expression. Still, it's a challenge to try to work primarily with the harmonic moves described in the above list.

Here's one of the millions of possible re-harmonizations that you can create using these techniques. Please notice that in the re-harmonization below even though many of the harmonic moves are not functional in a strict sense, I am working with "These Foolish Things" in Eb again, and there are many moments where that tonality can be heard. This is fairly typical of the way many jazz players employ these techniques, where tonality is stretched and played with, but not abandoned. How far you take these non-functional approaches is up to you and a matter of your own personal taste and of course, will vary tune to tune and performance to performance, depending on the effect that you are trying to create.

CONCLUSIONS   CHAPTER 23

(CD Track 117)   These Foolish Things   Music by Jack Strachey

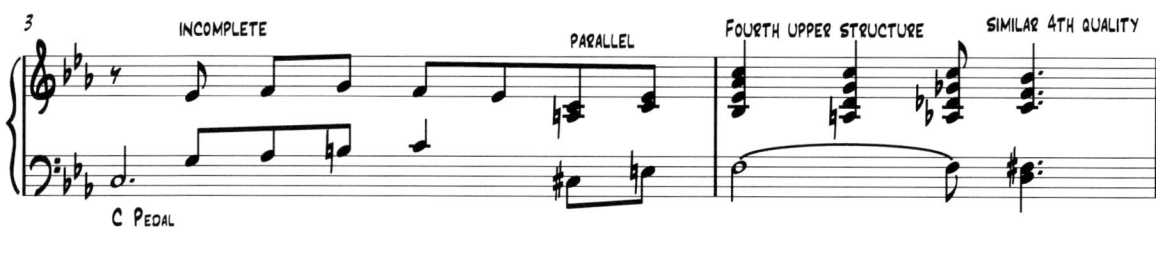

©1936 by Boosey & Co., Ltd. Copyright renewed. This arrangement ©2013 by Boosey & Co., Ltd. All Rights for USA, Canada & Newfoundland assigned to Bourne Co., New York. All Rights Reserved. International Copyright Secured.

Chapter 23

Conclusions

184

CONCLUSIONS CHAPTER 23

185

Chapter 23 — Conclusions

I urge you to try these for yourself. Let your mind run free and then go back and work out some more diminished passing chords or tritone substitutes. One great lesson I learned from working with Tom Harrell over the years is that as a composer or arranger, one can never use up any particular kind of harmony. At any number of rehearsals, Tom would bring in four or five new tunes he had just composed. The first tune might be all ii-V harmony and sound very be-bop-ish. The next tune would be a ballad with a little bit of a Duke Ellington/Billy Strayhorn sensibility. The next tune would be pretty atonal feeling with complex written-out voicings. Another would sound Brazilian and modern or Afro Cuban and mambo-ish from the fifties. Another would be kind of 70s-ish, bluesy harmony and have a kind of boogaloo feel. Of course, a lot of his music couldn't be so easily categorized and I don't mean to do it a disservice by making it sound as if he just writes in "bags" or styles like a commercial writer does. My point is, that in his writing no kind of harmony was off-limits or out-moded. He can revisit ii-V I harmony in one tune and contemporary classical harmonic sounds in the next. Or perhaps find a way to use both in one tune.

After a rehearsal of some of my music, Tom said, "You like the harmony of the sixties a lot." And I said, yes, I did. "But the 60s were pretty difficult times for a lot of people," he said. "Bebop harmony is a lot happier." I took this to mean that all the different kinds of harmony are different colors to paint with, so why limit yourself to just one color or emotion?

At this point in my class, I ask students to again transcribe something. This time, I ask them to transcribe a pianist, guitarist or large ensemble arrangement to see some of these non-functional approaches in action, just as we did at the end of the first section of the book, where they did a transcription that had a lot of functional harmonic moves in it. Usually students pick something modern, late-60s Miles Davis bands or contemporary players who push the harmonic envelope such as Jason Moran, Richie Beirach or Herbie Hancock. Several students have transcribed a wonderful Herbie Hancock solo piano version of "My Funny Valentine" from his recording, "The Piano." This gorgeous performance contains pretty much everything that we've discussed in the second half of this book, all performed with so much feeling and mystery that I am amazed every time I hear it. But that's just the tip of the iceberg. There are so many fascinating harmonic options by brilliant pianists, guitarists, composers and arrangers stretching and helping to enrich the jazz tradition.

Good luck with your own harmonic explorations.

David Berkman, January 2014

APPENDIX A – TIPS FOR COMPOSERS

If you are a pianist, guitarist or vibraphonist, your connection to harmony, particularly the processes of re-harmonization outlined in this book, is obvious. If you are not a chordal instrument player, there are three reasons why you need to study harmony. One reason is to give yourself more harmonic options on songs. Re-harmonization can lead to superimposition of new chords over progressions, lines based on substitution or passing chord harmony. A second reason is that you will become more aware of harmony when you play with chordal instruments. Understanding the harmonic choices that these players make in comping situations will make you more attentive and connected to the band and give you the ability to take harmonic suggestions and incorporate these colors into your solos.

But perhaps the most important reason that most non-chordal instrument players need to study harmony is because they are (and want to develop further as) composers and arrangers. One of the extremely liberating things about jazz music is that each musician is often a music director, arranging, composing and performing his or her own pieces. A well-known pianist, coming from a gig led by a somewhat inexperienced composer/bandleader told me: "Only pianists should be allowed to write music." (Of course, the pianist mentioned above was being facetious—great composers and arrangers have played every instrument: Thad Jones, Duke Ellington, Tony Williams, Miles Davis, Wayne Shorter, Benny Golson, Charles Mingus, and on and on.)
Still, I know what he meant: if someone is going to write chord changes for me to play, I hope they have a strong idea of how changes work. (On the other hand, I heard that Herbie Hancock once said that only a drummer could have written the tune "Sister Cheryl" (by Tony Williams) because the chord progression is so beautifully un-pianistic.)

With that in mind, I thought I'd include a short appendix about composition, since I think many of you will be interested in this. My own career as a composer continues, I've written 7 records of original music and participated in many others as an arranger and composer. (Those interested in my compositions can check out my music at **www.davidberkman.com** or what, the heck, you can always buy a CD, as old fashioned as that sounds.)

When my first record as a leader came out, I was with a label that did a fair amount of publicity and we got some good reviews and a number of them talked about my compositions. One thing about first records, you can record all the music you've had lying around for years. I had recorded all the tunes that I knew worked well and so after that record was finished I had only a year to write the new music I'd need for the next record. Today, that seems like enough time to write the music for four or five records, but at the time I ended up with a bad case of writer's block because I was sure that the new music I was writing wasn't going to measure up to things I had already written for the last recording. (After all, those were my favorite tunes going back as many as 10 years before we recorded them.)

I know a lot of would-be composers feel writer's block. I have a lot of students who tell me that they have written the first three bars of a tune, in fact they have the first three bars to many, many tunes but they don't know how to finish them. I think that often these tunes remain unfinished because of self-imposed pressures: the pressure to write a certain kind of tune or some other expectation that creeps into the writing process and hinders the free flow of ideas when composing.

APPENDIX A   TIPS FOR COMPOSERS

The mental pressure to write, or any feelings that you have about limitations you have in this department, mask the simple fact about writing music—which is it's easy to do. Writing GREAT music might be more difficult, but since you don't want to set out to write great music—you just want to keep writing and figure out what you like later—there's no problem there.

Anyway, a few of the things that I did to overcome my writer's block might be helpful to you. Even if you don't have writer's block, analyzing the process of composing might be something that will help you write more easily, or allow you to vary the kind of music you are writing.

The first thing that I did was to try to look at the process of being stuck. Being stuck is a little like having a small editor sitting on your shoulder, watching you write down a few notes and shaking his head in disappointment at the way things keep turning out. The problem there is that you really don't want to edit as you write. There's a saying I've heard in the fiction-writing world that first drafts should be sloppy and terrible. You just have to get it all out and it doesn't really matter what your personal taste is at that point.

I like something that I heard the short story writer George Saunders say in an interview. The interviewer asked him why his writing often took an absurd, or science fiction-y twist. Didn't he ever want to write something that just told a story beautifully without going in some oddball kind of direction? Saunders said that he thought of his talent for writing as like a dog playing fetch on the beach. You send the dog out, tell it to bring you back something beautiful (I know this isn't how you play fetch, but bear with me, this is how I remember the story, although I may have it wrong by now) and it trots off and then comes back with a broken Barbie doll with one eye missing. You just have to accept what your talent brings you—you can't tell yourself what to write.

I think that this is as true for writing music as it is for writing fiction. You can't tell yourself what to write. So in my case, my first job was to figure out what tune I was avoiding writing. I wasn't **really** stuck, **something** kept coming out—it's just that I didn't want to write the song that kept asserting itself to be written. In my case, there were two sides to this problem. One was that the songs that I seemed to be drawn to writing were not very lyrical, mostly in a constant rhythm (all 8th notes, all half notes, all quarter notes) that outlined some sort of harmonic progression. The other side of the problem was that I was fixated on a tune from my last record, the song I included a part of earlier in our discussion of non-functional chord progressions, "Tom Harrell." I liked this tune because I thought it walked the line between a lyrical, sing-able melody and interesting harmony. There's often that moment after you've written a tune when you play it with a band, and if it's something that really works and you are satisfied with it, sometimes there's a feeling of, "Wow, did I really write this? I really like it." This feeling is a little bit dangerous. It's certainly good to like what you write (if you don't, who will?) but you don't want to like anything you write too much, because it can slow down the process of writing more music. (On that score, Duke Ellington, a genius and a profoundly wise man, was asked what his personal favorite was of all the songs he'd written and he said, "The next one.")

Okay, so these were my two issues, I didn't like these somewhat obsessive, non-lyrical tunes I was writing (I say "I was writing" but like some of you, I wasn't really writing these tunes—I would only write the first few bars and then stop and start again), and I wanted to write "Tom Harrell" again. So I gave myself a task. What is the tune that keeps coming out? Can you describe it? Yes, it is one rhythmic value and it moves somewhat chromatically through some kind of chord progression. Okay. Now there's nothing intrinsically wrong with songs based on one rhythmic value. Perpetual motion fugues by Bach are one rhythmic value (one of my favorite pieces in the world, the E minor toccata is all 16th notes) as are many of his preludes, Chopin etudes, and so on. So I assigned myself the job of writing as un-lyrical a tune as possible. Write this tune, the one that you are afraid of. I ended up writing four or five of these tunes ("Communication Theory #1," "Blue Poles," "Blutocracy (included in Chapter 20)," "Colby" and a similar one-rhythm idea tune called "No Crosstalk") for my next CD, "Communication Theory." I wrote them pretty easily and they took me in another direction, although at the time I didn't feel quite so relaxed about it.

I eventually went back to "Tom Harrell," analyzed a couple of aspects of the harmony to write tunes that were based on those devices. Again, I gave myself assignments. Describe a certain feature or something about the tune that you want to explore. And then write that.

For me, having some kind of plan or jumping off place for the writing—some kind of idea of what the tune might be about—was a useful device to de-throne the editor and rid myself of writer's block. Hey, it doesn't matter if you like this thing or not, I'm just filling the contract here: one tune, based on one rhythmic value. Taste doesn't enter into it.

Many musicians write intuitively and that's fine. I often write intuitively myself. But what I've noticed is that if you want to write something very different from what you've written in the past, or if you are having trouble finishing something, you might want to employ a different methodology.

I am contrasting writing from a game plan of sorts to writing intuitively and that over-simplifies things a lot. I sometimes use a method or a plan as a jumping-off point, but I can always abandon my approach and let my intuition lead me. About half of the time I'm writing (and a lot more if I feel stuck in any way) I'd say that intuition is working with an approach I'm trying, shaping decisions, but freed of the responsibility of evaluating how the work is going.

So, this is how I dug myself out from under my writer's block: the first thing I did was to imagine all the possible tunes that I could write. I made a list of 30 or 40 types of tunes I could write, kept the list on the piano, applying myself with conviction to any one of those ideas that interested me, not caring much about the results of these assignments.

Since that time, I've come up with many versions of The List. I still sometimes use it to aide me in my writing projects.

There are really two kinds of ideas on The List of Possible Tunes I Could Write. One is based on musical content and contains things like: 'write a tune based on one chord', or a 'blues with no IV chord' or 'write a new melody on the chord progression of a standard'. The other kind of idea is based not so much on musical content but on the compositional process itself, the "how" of composing rather than the "what" of composing. Compositional processes are things like: write the melody first and add chords later, or write the chords first and add a melody later. Compose something away from your instrument by singing it. Write down 10 chord names and place them on strips of paper in a hat and then write down 10 intervals on paper strips and put them in an-

APPENDIX A   TIPS FOR COMPOSERS

other hat. Then pick intervals and chords out of the hat and start the tune there. Take the digits of your phone number as a melody using scale degrees of a major scale or a major bebop scale or a diminished scale. And so on.

Together, the ideas based on content or the ideas based on processes answer that question that has nagged at so many would-be composers—what do you do with those fragments of tunes that you can't finish? A content-oriented answer would be something like: analyze the melodic or harmonic material and write 3 variations on that same material to connect to your fragment. A process-oriented answer to that question would be something like: 'write down a series of note names, and then pick them at random to add to your fragment'. Or 'sing the fragment and then sing the first phrase that pops into your head,' or 'play the fragment and then play it backwards starting with the last pitch'. These processes are things that you can do to your fragment—kind of like games or functions in math. The main point is that there is a way to finish all of those fragments as long as we are willing to give up the dream of the amazing tune that you were going to write and write the tune (amazing perhaps, or not) that you are actually going to finish. The best and most promising three bar fragment isn't worth as much as a mediocre complete tune. So, finish all your fragments even if you end up writing the musical equivalent of a broken Barbie doll with one eye missing.

So here is yet another version of The List. I've broken it down into categories and into two broad sections, one for musical content-based ideas, or tunes you can write, and another for processes, or ways to write a tune.

    I. MUSICAL CONTENT-BASED IDEAS
       a. Single line melody
          i. Write a melody based on a major scale (like chant)
          ii. Write a melody based on each mode of the major scale (like chant or modal jazz tunes.)
          iii. Write a melody based on the melodic minor scale and each of the modes on this scale
          iv. Write a melody based on any other scale such as augmented and diminished scales
          v. Write any of the above melodies based on scales but add a note that's not found in the scale
          vi. Write a melody that is only pitches with no rhythm
              1. Develop this melody by adding rhythm to it—first have all the notes have the same rhythmic values
              2. Then try putting rhythmic values to the melody intuitively
              3. Then try putting rhythms to the melody using a repeating rhythmic pattern
          vii. Write a melody that has only rhythms and no pitches
          viii. Write a melody that is based on one interval
          ix. Write a melody that is based on more than one interval such as whole steps and fourths
          x. Write a melody that is based on a pentatonic scale
          xi. Write a melody that is based on more than one pentatonic scale

xii. Make a set of pitches that you like, but one that is specifically not a common scale you can easily name. Write a melody based on your scale.
xiii. Write a melody that is based on any of the above harmonic devices used in combination, such as two different scales, a pentatonic scale and an augmented scale and so on.
xiv. Write a melody that is based on the chromatic scale
   1. Write a tone row (each chromatic pitch is used once). Develop the melody by using the retrograde form of the tone row.
   2. Write a tone row. Develop the melody by using a transposition of the tone row.
   3. Write a tone row that is 8 notes long (8 notes, none repeated and a non-scale, meaning something chromatic) Develop as above.
   4. Write a melody based on the chromatic scale that isn't a tone row—repetition of notes is fine and you don't have to use all 12.
xv. For any of the above melodies add rhythm as you did in v
xvi. Write a melody that never settles into one scale
xvii. Write a melody that is based on arpeggios
xviii. Write a melody that is based on arpeggios but uses fourths instead of thirds
   1. Write a melody that is based on triadic sounds
      a. In a key
      b. In a chromatic open harmonic situation
      c. In multiple keys
   2. Write a melody that is based on 7th chord sounds
   3. Write a melody that is based on a particular 7th chord sound
   4. Write a melody that is based on approaches 1, 2 or 3 above, but add a note not found on the triad or seventh chord.
xix. Write a melody that is based on chromatic approach note patterns
xx. Write a melody that is based on a particular instrument, such as a flute or a bass line
xxi. Write a melody that is all one rhythm
xxii. Write a melody that is based on a repeating rhythmic pattern
xxiii. Write a melody that is mostly composed of rests
xxiv. Write a melody in an unusual meter
xxv. Write a melody in mixed meter
xxvi. Write a melody that is triumphant
xxvii. Write a melody that is sad and introverted
xxviii. Write a melody that is mostly long notes
xxix. Write a melody that is composed of busy fast note passages followed by rests
xxx. Write a melody in which every phrase ends in a question
xxxi. Write a melody that has a lot of repeated notes
xxxii. Write a melody that modulates and repeats itself in another key
xxxiii. Write a melody that repeats itself many times with variations
xxxiv. Write a melody that is one long phrase
xxxv. Write a melody that is many short phrases

APPENDIX A

TIPS FOR COMPOSERS

    xxxvi. Write a melody that is one long phrase followed by pieces of that phrase
    xxxvii. Write a melody that is based on question and answer
    xxxviii. Write a melody that is all questions and no answers
    xxxix. Write a melody that is all answers and no questions

b. Writing Chord Progressions
    i. Write a chord progression in one key
    ii. Write a chord progression in two keys
    iii. Write a chord progression that modulates all the time
    iv. Write a chord progression using all one chord quality
    v. Write a "Giant Steps" type chord progression
        1. Write a "Giant Steps" progression, independent of any standard (like "Giant Steps" by John Coltrane)
        2. Write a "Giant Steps" progression, based on a standard (like "26-2" by John Coltrane)
    vi. Write a color chord progression
    vii. Write a progression that is all slash chords
    viii. Write a progression that is all incomplete chords
    ix. Write a progression that is all chords with unavailable tensions
    x. Write a chord progression that uses a lot of parallel chords
    xi. Write a chord progression that uses a lot of diminished chords
    xii. Write a chord progression that uses as many modal interchange chords as possible
    xiii. Write a chord progression that has many ii-Vs in different keys
    xiv. Write a chord progression that has very few chord changes
    xv. Write a chord progression with a lot of tritone substitutes
    xvi. Write a chord progression that never feels like it's in a particular key
    xvii. Write a chord progression that never has a V7 to I relationship
    xviii. Write a chord progression that is drawn from a standard but substantially altered
    xix. Re-harmonize a standard. Write a new melody over that re-harmonization
    xx. Write a chord progression that is based on the bridges of two different standards
    xxi. Write a chord progression that feels like it starts in the middle
    xxii. Write a chord progression in which every chord feels like a surprise
    xxiii. Write a chord progression in which every chord feels wrong and clashes with the one that came before it
    xxiv. Write a chord progression where there are islands of harmonic busyness and long periods with fewer chord changes
        1. Write a song in two sections. In the first section each chord lasts for four bars and in the second section each chord lasts for one bar
        2. Write a song in which the chords that last a long time have one type of harmonic relationship and the chords that last a short time have another type of harmonic relationship
    xxv. Write a chord progression that feels circular
    xxvi. Write a chord progression that has important destination chords every four

	bars, or every eight bars
xxvii.	Write a chord progression that has important destination chords every 5 or 7 bars (or any other odd number of bars.)
xxviii.	Write a chord progression that sounds like a pop ballad
xxix.	Write a chord progression that you like to solo over
xxx.	Write a chord progression in which all of the chords are near neighbors of each other
xxxi.	Write a chord progression that is confusing
xxxii.	Write a chord progression that sounds like a maze

c. Combining Melody and Harmony
   i. Combine any of the above melodic concepts with any of the above chord progression concepts
   ii. Write a tune that is all melody, doubled in the bass
   iii. Write a melody and a counterline (like "Chasing the Bird" by Charlie Parker)
   iv. Write a melody and a counterline over a pedal
   v. Write a melody and a counterline over any of the chord progressions mentioned on this list in the sections above
   vi. Write a melody over a pedal (like "Phantoms," by Kenny Barron)
   vii. Write a melody over rhythm changes (like "Anthropology," by Charlie Parker)
   viii. Write a melody over a standard (like "Ornithology," by Charlie Parker)
   ix. Write a melody that is based on the blues
   x. Write a melody that is based on minor blues
   xi. Write a melody that is based on blues or minor blues but goes somewhere outside of the form that is harmonically unexpected
   xii. Repeat the above step xi on rhythm changes or a standard
   xiii. Write a blues with no IV chords in it
   xiv. Write a blues with no V chords in it
   xv. Write a blues with no dominant 7th chords in it
   xvi. Write a melody over one chord on the A sections and over a different chord on the bridge (like "Milestones (new)" by Miles Davis)
   xvii. Write a melody over a chord progression in which the melody is always a chord tone of the chord
   xviii. Write a melody over a chord progression in which the melody is always a tension of the chord
   xix. Write a melody over a chord progression in which the melody is always a suspension and resolution of the chord
   xx. Write a melody that is a rhythmic and melodic cell that moves through a chord progression altering the melody to fit the chord change (like "Prelude in C" from "the Well-Tempered Clavier," by J.S. Bach and like "Fairy Tale," by David Berkman)
   xxi. Write a tune that sounds like a folk song
   xxii. Write a tune that sounds like a hymn
   xxiii. Take a motive from a very famous tune and write a song around it

APPENDIX A

xxiv. Write a tune that sounds like a bebop tune
1. With non-functional harmony
2. With bebop type harmony
3. Over a pedal
4. Over a series of pedals
5. Over a series of extremely dissonant voicings

xxv. Write a tune that sounds like a standard
xxvi. Write a tune that has many harmonic sequences
xxvii. Write a tune that sounds militaristic
xxviii. Write a tune that sounds like the film score to a romantic movie
xxix. Write a tune that sounds like a film score to a horror movie
xxx. Write a tune that sounds like a film score to a science fiction movie
xxxi. Write a tune that sounds like a tune by any of your favorite composers

d. Forms
 i. Write an AAB tune
 ii. Write an AABA tune
 iii. Write and AABAB tune
 iv. Write an ABAC tune
 v. Write a tune that is only 6-11 bars long
 vi. Write a tune that is one phrase repeated
 vii. Write a tune that has repeated phrases, each harmonized differently than the last
 viii. Write a tune that never repeats
 ix. Write a tune that has a bassline, a counterline and a melody line, and they each enter separately
 x. Write a tune that is a theme and variations
 xi. Write a tune with an odd number of bars in one of the sections of the tune: the A sections or bridge
 xii. Write a tune that is really just an intro for a tune
 xiii. Write a tune in which every phrase is a different number of bars
 xiv. Write a tune that is extremely repetitive
 xv. Write a tune that is a vamp, but an extremely complex vamp
 xvi. Write a song where the melody and the harmony are at war with each other

II. PROCESSES
 e. Write a song away from your instrument singing all the notes
 f. Write a song at your instrument, but whenever you get stuck, sing the next pitch to determine where to go
 g. Write a chord progression first, then put a melody over it
 h. Write the melody first and then add chords
 i. Write four bars of a melody. Go back and add bass notes to the melody. Write the next four bars of melody followed by the next four bars of bass notes. Continue in this manner alternating between melody and harmony
 j. Write down a chord quality for each note of the chromatic scale. These chords are the chords you'll use in this piece

- i. Combine them into a progression or several progressions using a random process (drawing chords out of hat, alternating, every third or whatever)
- ii. Combine them into a progression or several progressions using your taste—what sounds best to you
- iii. Pick a change and start writing a melody over it. Whenever it feels like it's time for a new chord change, pick from the chord changes you have left on your list.

k. Compose a rhythm. Make it something you like.
   - i. Put pitches to this rhythm using your intuition and imagination
   - ii. Put pitches to this rhythm using a combination of random intervals
   - iii. Put pitches to this rhythm using some predetermined harmonic device or scale
   - iv. Figure out the harmonic rhythm before you figure out the melody, put an x over each place where you think a downbeat ought to go

l. Appropriate (steal) the rhythm of a song you like. Put new pitches and harmony to it

m. Analyze a song you like (something by a famous composer, any style of music)
   - i. Try to write a song that uses a similar rhythm-based idea
   - ii. Try to write a song that uses a similar harmonic idea
   - iii. Try to write a song that uses the same phrase-lengths

n. Analyze one of your own tunes. Try to figure out what you like about this particular piece. Write a song that employs that same device.

o. If you drink, write a song when you've been drinking

p. Write a song when you first wake up in the morning

q. Write a song right before you go to sleep at night

r. Write a chord progression or a chord progression and melody together that is 100 bars long. Cut out all the parts you don't like and see what you have left.

s. Write a song only thinking about voice-leading and counterpoint and let the harmony fall where it falls

t. Write a series of chords and voicings for those chords without rhythm. Decide how long each chord feels like it should last. The top note of each voicing is your melody. Ornament it as you wish.

u. Play a voicing in your left hand. Sing something over it. Write it down. Repeat these steps as many times as necessary.

v. Write a series of pitches, by singing. Add bass notes. Define chord qualities. Add measure lines. If necessary edit until you are satisfied.

w. Improvise at the piano (whether you are a pianist or not.) Record it. Listen back and write down any motives you like.

x. Improvise on your instrument if you are a non-pianist. Record it. Listen back and write down any sections you like.

y. Keep a notebook of motives you like. Assemble as the spirit moves you.

z. Write every day at a specific time of day

aa. Write every day at various times in the day

ab. Write in a notation program as fast as you can, hearing little or nothing of what you are writing. Edit later to see if there's anything in there worth keeping.

ac. Hear a whole symphony in your head, imagining all of the parts perfectly from the beginning to the end. Write it down when you get a chance. (This is especially

effective if you are Mozart.)
- ad. Write to accompany a picture, story or mood
- ae. Write something you think your mom would like
- af. Write something that sounds like it's from a foreign culture
- ag. Go on a trip somewhere. Walk around. Drink coffee. Go back to your hotel room and write something that feels like that place.
- ah. Study the rhythm of a musical style that is foreign to you. Use an element from this new rhythmic approach in a composition.
- ai. Write something that feels like a game. Like the game "tag" with lots of space.
- aj. Write down a number of places in the measure (the and of three, the and of four, one.) Write phrases that begin or end on these pitches.
- ak. Write something that feels like it's improvised
- al. Improvise something that feels like it's composed
- am. Write something that feels like it goes someplace completely different from where it started
- an. Write a series of pieces all based on one motive or one chord progression
- ao. Write a song three times. Throw out the first two versions.

I guess that's enough. Maybe you are getting the idea. I think that if you approach composing in many different ways, you'll get many different kinds of tunes. I don't know why it's hard for some people to write, although I CAN relate. Sometimes it's been hard for me to write and I didn't really know what to do about it so I've come up with a lot of ways to kick-start the process.

I don't really believe in waiting around to be inspired. I think people who do that are kind of like Sunday afternoon painters. They might get some great or inspired tunes that way, but I want to try more varied approaches than that. I like giving my inspiration something to sink its teeth into. Maybe some of those above ideas are stupid. Certainly I don't think they'd all work for anybody. But having a list of ideas is convenient. I used to keep my old list (it was a lot shorter) on my piano and sometimes I'd glance at it and try something that I hadn't tried in a while.

Make your own list. Pick some of the above ideas that interest you and add more of your own. Analyze the ideas you've used in previous tunes you've written and revisit some of them to see if you can make something new.

One thing about analyzing tunes, yours or someone else's. If I have a tune I like: "Nefertiti" for example, I don't necessarily want to write something that sounds like it, but maybe I could analyze it and find something there—an approach to melody, an interval or harmonic movement from one chord to the next—something that I can steal, or some kernel that will start me on my own creative process.

Fortunately for me, I like a lot of different compositions: from "Nefertiti" to "Embraceable You", from "Friday the 13th" to "Survivor's Suite," "Ludus Tonalis," "Atlantis", "Death and the Maiden," "Smile, Please," "We Shall Overcome, "The Face of the Bass," "Free for All," "Satellite," "Blood Count," "Can't Hide Love," "Toys," "Cheio de Dedos," "Passarim" and about a million others. And they all use different methods and harmonic techniques, and I am free to try out any of them. And of course, so are you.

APPENDIX B – PIANO BASICS

Students who attempt to learn jazz harmony without piano skills are facing a daunting task. (Guitarists and vibraphonists fare better of course, but also usually benefit from learning harmony on a keyboard without the inherent limitations of their instruments. Sorry, but it's just easier to find all the notes on the piano especially if you are playing 7-note chords or chords with a lot of seconds). Each time I write something about harmony, I find myself trying to condense basic jazz piano study into a shorter and shorter primer. Students who can play the piano with a minimum level of competence will usually have a more nuanced sense of harmonic possibility. (In a much repeated story, a young Miles Davis supposedly asked his mentor and hero Dizzy Gillespie where he found all those crazy notes that he played and Dizzy, pointing to the piano responded, "There.")

So, studying the piano is of paramount importance to developing a more refined understanding of harmony. Fortunately, becoming a piano virtuoso is not required (although more power to you if you do become one—maybe it's the aging process but I seem to encounter more of them every day.) Students studying the piano often lose focus on what they are trying to learn and waste time in technical drill or classical piano repertoire. (I'm using the phrase "waste time" in a very specific way here. Nothing is a waste of time if you are pursuing your interest or passion and developing piano technique and studying classical repertoire is all to the good if you are enjoying it. However, many students bristle at the idea that they need to learn another instrument in addition to the one they are already working on and approach the piano with fear and loathing. These are the students that I am addressing in this chapter on piano playing.)

So what piano skills do you need to continue your studies in jazz harmony? First and foremost is the ability to play a reasonably pianistic version of a jazz standard from a lead sheet. "A reasonably pianistic version" means playing the kind of voicings that sound clear and resonant on a piano, with the appropriate chord tones or tensions that are commonly associated with the chords on the page in a good register of the instrument.

This may sound difficult, but, at least conceptually, it's pretty simple. A good voicing of a chord usually has the root fairly low on the piano (in the range from roughly a fourth below middle C to about an octave below that, give or take a few notes), and the 7th and 3rd of the chord above the root—although not TOO far above. If you are playing a diminished7 or minor7b5 chord you need the flatted fifth in the voicing as well. Put the melody on top of it (if you are playing a tune), add a tension above the chord tones (or possibly below, if the tension is a 9th) and you're sounding like a functional pianist. Congratulations!

Of course, there's more to acquiring the basic piano skills you need than just understanding the basic concept. Mainly, you have to familiarize yourself with the way the piano looks and sounds, and deal with the challenging reality that every key looks and feels a little different on the piano keyboard.

Beginning students of the piano can break down the process into these steps:

APPENDIX B

1. Finding the chord tones of common chords (in all keys). Play them in root position.
2. Playing the chord tones of common chords in "open" root-based voicings (in all keys).
3. Finding the most commonly used tensions associated with chords (in all keys). Play them in stacked thirds.
4. Playing combinations of chord tones and tensions of common chords in "open" root-based voicings (in all keys).
5. Playing songs with the melody as the top note of the voicing, the 3rd of the chord below the melody in the right hand, the root as the bottom note of the left hand and the 7th or 6th (or 5th if the chord is a triad) as the top note in the left hand.
6. Playing songs as described in step 5, but adding tensions in (primarily, but not exclusively) the right hand below the melody and above the 3rd (9ths can be played above or below the 3rd.)
7. If students wish to go further, they can make adjustments to the above methods based on voice-leading considerations and variations in the left hand.
8. If students wish to go further, they can learn some common root-based voicings with upper structure triads.
9. If students wish to go further they can learn some non-root left hand voicings to be used with bass player accompaniment, or as right hand voicings with bass notes in the left hand.

And that's it. Piano mastery is right around the corner. You can do lots more, as you've already gathered if you've read this book. But, if you don't love working on the piano but have minimal knowledge of the instrument, focus very clearly on what you need to know to aid yourself in arranging, composing and the harmonic study that will carry over to improvising on your main instrument. Stay away from scales, arpeggios, soloing and piano technique exercises such as Czerny or Hanon and concentrate on learning enough about voicings that you can hear what chord progressions sound like. (Let me repeat once more what I said above. If you enjoy working on that stuff, go for it. Technical exercises will help you become more familiar with the instrument and make you a faster learner. This kind of basic piano study is certainly a good thing, but if you are going to dabble and then leave piano study without gaining a repertoire of acceptable voicings, then you haven't gotten the basic harmonic control of the instrument that you need to study harmony on the level that we are dealing with in this book.)

Having a competent repertoire of piano voicings will change your re-harmonizations. If you can't make good sounding basic voicings at the piano, it's very likely that you will seek out more abstract sounds, making re-harmonizations that are extreme because a C major7 sounds bland and uninteresting to you. If you understood more about voicings, you could make a lot of different sounding voicings for a C major7, each with its own color and nuance and you'd be less inclined to search farther afield. It's like the difference between sculpting with a chain saw or a wood chisel.

So let's begin.

1. Finding the chord tones of common chords (in all keys). Play them in root position. I have them here in C and F, two keys far enough apart that they will present different problems in registration, which in this context means: finding a good place for the root. Transpose these root position chords into all keys but don't play roots much below the C voicings (they start to sound muddy) and don't play roots much above the F voicings (the bass notes start to sound thin, more like part of the upper structure of the chord and less like a complete root-based chord.) The best

PIANO BASICS   APPENDIX B

way to practice these chords is to play each chord quality around the circle of fifths, rather than playing all the qualities in one key and moving on to the next. (They are written here like that to present them in two keys for registration purposes as mentioned above.)

[Musical notation: Chord voicings in C: C△7, C6, C△6, C-7, C-6, C-7♭5, C°7, C7, C-△7, C7sus4, C△7♯5]

[Musical notation: Chord voicings in F: F△7, F6, F△6, F-7, F-6, F-7♭5, F°7, F7, F-△7, F7sus4, F△7♯5]

2. Play the chord tones of common chords in "open" root-based voicings (in all keys).

Usually, root position voicings are somewhat problematic, often sounding ungrounded if played high up on the instrument because then we are missing the bass function that gives us a clear sense of the root of the chord. Lower on the instrument these chords can sound muddy because of the low thirds in the voicing. Root position 1,3,5,7 voicings are often used by beginning pianists because they are easy to find, but students should try to move to more open pianistic voicings as soon as they can. The voicing of 1 and 7 in the left hand and 3 and 5 in the right hand will provide a more pianistic approach to the above chords and sounds better, clearer and more resonant. Once again, they should be played in all keys. (As noted above, I am giving you examples in C and in F so that you can see where you need to change octaves to find the right register on the piano. Once again, practice each chord quality around the circle of fifths before moving on to the next chord quality.)

[Musical notation: Open root-based voicings in C: C△7, C△6, C-7, C-6, C-7♭5, C°7, C7, C-△7, C7sus4, C△7♯5]

[Musical notation: Open root-based voicings in F: F△7, F△6, F-7, F-6, F-7♭5, F°7, F7, F-△7, F7sus4, F△7♯5]

Please note: if this is all you can manage, it's adequate. Students who stop at this level, have the ability to play reasonable voicings for all of the common seventh chord types. You can play through tunes singing or humming the melody. It would be very valuable for you to go through a fake book now and play through any standards you know in time. Keep doing this (a few minutes each day, or more if you are enjoying it) until these voicings are available to you in real time while sight-reading chord progressions.

3. **Finding the available tensions associated with common chords (in all keys). Play them in stacked thirds.**

Here are the same chords with tensions stacked above chord tones.

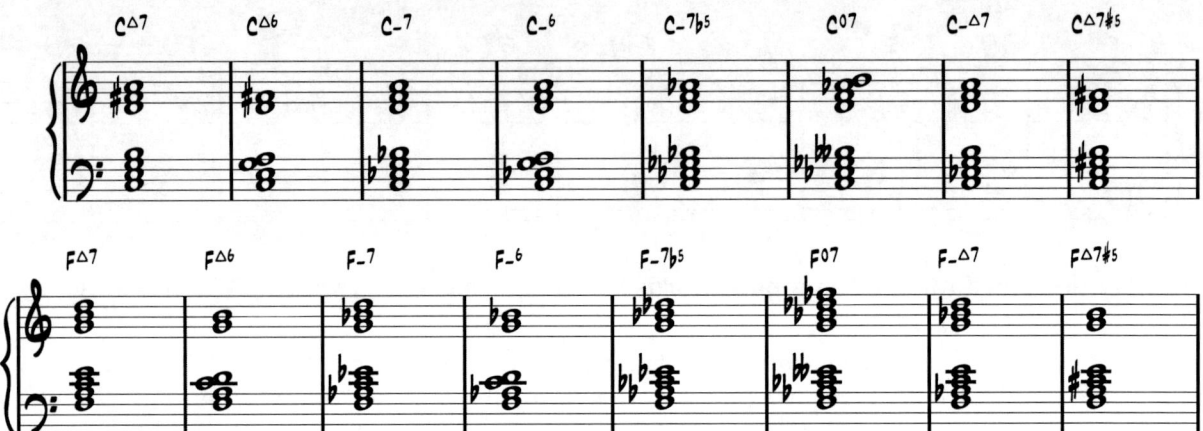

Missing from the above chords are dominant 7ths and dominant 7th sus4 chords. These chords have more than one choice of available tensions and are given below.

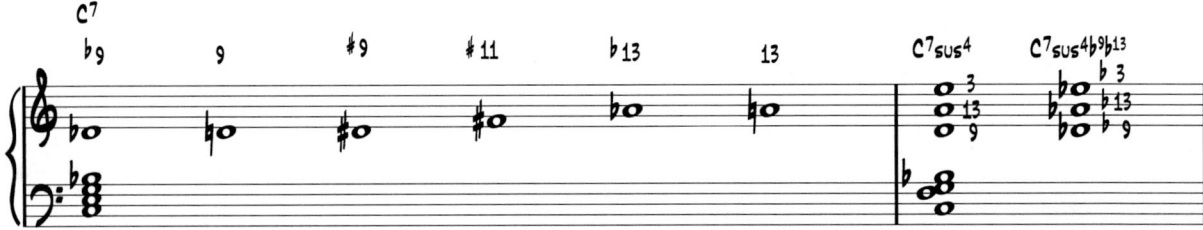

In the case of dominant sevenths, these six tensions are available although certain combinations are almost never used, namely, any combination that creates the interval of a b9 between any chord tones and tensions other than the root of the chord. Examples of these avoided combinations are natural 9 and b9 or #9, 5 and b13 and 13 and b13. In the case of dominant 7sus4 chords, they are either harmonized with natural tensions or flat tensions, but not both. Also notice that the third of the chord is available as a tension on dominant 7sus4 chords (sometimes called the 10th).

You'll notice that we're back to root position 1,3,5,7 voicings in the left hand for all of the above voicings (as opposed to 1 and 7). This means that we are playing these voicings not so much to find ways of comping on tunes (although when played in a good register of the piano they can sound fine), but more as a mental exercise to help improve your ability to find all seven available notes on a chord quickly. To repeat a concept I mentioned earlier, the more you are able to add colors to your chords, creating variations on major7ths by adding 9ths, #11ths and 13ths (for

PIANO BASICS   APPENDIX B

example) the more likely you will be to make subtle choices based on harmonic nuance. If you want to improve these voicings a bit, you can start by leaving out the fifths in the left hand (except on diminished7ths, minor 7b5 chords and major7#5 chords). That will decrease the muddiness of the above voicings by leaving out this (usually) unnecessary chord tone.

4. Playing combinations of chord tones and tensions of common chords in "open" root-based voicings (in all keys). I can combine approaches 2 and 3 and improve my voicings further. I will use 1 and 7 in the left hand and 3 and each tension separately in the right hand. Feel free to place 9ths up an octave. 1, 7 and 3 plus one tension is usually a pleasant sounding colorful voicing. It has the added benefit of limiting the random doubling of notes in a chord that plague many beginning students' piano playing.

5. Playing songs with the melody as the top note of the voicing, the 3rd of the chord below the melody in the right hand, the left hand is 1 and 7 (6 replaces 7 for 6th chords and the 5th replaces the seventh for triads.) Here are the first four bars of "Here's that Rainy Day" with 1 and 7 in the left hand and the melody and the third of the chord in the right hand. Please note again, that this gives a clear harmonic picture of the tune. Obviously, you should play the rest of the song in this manner. Then repeat the process using tunes from your fake book. You want to become competent at playing these voicings at sight with minimal effort. (Please note that the grand staff below covers the area where voicings are played. While the treble clef is often thought of as "the right hand" and the bass clef as "the left hand", that is just a convention. So in bar 1, you should play the "B" and the "D" in your right hand and the "G" and "F#" in your left hand.)

6. Playing songs as described in step 5, but adding tensions below the melody (usually, but not exclusively) in the right hand. Step 5 is mostly mechanical, by which I mean, you have very few choices to make—just where to put the root and by now that should be obvious in many cases to you. While the voicing structures in Step 5 give you a competent reading of the basic harmony of the tune, tensionless voicings are somewhat colorless and only tell part of the harmonic story. In step 6 you are adding color. At this point, it should be fairly easy for you to identify the available tensions for these chords, at least if you've spent time on steps 3 and 4.

201

Now you need to go through each voicing and decide which tensions you want to add. Be sure to check out all of the possibilities, which means that you can add a ninth on the third beat of the second bar and change it to a b9th a beat later. You can also decide if you want to add chord tones (such as the fifth) or if you want to double a chord tone which can be very effective, particularly if the chord tone is the melody note). The only chord tone you should avoid doubling is the root since it just adds weight to the chord and no new color (and there's always a 9th near it which is probably the most often added tension.) Here are the first four bars of "Here's That Rainy Day" with added notes, tensions and chord tones. You should, of course, find your own voicings for these bars and then go through this process for the whole song. Getting to this point gives you a competent and complete arrangement of the tune and, needless to say, repeating this process on many songs would help solidify this skill.

7. If students wish to go further, they can make adjustments to the above methods based on voice-leading considerations and left hand variations. That sounds pretty general. To make things simpler, let's put it this way: after you've been through steps 5 and 6 you will have a complete harmonization of the song. Now go back and see if any voicings aren't really working for you. It may be that the limitation of always having 1 and 7 in your left hand is starting to bother you. It's a very effective approach to hearing the chord sounds in a pianistic way, but it's limiting to have a seventh interval at the bottom of every single chord. So, pick a few voicings that you still aren't satisfied with and see if changing the left hand voicings helps things. You can use 1 and 5; 1, 5 and 9; 1, 5 and 10 if you can reach it; 1 and 6; 1 and 3; 1, 3 and 7; really, just about anything with the root at the bottom of the chord. A ii-7 with 1 and 7 in the left hand followed by a V7 that is voiced with 1 and 3 is often a good choice because the 7th of the ii-7 leads by half step to the third of the V7. This is a very common voice-leading choice and one that you can practice.

To return to step 7, here is the adjusted version of the first four bars with some left-hand variation.

PIANO BASICS   APPENDIX B

(Please note that some of the above voicings might be hard for people with small hands. You can always leave out notes if you wish or break up the left hand notes in an arpeggio with the sustain pedal held down. You don't need voicings with 7 notes in them. Try to play what's comfortable and sounds good to you, but make sure that you check out all of the possibilities when adding tensions to chords. In general, try to avoid large "holes" or big spaces in the middle of your voicings in favor of an even spacing of notes in the right hand. That tends to sound resonant and full on the piano.)

As you look over your voicings for this tune—voicings that were constructed primarily vertically, building up from the root and down from each melody note at the point of a chord change, you might notice if there are ways to create smooth voice-leading with some of the internal voices of the chord. Look over the four bar passage above starting with beat 4 of the first bar. The C# below the melody on this G major 7th moves down a step to a C on the first beat of bar 2 on the F-7 chord change. The C moves down a whole step to the Bb on beat 2. On beat 4 this note moves down to a Cb or B natural—the b9 on the Bb7 chord. That leads to the C on bar 3—the 6 on the Eb chord. This kind of voice-leading makes one chord lead logically to another. Listening to solo recordings of Bill Evans, a master of this technique, will help develop your awareness of this aspect of harmonizing songs on the piano.

Repeating steps 5,6 and 7 with many tunes is without a doubt the single most valuable thing that you can do to develop a repertoire of piano voicings (in my opinion.) Working through the voicing possibilities on your own, rather than learning pre-set voicings, allows you to make voicing choices and develop your ear. As long as you stick to available tensions, you should be making clear voicing choices and learning more about the colors available to you on seventh chords. I can't possibly over-emphasize the value of this.

8. If students wish to go further, they can learn some common root-based voicings with upper structure triads. Let's look at some ii-V voicings here. For the minor chord we'll use a common upper structure, a major 7th chord built on the minor third of the chord.

203

APPENDIX B

On dominant7ths there are four common upper structure major triads that are often used: the major triad built on scale degree 2, the major triad built on scale degree #4, the major triad built on scale degree b6 and the major triad built on scale degree 6.

Dominant7th voicings with their many possible tension combinations are among the most iconic sounds in jazz harmony. Adding these upper structure voicings to your repertoire will give you more options when playing ii-Vs and help make your chords richer and more interesting when you are comping through the changes of the tune without the melody.

9. If students wish to go further they can learn some non-root left hand voicings to be used with bass player accompaniment, or as right hand voicings with bass notes in the left hand. As I said above, constructing your own root-based open voicings is probably the most valuable things that non-pianists can do to further their keyboard/harmony knowledge. Having said that, knowing a few "stock" voicings is helpful. The following voicings are very self-contained, possessing all the important harmonic colors of the chord (except the root) and they have nice voice-leading (meaning the hand doesn't have to move much to play them). They are: ii minor7th: 3, 5, 7, 9; V7: 7, 9, 3, 13; I major 7th: 3, 5, 7, 9. These are sometimes called "A" voicings.

These voicings should be practiced in all keys. It's important to pay attention to register with these voicings. You can see that the first and third voicings above are the same structure as a root position major 7th chord and a root position minor 7th chord, respectively. The second voicing is the same structure as a major7 b5 chord.) The lower these voicing are on the piano, the more the bottom voice of the chord sounds like the root of a muddy root position voicing for a major 7th and the less it sounds like a minor 7th starting on the 3rd. For registration reasons, there is an inversion of these voicings that is also commonly used. These are called "B" Voicings.

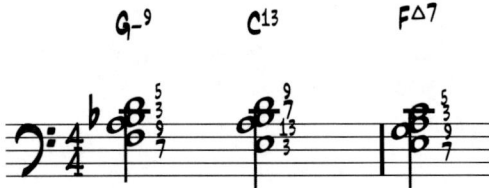

These should also be practiced in all keys. The point of having these two inversions available is that in certain keys, an "A" voicing is either two high or two low on the piano. If I am playing very high up on the piano some of these high voicings might get used, but for a lot of playing situations, I'll need something in a different register. For example, the "B" voicings for ii-V I in C are (usually) not as useful as the "A" voicings are, at least when using these voicings in the left hand while playing a melody in my right hand. That's because, either these voicings will be low and muddy, confusing our sense of the root of the chord, or they are so high that they'll get in the way of the melody being played in the right hand.

So we can switch back and forth between "A" and "B" voicings to keep these non-root left hand voicings in a kind of "sweet spot" on the piano, not going below D or Db below middle C as the lowest note of the voicing. Where the highest note of these voicings should fall really depends on what I am doing in my right hand. If I am playing a melody, a scale or soloing then I'll want my left hand to be out of my way, not interfering.

These voicings can also be used as two-handed voicings by playing roots in your left hand and the voicing in your right hand. In this case, range considerations are just the opposite, I want to have the right hand voicing low enough on the piano to sound functional and strong, but I probably will allow it to go a little higher up on the instrument than when I am playing this voicing as a left hand accompaniment.

When I use these voicings, I can create more variety by altering tensions on the dominant7ths as I want. (Please note, in the example below, I'm not carrying over accidentals.)

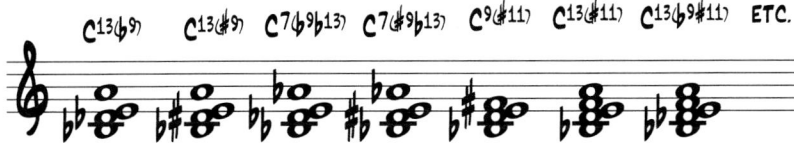

The above voicings should be practiced both in their A and B forms.

I also need to consider these voicings in minor ii-V7 I situations.

APPENDIX B

You'll notice that even though we are calling these non-root voicings, I've added the root to the minor7b5 chords (as the top voice (or soprano) in the ii-7b5 chord in the "A" form of these voicings, as the 3rd voice (or tenor) in the "B" form of these voicings.) In major ii-Vs that voice was playing the 9th of the chord, but I am replacing the 9th with the root of the chord on minor7b5 chords. The 9th IS available to me on minor7b5 chords, however, the natural 9 (which is the major 3rd in the key) isn't a note that I'd want to use in all minor situations—it's a beautiful sound, but it's not as harmonically neutral a note as it is on a minor7 in a major key context. For that reason, I've replaced it with the root, which is harmonically neutral. However, it's a great variation and you should use the natural 9 to replace the root whenever you want that sound.

If you've hung in this far and done the work, you are well on your way to becoming a functional pianist. Doing the work of this chapter, as well as playing and studying the piano arrangements in the preceding chapters, should give you the tools you need. By now, you are playing what is sometimes called "arranger's piano" and it's important for serious jazz players on any instrument to achieve this level of pianistic ability if you want to be able to use the piano as a composing and arranging tool.

To become really comfortable at the piano you need to keep playing songs, voicing chords and finding harmony. Doing this repeatedly will get you over the hump and allow you to enter the exciting world of harmonic discovery.

SHER MUSIC CO.
The World's Premier Jazz & Latin Publisher!

BEST-SELLING BOOKS BY MARK LEVINE
- The Jazz Theory Book
- The Jazz Piano Book
- Jazz Piano Masterclass: The Drop 2 Book
- How to Voice Standards at the Piano

THE WORLD'S BEST FAKE BOOKS
- The New Real Book - Vol. 1 - C, Bb and Eb
- The New Real Book - Vol. 2 - C, Bb and Eb
- The New Real Book - Vol. 3 - C, Bb and Eb
- The Real Easy Book - Vol. 1 - C, Bb, Eb and Bass Clef (Three-Horn Edition)
- The Real Easy Book - Vol. 2 - C, Bb, Eb and Bass Clef
- The Real Easy Book - Vol. 3 - C, Bb, Eb and Bass Clef
- The Latin Real Easy Book - C, Bb, Eb and Bass Clef
- The Standards Real Book - C, Bb and Eb
- The Latin Real Book - C, Bb and Eb
- The Real Cool Book - West Coast 'Cool' Jazz Octet Charts
- The All-Jazz Real Book - C, Bb and Eb
- The European Real Book - C, Bb and Eb
- The Best of Sher Music Real Books - C, Bb and Eb
- The World's Greatest Fake Book - C version only
- The Yellowjackets Songbook - (all parts)

DIGITAL FAKE BOOKS (at shermusic.com only)
- The New Real Book - Vol.1 - C, Bb and Eb
- The Digital Standards Songbook
- The Digital Real Book
- The Jazz Songbook Series

LATIN MUSIC BOOKS
- Decoding Afro-Cuban Jazz: The Music of Chucho Valdés and Irakere - by Chucho Valdés and Rebeca Mauleón
- The Salsa Guidebook - by Rebeca Mauleón
- The Latin Real Easy Book - C, Bb, Eb and Bass Clef
- The Latin Bass Book - by Oscar Stagnaro and Chuck Sher
- The True Cuban Bass - by Carlos del Puerto and Silvio Vergara
- The Brazilian Guitar Book - by Nelson Faria
- Inside the Brazilian Rhythm Section - by Nelon Faria/Cliff Korman
- The Conga Drummer's Guidebook - by Michael Spiro
- Language of the Masters - by Michael Spiro
- Introduction to the Conga Drum, DVD - by Michael Spiro
- Afro-Caribbean Grooves for Drumset - by Jean-Philippe Fanfant
- Afro-Peruvian Percussion Ensemble - by Hector Morales
- Flamenco Improvisation, Vol. 1-3 - by Enrique Vargas

Bilingual or Libros en Español
- The Latin Real Book - C, Bb and Eb
- 101 Montunos - by Rebeca Mauleón
- Muy Caliente! - Afro-Cuban Book Play-Along CD
- El Libro del Jazz Piano - by Mark Levine
- Teoria del Jazz - by Mark Levine (digital only)

ALL METHOD BOOKS ALSO AVAILABLE IN DIGITAL FORM ONLINE

JAZZ METHOD BOOKS
BASS
- The Improvisor's Bass Method - by Chuck Sher
- Concepts for Bass Soloing - by Marc Johnson & Chuck Sher
- Walking Bassics - by Ed Fuqua
- Foundation Exercises for Bass - by Chuck Sher

GUITAR
- Jazz Guitar Voicings: The Drop 2 Book - by Randy Vincent
- Three-Note Voicings and Beyond - by Randy Vincent
- Line Games - by Randy Vincent
- Jazz Guitar Soloing: The Cellular Approach - by Randy Vincent
- The Guitarist's Introduction to Jazz - by Randy Vincent

PIANO
- Playing for Singers - by Mike Greensill
- An Approach to Comping: The Essentials - by Jeb Patton
- An Approach to Comping, Vol.2: Advanced - by Jeb Patton
- Wisdom of the Hand - by Marius Nordal
- Intro to Jazz Piano, A Deep Dive - by Jeb Patton

OTHER INSTRUMENTS
- Inner Drumming - by George Marsh
- Method for Chromatic Harmonica - by Max de Aloe
- Modern Etudes for Solo Trumpet - by Cameron Pearce
- New Orleans Trumpet - by Jim Thornton

FOR ALL INSTRUMENTS
- The Jazz Harmony Book - by David Berkman
- Jazz Musician's Guide to Creative Practicing - by D. Berkman
- The Jazz Singers Guide Book - by David Berkman
- Metaphors for the Musician - by Randy Halberstadt
- Forward Motion - by Hal Galper
- The Serious Jazz Practice Book - by Barry Finnerty
- The Serious Jazz Book II - by Barry Finnerty
- Building Solo Lines From Cells - by Randy Vincent
- The Real Easy Ear Training Book - by Roberta Radley
- Reading, Writing and Rhythmetic - by Roberta Radley
- Minor is Major - by Dan Greenblatt
- Jazz Scores and Analysis - Vol. 1 - by Rick Lawn
- Essential Grooves - by Moretti, Nicholl and Stagnaro
- The Jazz Solos of Chick Corea - transcribed by Peter Sprague

FOR STUDENT MUSICIANS
- The Blues Scales - by Dan Greenblatt - C, Bb and Eb
- Rhythm First! - by Tom Kamp - C, Bb, Eb and Bass Clef
- The Guitarist's Introduction to Jazz - Randy Vincent
- Jazz Songs for Student Violinists - by Keefe and Mitchell

CDs
- Poetry+Jazz: A Magical Marriage
- The New Real Book Play-Along CDs (for Vol.1) - #1, 2 and 3
- The Latin Real Book Sampler CD
- The Music of Charles Stevens

For more info, see SherMusic.com